A GUIDE TO

Learning
Independently

D1396448

A GUIDE TO

learning
independently

Lorraine Marshall &
Frances Rowland

3rd edition

Open University Press

Published in Great Britain by
Open University Press
McGraw-Hill Education
McGraw-Hill House
Shoppenhangers Road
Maidenhead
Berkshire
SL6 2QL
UK

and

Two Penn Plaza
New York, NY10121-2289, USA

email: enquiries@openup.co.uk
world wide web: http://www.openup.co.uk

Copyright © 1998 Addison Wesley Longman Australia Pty Limited

First published 1981
Reprinted 1983, 1989
Second edition 1993
Reprinted 1996
First published in this third edition 1998
Reprinted 2003
Reprinted 2004 (twice)

A catalogue record of this book is available from the British Library.

ISBN 0 335 20366 3 (pb)

Printed by Bell & Bain Ltd., Glasgow

CONTENTS

LIST OF TABLES

THANKS

We would like to thank the people who gave us encouragement and advice on the first edition, especially those who put time into reading the manuscript—Simon Avenell, Michael Booth, Mary Dale, Patsy Hallen, Richard Jakob-Hoff, Jim Macbeth, John Raser and John Webb. For comments on the section on using libraries, thanks to Tricia Cawley, Nancy Lane and Hugh Malcolm. We would also like to thank our typists/secretaries Anne Francis, Leonie Pimm, Annette Ritchie, and especially Meredith Beevers for burning the midnight oil.

For the third edition we thank those who helped and supported our writing: Marie Arandiga, Allison Brown, Deidre Stanton, Grant Stone and Sarah Veitch. A special thanks to Colin Beasley for his work on the chapter on conventions and to Marian Kemp for her input on numeracy.

Thanks to my parents for their encouragement—to my father who gave so much and would have been so proud to have his copy of this book, and to my mother for her continuing support. Thanks to Al for the spark that led to this book. And last, but in fact first, special thanks to Jim for his patience and support throughout, for his endless reading of the drafts and for saving my sanity at sea. And for the second and third editions, thanks again to Jim and also to Suzannah who although not involved in the first edition has helped with these.

Lorraine Marshall

My personal thanks to John Holt, who reminded me of what I believe about teaching; to Ann, who taught me about learning; and to Ann's babysitters, without whom I wouldn't have written this book. And thank you to John.

Frances Rowland

PREFACE TO THE third edition

This third edition is one to take with you into the twenty-first century. This revision of *A Guide to Learning Independently* has added new information and techniques and integrated new ideas.

- The major technological changes of the 1990s which affect learning have been taken into account. While we would argue that technology should support rather than direct learning, computer-based technology is changing the way students learn and is transforming the life of every student. For example, libraries now access information electronically, and increasingly students are taking mixed mode courses with many students learning online.
- Much of the new material springs from changes in higher education and from recent philosophical and theoretical bases.
- Some sections of the book have been updated, such as the chapter on conventions and the further reading lists at the end of each chapter.
- Material has been modified in the light of experience. For example, as a result of extensive use by students and lecturers at Murdoch University, the chapter on 'Choosing and Analysing a Topic' has been streamlined in ways that work better for students.

It is over seventeen years since the first edition of *A Guide to Learning Independently* was published. Some of the ideas it contains were first formulated and written in the 1970s when access to higher education was expanding in Western societies. At this time of structural and social change it seemed possible for many motivated individuals to achieve whatever level of education they desired. It was a time of focus on individual growth and *A Guide to Learning Independently* with its emphasis on 'you' grew out of that time.

In the 1990s the emphasis has been different—it is now all too clear that for some groups in our society all the determination and effort they can muster is unlikely to get them where they would like to be educationally. There is increasing recognition of what it means to live in a culturally diverse society and of the influence of gender, race and class on people's opportunities.

However, *A Guide to Learning Independently* still rests on the premise that it is possible for a person to change the way they approach their learning; and it is directed to the individual student because it is the individual who must write the essays and reports, pass the exams and organise themselves in order to be successful in the tertiary education system. The book still offers techniques to help you do what is expected of you by your teachers. But rather than providing a guide which only sets out to help you jump successfully through the hoops held by other people, we still argue that your learning should be centred on you and on your purposes for learning.

To some academics (and possibly some students), this approach may seem out-of-touch with the realities of budget cuts and institutional 'rationalisations'—and this third edition of the *Guide* takes account of current factors such as worsening staff–student ratios. But we claim that it is even more important in such times for students to try to take charge of their own learning as much as possible; and any help that this book can give with this is worthwhile.

So the conceptual framework of the book retains key elements from the first edition, but themes which have acquired increased relevance in higher education have been re-emphasised—themes such as lifelong learning, collaborative learning, the role of reflection and learning independently. In addition, the content takes into account some of the recent developments in educational theory; changes to our own thinking; recent changes in emphasis within higher education; and the increasing impact of higher education being offered globally and by providers other than universities. Some examples follow.

- The role of culture and society in shaping learning is explored particularly in Chapters 1 and 5; and the need for students to learn to operate in the culture of a tertiary institution is discussed in Chapters 1 and 3. In addition, throughout the book we have taken into consideration the diverse learning experiences of students from a range of different ethnic backgrounds.
- The development of students' learning has been more closely framed within a critical thinking context. For example, the chapters that deal with essay writing have been rewritten to highlight the need for developing an argument. Chapter 12, 'Participating in Discussion Groups', focuses on discussions that allow interchange between different world views. The book reinforces the centrality of reflection for thinking critically, with a discussion of reflection in Chapter 1 and more direct entreaties to students to take time to make this activity part of their learning.
- Changes to the nature of learning brought about by the increased use of technology are dealt with in the appropriate chapters. For example, the chapters on researching and using information sources deal with accessing information online and using libraries electronically. The chapter on discussion groups has widened its scope to include online discussions. Throughout the book we also draw attention to the possibilities that computer-mediated communications offer for student–student interaction and for more flexible learning.

- Chapter 3, 'Becoming an Independent Student', exemplifies an approach in which we no longer assume that students will enrol in and connect with a single institution.
- Numeracy as a literacy skill has been given more prominence in this edition, particularly in the chapters on reading and on writing scientific reports.
- The challenges posed by feminist methodologies and postmodern thought to the fundamental paradigms of a range of disciplines are reflected in material such as that on subjectivity and objectivity.
- The chapters on writing, especially Chapters 12 and 13, meld the 'process' approach to teaching writing with ideas and suggestions from the 'genre' approach. Students are led from analysing a topic to researching, then to writing and rewriting a piece of work. While the demands of different disciplines and genres in which students are writing are taken into account, the writing chapters rest on the conviction that there is much to be gained by using elements of both approaches and not relying solely on one or the other. This conviction is based on extensive experience helping students with their research and writing.
- The role of collaborative learning has been emphasised because of its potential in online courses, to complement the focus on the individual student, and to help students cope positively with decreased access to academic staff. This emphasis can be found throughout the book and particularly in the chapter on discussion groups.
- In the first edition of the book, students were urged to link content with process—that is, to link what they are learning with how they learn it. Recent research into student learning has strengthened this basic premise, and it has been reinforced in this edition.

Many of the techniques we describe have not changed, although we have introduced some new ones. Much that was relevant in 1981 remains relevant for the turn of the century. What is different is the nature of the awareness that we suggest you bring to your learning.

Our thanks to the many people who have taken the time to tell us that they have found the earlier editions of the *Guide* helpful and to make suggestions for improvements. We hope that the third edition of the book will prove as useful.

READ THIS FIRST!

If you are looking for a book which does more than describe techniques to help you succeed in your formal education, *A Guide to Learning Independently* is the book for you. It will help you with learning tasks such as writing assignments, reading textbooks, making notes and concentrating when you study, and it presents a range of techniques to help you meet the requirements of your teachers and courses. However, *A Guide to Learning Independently* is also designed to help you discover your own learning purposes and how you learn best. It will help you articulate your knowledge about your own learning, that is, it encourages you to think about or to become 'metacognitive' about your learning. It doesn't set out to prescribe how you should learn, but offers a range of ideas and techniques from which you can choose. These alternatives are presented in the context of encouraging you to use tertiary institutions for your own purposes. To set the ideas and techniques in a broader framework, the book also discusses learning in general and tertiary education in particular.

This book focuses on you—who you are and what you bring to your learning. Throughout the book you are encouraged to examine your purposes and what you want to learn. You are also encouraged to reflect on how you learn informally, and to build on this self-knowledge in your formal learning. Implicit in this approach are the beliefs that there is no single way of learning which suits everyone and that it is your right and responsibility to shape your own learning.

So *the first five chapters* of the book concentrate on you—those aspects of your self and your lifestyle which affect your learning, when and how you study, and the decisions and adjustments you make when beginning tertiary studies. The importance of asking your own questions in your learning is emphasised, as is learning in ways that suit you so that you remember what you learn. *The next five chapters* look at how you can find, take in and evaluate information and ideas when pursuing your own and other people's questions. These chapters deal with analysing and researching a topic, finding and using a range of information sources, reading and listening to lectures. *The last six chapters* look at communicating, using, critiquing and presenting what you learn. They deal with participating in discussion whether face-to-face and online, with developing your writing, and with writing and presenting essays and reports.

You are encouraged to explore your past experience of learning, to clarify why you learn as you do. *Within each chapter* you will find questions and ideas about you as a learner. These are intended to centre the book on you and to help you discover your own purposes and methods for learning. Because the questions are based on the premise that only you can answer them, we don't prescribe one 'best' way to learn, but instead suggest alternative study techniques. We give reasons for these techniques so you can decide how useful they are for your purposes, and we encourage you to try them as you actually learn and study to find those which suit you. Often these techniques are presented in the framework of 'before', 'during' and 'after' stages of a learning activity, such as in the chapters on 'Researching a topic' and 'Reading'.

This book contains frequent *cross references* to other sections of the book. These direct you to another section within the chapter you are using to a section within another chapter, or to another whole chapter.

In case you wish to pursue a topic, question or skill in greater depth, we suggest *further reading* at the end of some chapters and the general bibliography. We also use *quotations* from a wide variety of sources to offer different perspectives, to reinforce what we say, and to entertain you.

Each chapter in *A Guide to Learning Independently* has a particular focus. However, the ideas and techniques mentioned in any one chapter cannot be neatly separated from those in any other chapter, any more than your learning can be segmented. Use this introduction and the 'What to do now' section to familiarise yourself with the whole book. Use the Contents list to become familiar with the controlling focus of each chapter. When working with a chapter, use the Index and cross references to move backwards and forwards through the book, to think about the ideas and techniques in different contexts.

This book is intended primarily as *a guide and reference* for people who have some opportunity for independent learning. It is intended for students who are past the age of compulsory schooling, and for people who want to discover how to use the resources of formal tertiary education for their own purposes in learning. However, the learning techniques presented in the book can be used in a range of structured classes, and sections of the book can be used by people who need help with activities such as journal writing, learning online, producing business reports and running discussion groups.

You are likely to find the book valuable if you are a student at university or college, especially in first or second year. You will find it useful if you are in the final years of high school, whether or not you are going on to tertiary study. If you have left school and are taking technical or training courses, the book can help you with basic learning skills. If you are a student who has little contact with teachers, perhaps because you belong to a large institution or because you are studying online, part-time and/or at a distance, the book offers information otherwise available from frequent face-to-face contact with teachers. If you are a student straight from a highly structured school situation, the book will help you adjust to taking responsibility for your studies. If you are returning to study after an absence from it, you can use our suggestions to help you gain confidence in yourself as a learner.

A Guide to Learning Independently can be used in several different ways, each of which involves actively trying the ideas and techniques in your learning and studying. Don't simply read the book. Acquaint yourself with its contents, and then use it as a guide and reference when the need arises.

Firstly, you can use the book *on your own*. Refer to it, for example, when you need help with how to use a library or write an essay. Read chapters such as 'Becoming an independent student', 'Learning and remembering' and 'Learning from evaluation' if you are thinking about the nature of formal tertiary education.

Secondly, the book can be used when studying and learning *collaboratively*. You might, for example, use the chapter on 'Developing your writing' to work on your writing with other students. The process of learning with other students can enrich your education and make it less solitary. You can also use the book when working on your learning skills with a teacher, so you can both relate our suggestions to your particular learning activity. For example, refer to the chapters on 'Choosing and Analysing a Topic' and 'Researching a Topic' and 'Writing Essays' when working on how to prepare and write an essay.

Thirdly, *teachers* can use this book too. A teacher within a course can refer students to sections of the book which would be most helpful to the particular individual or group. Learning skills advisers and counsellors can also use the book in their classes or with individual students.

However, all the ideas, information, techniques and suggestions we offer are of little value to you as a student unless you are reading, writing, listening, talking, asking questions, experimenting, stretching your mind—unless you are engaged in learning. Exploring and practising alternative approaches to learning and study provides a basis from which you can choose those approaches which are most effective and satisfying for you. This experience with alternative ways of learning is also essential if you are to change habits which no longer suit you. Such changes take time and practice, and suggestions which are easy for us to make may take courage and persistence for you to apply. But defining your purposes, reflecting on your learning, thinking critically, building on your strengths, and working on your weaknesses as a student are all crucial to learning independently. This book is intended to help you discover these challenges and pleasures.

■ ■ ■ ■ ■

'Students' minds are like containers to be filled.'
'Education is to sharpen that tool which is the mind.'
'Knowledge is to be built up, block by block.'

These are a few of the metaphors commonly used to describe formal education. But such metaphors describe learning as essentially confined and defined, rather than as a process of growing and changing.

Each of us is born with a great curiosity, and this curiosity is essential for us to survive and learn. We learn as we ask and think about what we need and want to know. We are learning all the time, whether or not we realise it. We learn from what we do, from what happens to us, from our jobs and our pastimes ... the list is endless. And we learn more easily when actively involved and when using what we learn in doing or talking, thinking or dreaming.

Learning is often thought of largely as an approved activity which happens in certain places (schools, universities and colleges) at certain ages (usually between five and twenty-one) and in certain ways (in classrooms, according to a curriculum taught by teachers). But this formal study is only one part of our learning, and is designed to achieve only particular objectives. At the heart of all of our significant learning, formal and informal, are the questions we ask because of who we are and what we need and want to know.

Formal educational institutions can help you ask and pursue your own questions and problems. There are teachers in these institutions who care about learning and about you as a learner, who can convey to you the fierce and gentle pleasures of the mind. Having teachers who help you ask your own questions, who share their knowledge and experience and who are also questioning and learning for themselves is an invaluable part of formal education. There are also students with whom to talk and argue, theorise and fantasise.

However, formal education can be one of the most effective methods for squashing curiosity or channelling it in artificial and unnecessary directions. And without curiosity, you are limited to learning what is presented to you rather than discovering how to learn, how to ask your own questions and communicate and exchange ideas. Knowing how to learn makes it possible for you to continue learning long after you finish formal education. Otherwise you are restricted to learning a particular body of knowledge, which may soon become outdated.

Using the resources of an educational institution for your own purposes entails thinking about what is expected of you—and why. Who decides what you should learn, and how and when this should be taught? Who decides when and how you should be required to prove what you have learned? These decisions, made partly by teachers, reflect what many others see as the purposes of a university or college in our society. These 'others' include government bodies, academic committees, administrators, professional organisations, employers, and individuals who hold power in our society. If you want to use formal education as part of your purposes for learning rather than simply following other people's goals, try to identify and examine and question the assumptions and purposes of the people who shape tertiary education. Will you accept what these people expect, what they require? If not, think about your options.

Formal educational institutions expect a lot of you. As with most work, sometimes you will be involved and enthusiastic, and sometimes you will have other priorities in your life which detract from your study. Learning is a personal process, not simply a commodity or a meal ticket which you will acquire after a set program of study, so keep your questions and your purposes in mind. Play with ideas—speculate, hypothesise, fantasise. Do the ideas offered excite you or make sense to you? If so, grab them with both halves of your brain. Read, write, draw, critique, experiment, for the sake of your own learning and for the pleasure and discovery of a craft. Learn how to communicate your own questions and ideas, and try hard to understand what others are communicating. Don't reject an idea or a topic or a course out of hand because of your biases or lazinesses or fears. Be willing to take a risk, to reach a little further than you think you can. Don't expect to understand all you read or hear.

Real, active learning of your own isn't easy—it's hard work. But the hard work is not that of a dutiful conscience, it arises from the joy of intense involvement. One of the greatest challenges you can take on is attempting to be aware of your purposes for learning, to reflect profoundly on what and how you learn, to communicate your ideas clearly, and to understand and critically evaluate the thoughts of others. This learning is a process of growing and changing, a process which is more exciting than filling bins or sharpening tools or building with blocks.

What to do now

1 Read through the Contents list.
2 Flick through the book and choose a chapter which would be especially useful to you now, or start with Chapter 1 'You' or Chapter 5 'Becoming an independent student'. Read thoroughly the chapter you have chosen.
3 Choose a topic which interests you, look it up in the Index, and read the relevant pages of the book.
4 Turn to Table 9.1, 'The anatomy of a book', and apply the questions in this table to *A Guide to Learning Independently*.
5 Look back over 'Read this first!'
6 Any questions or ideas? Ask someone else—another student, a teacher, or a friend, for their thoughts on your questions and ideas.

CHAPTER 1

YOU

This book begins with you. It begins with you because asking questions and thinking about yourself, your lifestyle and your background can give you insights into your individual learning style. You can then use these insights to make your learning and study more effective and satisfying.

Your body and your emotions, your cultural background and your beliefs, the people in your life, and where you study—all these affect your learning. Your physical state and your emotions influence your ability to learn, and too little sleep or exercise may affect your enthusiasm for and ability to study. A belief in the value of hard work may make you a conscientious student. An argument with the people in your household can create difficulties when you try to concentrate on study, and moving house or changing jobs can leave little time and energy for formal learning.

As people and as students we are all different. If you are a meticulous and deliberate thinker, a study task might take you longer. This may leave you feeling inadequate, or you might enjoy the leisurely savouring of new ideas. At the other extreme, if you have a high energy level and live at a fast pace, you might wish you could occasionally slow down enough to integrate in more depth what you learn, or you might enjoy the speed with which new insights come to you. There is no single way of learning and studying that suits everyone. And because you change daily, weekly and monthly, there is no one way of studying which always suits you. So you need to know more about these aspects of yourself, and examine how your culture and surroundings affect your learning.

This chapter contains three parts—your physical and emotional self, your cultural and social self, and your surroundings. Each section of the chapter gives you information, asks questions and makes suggestions. It is a chapter to work with, to take time with. Consider the questions and suggestions carefully. Here are some ideas on how to use them.

- Read each set of questions in turn and write down your answers or ideas on them, perhaps in a special notebook or a journal (see 'Learning journals or logs', Chapter 12). When you have read and thought about the whole chapter, look back over it and revise any notes.
- Read through the whole chapter and reflect on those questions and suggestions which are relevant to you at present. Later re-read the chapter and focus on other questions. Rethink your responses if you or your lifestyle have changed significantly.
- Discuss the questions with one or two friends or with a group of people (see 'Participating in discussion groups', Chapter 11).
- If you want to read more on a topic, check the further reading at the end of the chapter.

Your physical and emotional self

This section looks at aspects of your physical and emotional self that directly affect your learning and your study. As a first step to thinking about your self, centre your attention on your body. Stop for a few minutes. Centre your attention on your face—your forehead, eyes, nose, mouth, jaw. Are they relaxed? strong? tired? tense? Move your awareness down to your neck, shoulders, spine. Focus on each part of your body—down to your toes. How does your whole body feel now?

What do you like most about your body?

What do you like least?

How does your body feel now?

Now **stop**. Did you actually spend time thinking about and answering these questions, or did you just passively read them? If you didn't answer them, go back and think about them seriously. Get in touch with your body before you go on to the next set of questions. This chapter centres on you, but can only be effective if you become actively involved with the questions and ideas it contains.

Body rhythms

Certainly people show consistent, life-long predilections for morning or night activity. Physiological differences may be found in the circadian rhythms of the so-called lark people, who are most alive by morning, and the owls, who perform at their best late in the day, yet the owls are generally penalised by the usual scheduling of school hours. (*Gay Gaer Luce*)

Your body has many rhythms and cycles. Each day, for example, your temperature and pulse rate fluctuate slightly, and you pass through the same pattern of dreaming several times each night. Monthly cycles apparently occur for males as well as females. Perhaps you go through cycles where your desire for physical activity alternates with your desire for mental activity. One of the difficulties in studying for final exams can be that you often need to stay inside and be mentally active when you would prefer to be outside and physically active as the seasons change. If you are a night person you may be unwilling to leave your bed for an early lecture on a gloomy winter morning, or if you are a day person you may find it difficult to concentrate during an evening class. A cup of coffee may revive you for that evening class, but in the long run, regularly using stimulants to help you cope with study is self-defeating. Discovering your individual body rhythms can help you plan study times when you are more mentally active.

Are you a lark or an owl?

Are you aware of patterns in your body's needs for sleep? for exercise? for food? for sex?

How is your study related to these patterns?

- Determine the times during the day when you are usually most mentally alert and when you feel physically ready to study.
- Try to schedule your classes and your study during your alert times. If it is necessary to study when your energy level is low, plan to do work which demands less intense concentration.

Sleep

I haven't been to sleep for over a year. That's why I go to bed early. One needs more rest if one doesn't sleep. *(Evelyn Waugh)*

Sleep needs vary for different people. If you are frequently irritable and can't cope as well as usual with minor problems, you are possibly getting too little sleep. How well you concentrate on study is influenced by how much sleep you have.

Do you often sleep so much that your mind feels drugged?

What effect does a late night or interrupted night's sleep have on your concentration next day?

Can you think clearly after a nap? Does a brief nap or a couple of hours' sleep refresh you for long periods of study?

When do your sleep needs vary—when you are emotionally upset or physically active, for example? Do you often have to change your sleep times—because of shift work or a restless baby, for example? How do these changes affect your study?

- Determine your minimum sleep needs and the amount of sleep you think you need for a good night's rest. Think about a time when you have been very relaxed and were able to sleep as much as you needed.
- Think about your sleep patterns for the past two weeks and how they have helped or interfered with your learning.
- Try to plan your most demanding study periods for times when you are not short of sleep.
- On a night when you can't fall asleep, try deep breathing exercises and relaxing your body completely (see 'Tension and relaxation'). If this doesn't work, get up and do something rather than lying in bed and worrying about not sleeping.
- If you often have difficulty getting enough sleep, allow time to wind down before going to bed, and don't drink or eat foods that contain caffeine during the evening. Give yourself two or three periods of deep relaxation during the day. Relaxing your body fully from head to toe can be almost as refreshing as sleeping.

Food and drink

One cannot think well, love well, sleep well, if one has not dined well. (*Virginia Woolf*)

A breakfast which is more nourishing than tea and toast, or a lunch which is more than a bag of chips, a doughnut or a bowl of rice, helps you concentrate during class or private study. A light evening meal instead of a large dinner makes it easier to focus on your study or during an evening class. Studying is especially difficult if you feel tired and irritable because of poor eating or heavy drinking.

Do you prefer to eat one large meal a day or frequent small meals? Do you try to study after a large meal?

*When settling to study, does preparing something to eat or drink help
or hinder you?*

*Do you often drink so much alcohol that you cannot think clearly the next
day?*

*Are there some foods, such as certain additives, that adversely affect
your concentration?*

- Make sure your diet is well balanced, and includes protein,
  carbohydrates, and plenty of fruit and vegetables. Essential protein is
  available from complex carbohydrates such as beans or rice as well as
  from meat and dairy products, but refined carbohydrates such as ice
  cream, alcohol and soft drinks add little to your diet except kilojoules.
  If you generally lack energy, check that your diet isn't deficient in
  minerals and vitamins, particularly iron and the vitamin B complex.
  If you don't have much money or have dietary restrictions, eating
  properly takes more planning and a knowledge of nutrition, but it
  can be done.
- Avoid studying after a heavy meal.
- If you feel the need for food during a study session have a small
  amount of protein food, such as a piece of cheese, a glass of soy milk,
  or a handful of peanuts. Sugary food gives you a temporary lift then
  leaves you more tired than before.
- A judiciously chosen treat can help you when you settle to work or
  reward you when you finish.

Physical exercise

Not taking care of your body is like not paying the rent; you end up with
no place to live. (*Gayle Olinekova*)

Physical exercise can provide a welcome break from mental activity.
Exercise helps you study because it reduces tension, increases the oxygen
supply to your brain, improves your digestion and helps you sleep more
soundly. Long periods without exercising your body can make it difficult
to exercise your mind effectively. However, immediately after strenuous
physical exercise some people find it difficult to settle down to study.

*What form of physical exercise do you enjoy, for example, a team sport,
cycling, swimming, sailing, yoga, sex, dancing, table tennis, walking,
skating?*

*If you are a physically active person, do you find it difficult to sit still
for long periods to read, write or listen to a lecture?*

Does exercise usually refresh or fatigue you for learning?

*Do you renew your concentration during a study session by taking a
short break to move about?*

- Choose exercise that feels good to you and do it regularly. Include activity that exercises your whole body, including your heart and lungs, and activity which stretches your body and helps you loosen up.
- Plan to study and exercise when these two activities help rather than conflict with each other.
- If your work is physically tiring, allow yourself time to relax and eat something nourishing before you try to study.
- At times when you need to be especially mentally alert, such as during exams, regular physical exercise helps increase your alertness and concentration.

Senses

All creative activity, as well as much of your pleasure in life, depends on your sensory awareness. Even your ability to absorb and use second-hand information depends on your ability to relate it to your own first-hand observations. Yet, constantly exposed to second-hand information, you may forget to use your senses and may become, to some degree, cut off from the world immediately around you. (Fred Morgan)

Your earliest learning is through your senses, but as you come to rely more on abstract reasoning it is easy to forget how vital your senses are to your learning.

Stop for a moment. Shut your eyes. What can you smell? What can you hear? What tastes do you have in your mouth? What sensations do you feel on your skin? Now open your eyes. What can you see?

What is your strongest sense? Do you learn best by hearing, seeing, touching or a combination of these?

- At the end of each day ask yourself what you remember most vividly—which sight, sound, smell, taste or touch comes instantly to your mind? Conjure up these sense impressions as you drift off to sleep, or write a description of them in a daily journal.
- When you feel like relaxing, take a few minutes to become deeply aware of the smells, sounds, tastes, touch and sights you are experiencing.
- In your study utilise as many of your senses as you can. For example, when trying to learn something you find difficult don't just read it silently and use only your sense of sight. Speak it out loud so that you hear it, and make notes using patterns and colours so that you use your sense of sight more fully (see 'Patterns and principles', Chapter 5). The act of writing also uses the sense of touch.

Tension and relaxation

How did I live to be a hundred years old? Well, when I moves I moves slow. When I sits, I sits loose. And when I worries, I goes to sleep. (*Liz Carpenter*)

If you are reasonably relaxed you can learn more effectively. To relax and de-stress, you may need to put aside problems for a while, exercise more often, or learn how to relax your body consciously from head to toe.

Where in your body do you usually feel anxiety or tension?

Do you feel relaxed now? If so, why? If not, why not?

Can you study when you feel tense and stressed? If not, do you know how to relax?

While you are studying or listening to a lecture, do you occasionally check to see if any parts of your body are tense?

After a period of study or a session at a keyboard do you suffer from eye strain, headaches, or tension in your shoulder muscles?

Do you habitually rely on drugs to help you relax?

- Learn and practise relaxation techniques which help your whole body relax fully, for example, deep breathing, yoga, gentle exercise, massage, a hot bath.
- If you think your tension is due to physical causes such as eyestrain, seek appropriate help.
- When reading or writing or using a computer, stretch and change positions occasionally, rest your eyes by focusing on a distant object, and yawn and take several deep breaths to ease any tension around your mouth and jaw. There are 'on the spot' exercises that are quick to do and designed specifically to relieve keyboard stress.
- Get some whole body exercise following a long study session.

Emotions

> Last night I was seized by a fit of despair that found utterance in moans, and that finally drove me to throw the dining room clock into the sea. *(Marie Bashkirtseff)*

The ups and downs of your emotions influence your learning. If you are feeling cheerful you probably find it easy to study; if you are feeling depressed you may have difficulty concentrating or absorbing new ideas. Most students have emotional problems at one time or another— including anxiety or guilt about study.

What are the most positive aspects in your life at present? List these.

What are the most positive aspects of your studies?

What are you most worried about? List these worries.

Which aspects of your studies worry you the most?

How do you deal with stress and anxiety?

- Write down what is worrying you before you begin studying or if you continue to be distracted as you study. Ask yourself if it is more urgent to go on studying or to tackle your worries. Plan another time to deal with whichever is less urgent.
- Spend five to ten minutes before you are fully awake each morning remembering your dreams. This becomes easier with practice, and reflecting on your dreams can help you understand your emotions.
- Allow yourself a set time during the day to think about your problems and try to put them aside for the rest of the day. Talk to a friend about them or write them out.
- Practise physical relaxation techniques or activities which help you deal with your emotions.
- Reading for pleasure can give you a respite from your worries and stress.
- Spend some time away from the place where you seem to worry most. Going for a walk or visiting friends can put the problems in perspective.
- If you have a persistent problem, discuss it with a close friend, a sympathetic 'outsider' or a trained counsellor.
- If your difficulties are connected with your learning or lack of it, do some work. A few hours of concentrated study often works wonders if you are feeling overwhelmed with study demands. If you are stuck on a problem, discuss it with your teacher or with other students— often other people have the same problem. Read the relevant sections in this guide for some useful suggestions.
- If you are anxious about a responsibility such as taking an exam or giving a seminar paper, find out as precisely as possible what you want to know about your subject, and study it as thoroughly as you can. Talk to someone with experience in the techniques of exams or seminars, or read the relevant sections in this book. A certain amount of anxiety and tension can help motivate you to learn.

Reflections

Never do I close the door behind me without being conscious that I am carrying out an act of charity towards myself. *(Peter Hoeg)*

Reflection is one of the keys to understanding, to remembering, to learning, and to thinking critically. It is a key to integrating what you learn into your existing knowledge and belief system, and in deciding how to act. Thinking about your own thinking, or metacognition, will give you insights into how you go about your learning, and is important if you want to change or adapt study behaviours.

Do you enjoy spending time alone?

Are you able to spend enough time with your own thoughts?

Do you write down your reflections? Do you share them with someone else? With whom?

Do you live life at such a fast pace that you have no time to make sense of your experiences and learning?

How do your emotions influence your reflections?

Can you think of recent examples where your reflections have led you to act differently?

- If you can manage to have time alone without interruption, reflect on your life, your interests, your concerns and your learning. Try to set up both intellectual and physical space to reflect on what you are learning.
- Spend time directing your reflections towards a purpose.
- Document your reflections in a personal or learning journal (see Chapter 12, 'Developing your writing').

Your cultural and social self

This section encourages you to consider the impact of your cultural and social background on your thinking and learning, your beliefs and values and your relationships with others and how this affects your study.

Stop for a moment and think about your cultural background in your wider society and then within your tertiary institution.

Which cultural groups have been influential in shaping who you are? Do you identify with a strong cultural group in your country?

Were you born in this country or are you a migrant or an overseas student? If you were born here, for how many generations has your family been in this country?

To what socio-economic class does your family belong?

Are you from a group whose numbers in this society are small, for example, a recent migrant group?

Are you from a town or from the city?

For many years, most tertiary education communities in countries such as Australia and the UK consisted of school leavers from affluent families. This has changed, and university communities have become more varied. There has been an influx of students from overseas, and tertiary study now attracts students from diverse backgrounds, including mature-age people, Aboriginals, migrants, minority ethnic groups, and people from lower socio-economic groups.

Ways of thinking and learning

All of us are living and thinking subjects ... Everybody both acts and thinks. The way people act or react is linked to a way of thinking, and of course thinking is related to tradition. *(Michel Foucault)*

It is valuable to spend some time thinking about how your cultural and social background might influence your thinking and how you go about your learning.

Do the cultural groups with which you identify value learning?
How has your background helped or hindered you in your desire for a tertiary education?

With which cultural groups in the university or college community do you identify?

How does your background affect your view of the world? How has this world view affected your study? For example, how is your interpretation of what you read and hear different from that of other students?

How does your background give you particular strengths in your learning? Do you ever feel that there are gaps in your learning because of your background?

- If you are studying because it is a cultural or social expectation and not because you want to, think about your alternatives. If you are to continue with a formal education, you need to work out your own purposes for your learning so that the time and effort you invest does not seem like a waste of time (see 'Choices and decisions', Chapter 3). If you want a tertiary education but in pursuing this you are at odds with others in your cultural or social group, consider how you can handle this opposition and look for support from within your university or college (see Chapter 3, 'Becoming an independent student').
- Try to identify how your background might contribute strengths to your learning at university or college, and how it might leave you with areas on which you need to work. For example, if you come from a family with experience of books and academic learning, you may have an understanding of the approaches to study expected of university students, but you may also be subject to family pressure to achieve at a high level. If you come from a society where teachers are highly respected and where questioning the teacher is not acceptable, it may take you time to become accustomed to more informal teacher–student interactions, but your respect for teachers perhaps means that you are more ready to listen carefully in lectures. If you are a student from a developing country, your formal education may have suffered because of large classes and limited books and resources, but your learning is enriched by the cross-cultural comparisons you

can make. If your background includes experience with questioning and critiquing the world around you, you will find the critical culture of the university easier to adapt to.

- Once you become involved in your studies, you will find that your way of interpreting what you read and what is discussed in tutorials sometimes differs noticeably from that of other students. This difference reflects your background, experiences, world view, interests, and previous schooling. You are entitled to your own interpretation, which should be supported by evidence, examples and reasons. If you are a lone voice presenting a particular point of view, you need to think through your interpretation as fully and critically as possible, and you may have to work harder to have your ideas considered or accepted. Remember, however, that diversity of opinions is an important part of the intellectual debate in a university, and that everyone has a contribution to make.

Beliefs and values

Ideally, our choices will be made on the basis of the values we hold; but frequently, we are not clear about our own values. *(Sidney B. Simon et al.)*

What you believe and value directly affects your learning. It can affect your choice of courses, your work within courses, your open-mindedness and how you relate to other students and to teachers. For example, if you are concerned about the environment you might write your assignments on topics related to this area. If you are from a religious family and you don't believe in genetic engineering, you may find yourself in conflict with teachers in a biology course whose different world view means that they see no harm in this area of research. If you are a Marxist you may have little sympathy for a lecturer who is a postmodern thinker. Examining your world view with its values and assumptions is essential to critical thinking, and learning to think critically is an integral part of university study.

At times your views and values conflict with your learning. For example, a course on Eastern religious philosophy may affect your belief in a Western ethic which is goal-oriented. You may find yourself disillusioned with the studies required for a long dreamed-of profession, or with the realities of formal education. Perhaps you are confronted with a challenge to a cherished prejudice about the superiority of the male sex or of white-skinned races. A new insight into personal relationships can create dissatisfaction with your belief in the nuclear family.

How would you complete the following sentences?:
'I believe that humans are essentially ...'

'I believe that our society should be organised so that ...'

'What I believe about humans and our society is based on the assumptions that ... '

How does what you believe and value affect what and how you learn?

- Try to work out which beliefs are most important to you, and try to identify their source, including those embedded in your upbringing.
- If a conflict of beliefs and values is seriously affecting your study, talk it over with a close friend or a counsellor. If this conflict is related to a course, talk to a teacher in that course if possible.
- Think about the beliefs and values of the other people with whom you have frequent contact—your friends, a partner, your teachers, fellow students. Try to work out why they differ from or are similar to your own.
- Take a course in critical thinking to help you clarify the place of values and assumptions in academic argument (see 'Thinking critically', Chapter 3).

Social groupings

It isn't the work that is going to be hard in college. It's the play. Half the time I don't know what the girls are talking about; their jokes seem to relate to a past that everyone but me has shared. I'm a foreigner in the world and I don't understand the language. It's a miserable feeling. I've had it all my life. At the high school the girls would stand in groups and just look at me. I was queer and different and everyone knew it ... *(Jean Webster)*

Think back for a moment to times in your life when you have been the only different person in a group; for example, if you were the only young person in a group of older people, or when you were with others all of whom spoke a different language, or when the others all had different beliefs from yours.

- If you feel different and isolated from other students, find some who understands how you feel and share with them your experiences and your problems with learning. At the same time remember that you have much to offer to other students, and contribute your perspectives in formal and informal discussions.
- If you have rarely thought about what it is like to be on the outside, the chances are that you are a part of a particular majority group. Make an extra effort to listen to and learn from students who are from different backgrounds, especially those who are part of a minority group. Show respect for their opinions and ideas.
- Take advantage of the richness and variety of experience available in the diverse cultural and social groups within the student body. Being open to different world views and new ideas and perspectives, perhaps through informal social interactions with other students, is an important part of your formal learning and is essential to thinking critically.

Your surroundings

The environment in which you work and play and eat and sleep influences your learning. If you are a full-time student and your friends frequently drop by, your approach to studying will differ from that of a parent with young children who is studying part-time and taking evening classes, or that of a distance education student who lives and works on a farm. If you have a room of your own, you will organise study sessions differently from a person who works at the kitchen table or in a library. It is not essential to have ideal surroundings before you can study effectively; but often you can make changes which improve your study situations considerably.

This section looks at two aspects of your surroundings which directly affect your learning—the people in your life and the places where you study—and suggests alternatives which can make study easier.

The people in your life

On Mondays mum has a tutorial, so I have to go around to Grandma's place for tea. That's all right. She lets me watch television. *(8 year-old girl)*

In your household, the time and energy you have for study can be dramatically increased if you manage to work out a satisfactory living pattern with the other people. This usually takes time, and even if you have a comfortable arrangement, there will be difficult periods as you all adapt to the inevitable changes in your lives. But any time and effort in this direction is well spent to increase your enjoyment of formal learning. If the people with whom you live co-operate in making your study effective, you will have more energy and enthusiasm for study.

Do you live on your own, or with others—parents, relatives, friends, other students, a partner/spouse, children? Does your 'household' extend to daily contact with people who live in a different location, such as an elderly parent or a close friend?

Do your working hours coincide with those of the other people in your house?

Are the others also studying, or do they have some idea of the demands of being a student? Are they considerate of your study needs? Do they resent the time you spend studying? How do you arrange time with them and time to study?

Do you have responsibilities in your household, such as domestic chores, financial burdens, or caring for young children or a sick relative? Do these responsibilities leave you little time and energy for study? How might they be reallocated?

Are you under pressure from people such as your partner or your parents to succeed in your studies? Why? Are their criteria for success the same as yours?

- If there is a persistent or major problem in your living arrangements or personal relationships which makes it difficult for you to study, talk about it as soon as possible with the person or people concerned. Describe how you feel about the problem and suggest ways it might be handled, particularly what you can do about it. Listen to suggestions from others concerned and see if you can come to a workable compromise. If compromise doesn't seem possible, think seriously about the priority that formal learning has in your life (see 'All work and no play ...', Chapter 2).
- If you have friends who don't understand that study means you are less available for socialising and who think that because you are at home you can be interrupted, be firm until they come to understand that you now have to program your social arrangements. Ask friends to 'phone and not just drop in.

Where you study

If you are deeply involved with what you are learning, you can concentrate just about anywhere for short periods of time. However, in formal learning you also need to concentrate for sustained periods and to study subjects which aren't of immediate importance to you. It is then that your surroundings become important.

Location

Where do you prefer to study? Why? Does a relatively impersonal environment such as a library help you study?

Are the books and references you need readily available where you study?

Are there other people around where you study? Are they also studying? Do they help or hinder your learning? Why?

- Decide whether you study more effectively at home or elsewhere. If necessary, try to reorganise your time so that you can study in the location where you learn most effectively.
- If you have to work in a particular place, for example, because that is where your computer is located, it is important to make this environment as conducive to study as possible.

Study spots

You say I'm well read.
Thank you but—
I owe my deep and liberal knowledge
To the 100 watt bulb
in the loo
And not college. *(Margaret Norton)*

If you don't have a quiet study place at home where you can leave your work spread out, can you arrange one? How?

What objects on your work space help you study—a box of file cards, a dictionary, photographs, a collection of shells, a bunch of flowers? Why?

Can you study effectively outdoors?

The association of one place with a particular study activity helps you settle down to study more quickly and also enables you to leave it behind when you finish. You might choose a comfortable chair to read a book, but prefer a computer workstation in the library when organising essay notes.

- If possible, find or create one or two places where you can regularly study—a desk in your bedroom at home, a corner table in a library or a chair in a quiet room at a friend's house. You may be able to screen off a corner of a room or to move a table into one corner of a back-yard workshop.
- Create a work space which includes objects which prompt you to study and is organised according to your needs for space and order. Having your own work space, no matter how small, is much preferable to packing away your papers and books each time after you use them.

Comfort

You concentrate better on studying if you are physically relaxed (but not too relaxed!)—if you are sitting in a comfortable position, with lighting that cuts down eye strain, and without distracting noise.

Are you more comfortable when studying at a table or desk, or when sitting on a couch or bed? Do any of these positions help you study for a sustained period?

If your study places are too warm, too cold or too stuffy, how can you alter this?

What type of noise distracts you? How long can you concentrate fully with 'background' music playing?

Do you know which exercises help you loosen up after a stint at the computer?

Do you have ergonomically appropriate furniture?

- Prevent eye strain by avoiding glare or uneven lighting on your book or work surface. Try to use adequate direct and indirect light or an appropriate desk light. Light the whole room as evenly as possible, and position yourself so that light falls over the shoulder opposite your writing arm to avoid a shadow on your work space. Prop up your book at a constant angle so that your eyes don't have to accommodate to different distances.

- To reduce noise distraction, avoid irregular noise and exciting music, use ear plugs or headphones, or study when your household is at its quietest.
- Experiment with essential oils that can help you concentrate.
- If you are cold, put on an extra layer of clothes, wrap yourself in a blanket, or turn a heater on at a low setting rather than attempting to study in a stuffy overheated room. If the weather is hot, study at the cooler times of day.
- If you use a computer, ensure that the screen is placed so that you avoid eye strain and that you are sitting correctly. Make sure that you look away from the screen frequently and that you get up and loosen up from time to time. This is particularly important if you are using a computer for prolonged periods for a long assignment or if researching on the Internet.
- There is appropriate study furniture available for sale, for example, ergonomic chairs and special word processing tables. Even if you cannot afford these it can be worth your while to check them out and you may then be able to improvise with what you already have available.

■ ■ ■ ■ ■

The questions and suggestions in this chapter have focused on you—because you are central to this book and to what, why and how you learn. Reading and following guidelines which tell you how to make your formal learning more effective is useful only if you adapt these guidelines to your own personality, lifestyle and surroundings.

This above all; to thine own self be true. *(Shakespeare)*

Further reading

Faraday, Ann, 1976, *The dream game*, Harper & Row, New York.

Fossum, Lynn, 1990, *Overcoming anxiety: Effective solutions to a growing problem*, Crisp Publications, California.

Goodacre, Phillip & Follers, Jennifer, 1987, 'Communicating across cultures' in Terry Lovat (ed.), *People, culture and change*, Social Science Press, Wentworth Falls.

Iyengar, B.K.S., 1966, *Light on yoga*, Allen & Unwin, London.

Luce, Gay Gaer, 1973, *Body time: The natural rhythms of the body*, Paladin, Granada Publishing, St Albans, England.

Stanton, Rosemary, 1990, *Health and energy cookbook*, Murdoch Books, Sydney.

Wilson, Paul, 1995, *Instant calm*, Penguin, Ringwood.

CHAPTER 2

PLANNING WHEN AND HOW YOU STUDY

This chapter looks at planning when to study and at how to go about studying and concentrating. It begins with examining your life to determine where study fits in.

All work and no play ...

> It is impossible to enjoy idling thoroughly unless one has plenty of work to do. *(Jerome K. Jerome)*

As a student you are likely to be involved in campus or community activities, socialising, sport, hobbies, personal relationships, domestic chores, childcare or a paid job. These involvements may enhance your learning, for example if you are a keen athlete taking physical education courses, or if you are a parent studying child psychology. Possibly they may conflict with your study—your family may expect you to put their needs first, or your drinking mates might scorn your study.

Learning can be one of the most creative and satisfying pleasures you experience. However, there are inevitably times in your formal learning when you have to make yourself work—when you are not interested in a topic, when you have difficulty with an assignment, or when you have other things on your mind. At these times planning can be useful.

Planning how to spend your time can give you the opportunity to explore the pleasures of using your mind and can help you cope with occasions when it is difficult to study. If it suits you to study according to a timetable, don't make it too ambitious, and don't let it rule your life so that you rarely do anything spontaneously. Any schedule needs to be flexible.

Whether or not you like to plan your time, examining your objectives and workload for a year is important in relation to your reasons for studying (see 'Why are you studying', Chapter 3).

Planning a semester's study

The road to hell is paved with good intentions. *(Western proverb)*

Your objectives

Planning a semester's study involves formulating your objectives for the courses you will take, and drawing up a schedule of work to be done. For each course think about:

- where it fits into the overall objectives of your formal education
- how it is connected with your other courses
- your knowledge of the course content
- your interests or questions concerning the subject area
- skills you want to acquire, and
- grades you hope to achieve.

Your workload

Plan your workload for the semester, taking into account the time you spend in class, listening to tapes or reading course materials, preparing and producing assignments and reports, and reviewing material after a class or when preparing for exams.

One value of planning is that it minimises the stress that usually accompanies last-minute assignment writing or studying for exams. It is all too easy to delude yourself that there is ample time to complete an assignment or to study. Look realistically at your other study commitments for the same period and think about the stages necessary in preparing each assignment. Ideally, also allow 'just in case' time—just in case you have the 'flu in the week you plan to study, just in case your computer crashes, just in case you have an unexpected visit from an old friend when a major essay is due. Give yourself time for the serendipitous pleasure of exploring areas arising from your study but not directly related to your current goals, needs or pressures.

A method to use

Try the following method of planning your semester's study.

- At the beginning of a semester, find out as precisely as possible what work you want to do or are required to do in that period. Do you have exams, major and minor assignments, weekly preparation for tests or classes? Draw up a calendar, or buy and use a year planner—perhaps an appropriate software package—to show at a glance your overall study schedule and other definite commitments.
- For each assignment allow time for:
  - choosing and analysing a question
  - searching for and selecting material (including any field work)
  - researching, collecting and organising material
  - reading and notetaking
  - writing (taping or filming)
  - editing, and
  - reflecting on the finished product.

  Each of these is an activity in its own right and can require a deceptively large amount of time. Writing a report, for example, is not only a final chore to be hastily completed after your practical and field work is complete. If possible, allow more time than you think necessary for each activity.
- Estimate how much time you realistically have to devote to an individual piece of work. This largely determines your approach to the topic, as well as the quality of the end result.
- Allow time prior to each exam or test to revise your work.

Within the framework of your long-term plan, you can also plan for the short term.

Planning your week

'There's lots to do; we have a very busy schedule—
'At 8 o'clock we get up, and then we spend
'From 8 to 9 daydreaming.
'From 9.00 to 9.30 we take our early midmorning nap.
'From 9.30 to 10.30 we dawdle and delay.
'From 10.30 to 11.30 we take our late early morning nap.
'From 11.30 to 12.00 we bide our time and then eat lunch.
'From 1.00 to 2.00 we linger and loiter.

'From 2.00 to 2.30 we take our early afternoon nap.

'From 2.30 to 3.30 we put off for tomorrow what we could have done today.

'From 3.30 to 4.00 we take our early late afternoon nap,

'From 4.00 to 5.00 we loaf and lounge until dinner.

'From 6.00 to 7.00 we dilly-dally.

'From 7.00 to 8.00 we take our early evening nap, and then for an hour before we go to bed at 9.00 we waste time.

'As you can see, that leaves almost no time for brooding, lagging, plodding, or procrastinating, and if we stopped to think or laugh, we'd never get nothing done.' *(Norton Juster)*

To draw up a short-term study plan requires some knowledge of your lifestyle and of yourself as a learner, such as whether you often write with ease, or when during the day you are likely to be most alert mentally. Do you work best in bursts of intense activity for several days or weeks, with brief periods of relaxation in between; or do you prefer a regular daily or weekly work session?

Instead of planning for a week you may prefer to plan for a several days or a month. If you find it difficult to keep to a plan, try setting aside and using a regular time each day or week for concentrated study, combined with making and using a list of 'things to do'. This strategy can ease the worry of apparently having a lot of work and no time in which to do it. Use some of the suggestions in this chapter when your workload overwhelms you.

If you haven't thought much about how you spend your time, the following exercise will make you more aware of this. As it concerns a short period, the exercise is only an indicator of your current activities. But it can help you realise what priority study has in your life, how other activities can help or hinder your study, and where your time 'vanishes' to.

Time is like money. If you have lots of it to spare, you have more choice about how you spend it. If it is in short supply, knowing where it has gone can help you budget for the future. *(Anon.)*

1 Examine how you spend your time

For several days or a week, preferably near the beginning of semester or term, keep a detailed timetable of how you honestly spend your time. Record how much time is occupied by:

- formal required class activities at set times
- required course activities
- independent or private study
- paid or unpaid employment
- relaxing alone and/or socialising
- exercise and active recreation
- domestic chores and family activities

- travelling, and
- sleeping and eating.

Note particularly any activities which take up a lot of time. Look for time traps, such as watching TV or surfing the Net. Indicate the times during your private study when you concentrated at your best. Make sure your record is accurate—recording three hours' work on statistics is misleading if you spent part of that three hours on the 'phone chatting to a friend, shuffling desktop files, or watering the garden.

At the end of the week, estimate the number of hours you spent in each of the areas listed above, and ask yourself the following questions about your data.

Were there times when I studied more effectively, such as early in the morning or when I had the entire day to study? Why?

Did I work more effectively in some places than others, for example, in the library or at home? Why?

How did the amount of time I spent in required activities compare with the time I spent on independent study out of class?

Did I have a particularly heavy workload during this week?

Did I usually work more effectively in short periods and then lose my concentration, or did it take me a while to settle into study so that I needed longer periods for serious work?

Is my study connected with any of my other activities?

Did I prepare myself for long periods of serious study? How? Was this effective? Did I relax afterwards?

2 Give study the priority you want it to have in your life

Now that you have some data on how you spent a few days or a week, are you happy with how you spent your time? Would you like to make any changes? If so ...

- List four activities which take a lot of time and energy in your life at present. List four activities which you think *should* take the most time and energy, and four on which you *would like* to spend the most time and energy.
- Ask yourself if you spend enough time studying effectively. Do your non-academic activities and interests leave you sufficient time and energy for formal learning, and do they increase or decrease your satisfaction with that learning?
- If other involvements prevent you from learning as well as you would like, consider limiting these involvements, reducing the number of courses you are taking, or reducing the time and effort you put into a course.

- If there is a significant difference between your current involvements and those you feel you should or would like to have, consider changing your priorities. Think about why you are at university or college, and how important your formal learning is to you.

3 Map out next week's work
Take into account your findings and do the following:

- look at your long-term calendar and see what work is due soon
- chart in your short-term formal study commitments, such as giving a seminar paper or responding to a discussion list
- mark in any informal commitments connected with your study, such as an appointment with your tutor
- indicate your other commitments
- write out a list of what you want to accomplish during the week, and when.

    Then:

- plan to study when you are usually able to concentrate most effectively
- plan relaxation and social activities so that they complement your studies, and
- set aside time at the end of each day's study to review your work.

At the end of the second week, think back on how your week has resembled your plan. Don't expect to keep absolutely to your schedule—instead, examine why you did not. If you find you are spending lots of time glued to a computer screen, take time to reflect on whether this time is directed to your purpose at hand. Remember that working at a computer can be very addictive. If you are from a background in which the needs of your extended family network or your domestic responsibilities take precedence and you frequently find it difficult to meet the deadlines placed on you by the institution, discuss this with your teachers and with an adviser.

> Efficiency concerns the best ways of doing an assigned job. Effectiveness, on the other hand, concerns the best use of time—which may or may not include doing the particular job in question. *(Edwin C. Bliss)*

■ ■ ■ ■ ■

Both your long-term and short-term study plans need to combine flexibility and a commitment to realistic goals. You can best use your plans by reviewing them several times during a semester. Adjust them according to your current study needs and purposes, and to take account of other changes in your life. At the beginning of a course you need to explore and familiarise yourself with the topics and areas to be covered and the language used, so you probably spend a high proportion of study time in research and in classes. Half-way through a course you are likely to be relating new materials to what you have already learned, and to be planning and producing written work as well as attending classes and doing research. Near the end of a course you spend your time reflecting on and reviewing what you have learnt, and are probably involved in completing major assignments and preparing for exams.

Planning when to study is a beginning. To make full use of the time you have set aside, also think about how to study.

Concentrating while you study

'How can you go on talking so quietly, head downwards?' Alice asked, as she dragged him out by the feet, and laid him in a heap on the bank.

The Knight looked surprised at the question. 'What does it matter where my body happens to be?' he said. 'My mind goes on working all the same.' *(Lewis Carroll)*

Concentrating is not always something you have to work at—if you really want to know or do something you can concentrate easily, possibly for a long time. When concentrating fully you are so absorbed in what you are doing that you are unaware of time passing or of what is going on around you. Watch a small child building a sand castle, or two friends involved in an intense debate.

However, if you are required to learn about a topic which doesn't particularly interest you, or to study for a purpose which doesn't coincide with yours, or if you have to study at times or in ways which are difficult for you—then you have to make an effort to focus and sustain your concentration. Have you ever noticed that during a lecture many of the audience suddenly become restless, or that shortly before the end of a lecture many people change position, look at their watches and prepare to leave? The length of time for which you can concentrate fully depends on factors such as your enthusiasm for what you are doing, your skill at a particular task, your emotional and physical state, and your surroundings at the time.

You don't have to assume the position of a Zen Buddhist or a Rodin's Thinker or sit at a desk with pen in hand to concentrate. Why not let your ideas sort themselves out while you surf, watch the sunset, walk, or travel to college? When you do read and write, concentrating is not simply reading every word on a page or putting lots of words onto paper or a computer screen. Full concentration involves actively questioning and critically evaluating your material and integrating some of it into what you already know. This questioning, evaluating, and integrating helps you understand what you read and organise what you write; it also helps you when you share your ideas and knowledge with others.

This section suggests a step by step process for concentrating more effectively in study sessions of at least an hour. These sessions might include reading, notetaking, writing, working on a spreadsheet, organising or editing material, or listening to tapes. Concentration during class or while working with other people involves similar principles.

Experience as a mother has taught me a lot. Gone are the days of spending uninterrupted hours writing an essay or compiling a report. I'm lucky if I get half an hour now. But this maternal conditioning has its advantages. I'm now capable of making the maximum use of the time that is available and then switching off when family demands become pressing. Learning to use the available time to maximum advantage is one of the main secrets to success of the part-time student mother. *(Vivienne)*

Have you consciously thought about your study habits—when, where and how you prefer to study? How do you settle down for a study session? For how long can you concentrate fully? What do you do when you find it difficult to concentrate? There will be times when you can only concentrate for short periods, or when you can't concentrate at all.

However, you can concentrate for longer periods and more effectively if you know how to cope with distractions which can arise at certain points in your study. While you are warming up or preparing for concentrated study you might be prone to procrastination, and your mind could be partly elsewhere. After you have been concentrating intensely for a short time, you might suddenly become impatient with your task, be unable to capture a particular thought or think through a specific problem clearly, and you might begin to feel stiff from sitting still. After sustained concentrated work, you feel less mentally alert when you are reaching the end of your concentration span for a particular subject. When you can no longer concentrate at all, outside thoughts or events intrude and you feel generally tired.

Warming up

Demanding physical exercise requires a warm-up session; so does strenuous mental exercise and intense study. You can begin this mental warm-up during your previous activity. When travelling to the library, you can plan what you will research; while doing household chores you can mull over ideas for an essay; while finishing a task, visualise yourself sitting down at your desk with a hot drink and beginning to study. When you actually sit down at your study place, deliberately preparing your mind for study can motivate you, help eliminate conflict or anxieties from your mind, focus your thoughts on the task at hand, and increase your ability to understand what you learn so that you remember it more easily (see 'How you learn to remember', Chapter 5).

If you have difficulty settling down to study, the following suggestions may help.

1 Consider how you feel emotionally and physically. If you feel good, direct this energy to learning. If you are definitely not in the state of mind for studying, decide if you need to study at this particular time. If you don't, plan another specific time to work. If you do, use techniques that help you set your problems aside (see 'Emotions', Chapter 1). Try a brief energetic walk, a run around the block, a cup of tea, or a short chat with a friend.

2 Seat yourself comfortably, with everything you need at hand—books, blank papers, a drink, computer disks, or lecture notes (see 'Where you study', Chapter 1).

3 Decide on your time limits for this study session. Take into account your non-study commitments, then set a minimum study time to become involved in your subject. Set a maximum time, so you don't feel overwhelmed by apparently endless work and so you can focus your energy fully. Don't make these times so inflexible that you feel you must stop work precisely at the time planned. Plan to reward yourself after you have completed your study by doing something you particularly enjoy—go to the beach, visit a friend, watch a special TV program or prepare your favourite snack.

4 Decide what to study while your mind is fresh. Will you start with the subject or activity you find easiest? Will you tackle an assignment that has been worrying you or which you have been intending to do for a long time?

Think about the study activities you have to choose from. You might, for example:

- read for a tutorial paper or an essay
- find and bookmark an appropriate Web site
- edit the final draft of an assignment
- write the first draft of an assignment, a lab report, a short story or a journal entry
- prepare an annotated bibliography or illustrations for an assignment
- make a tape recording
- listen to a radio program or a lecture tape, or
- interpret information from a graph.

Set yourself a goal to accomplish. If you have a large task, planning to tackle it one section at a time makes it easier.

5 Begin your study with a *brief* warm-up task which helps you concentrate. Use this task only if it is necessary—not if it is a form of procrastination.

- Do some routine tasks which are part of the subject, such as filing lecture notes or compiling a list of important vocabulary.
- Revise previous work in the area, for example, summarise notes, or write comments on a discussion. This revision brings ideas to the

front of your mind, and can give you a sense of achievement if you are overwhelmed by the study before you.

- Foreshadow a topic by asking yourself 'Why am I studying this topic?' 'To whom do I want to communicate my ideas?' For example, are you studying to clarify ideas for your own benefit, or to prepare for a discussion group? Brainstorm your topic by jotting down as many ideas on it as possible—don't worry about the order of these ideas or how far-fetched they seem. Fill your mind with the subject.
- Preview a book you will use (see 'Previewing', Chapter 9), or read a section of the book and try to identify the central idea (see 'Reading for the argument or controlling focus', Chapter 9).

If you still have trouble concentrating, ask yourself why and what you can do about it. What must you change to help you concentrate better? (Try Chapter 1 for suggestions on coping with problems such as tension or a noisy study place.)

Sustaining your concentration

'Fan her head!' the Red Queen anxiously interrupted. 'She'll be feverish after so much thinking.' *(Lewis Carroll)*

Some people study mostly in short, intense bursts with frequent breaks in between; others need to study for long periods to become fully immersed in their task. Your concentration span also varies for different activities and how involved you are in what you are doing.

- When studying intensely, you occasionally become aware you are distracted by something and feel impatient with your work. Set yourself another five minutes in which to work. If your impatience still persists, give in to it. After the five minutes, take a short break while you physically loosen up—stand up and stretch, walk around, consciously relax. Leave your study spot for five minutes or so—get a drink, glance through a newspaper, organise your desk. Don't take a break for too long or you may require another warm-up.
- When you have been studying for a long time so that your concentration is diminishing and can't be rejuvenated by a short break, you need to recharge mentally. Re-motivate yourself by reviewing the material you have just covered and trying to get an overall picture of it. This often gives you a feeling of achievement as well as reminding you why you are studying a particular topic. Look ahead at what you intend to do next. Preview the rest of the book or chapter. Jot down or tape record ideas for the next section of an assignment. Switch to another subject and work on that until it becomes stale, then return to your first subject or go on to a third.

Losing concentration

Try to recognise when you can't concentrate any further. There is no point in believing you are studying when you are simply staring at the words on a page, when you repeatedly can't find the words you want, or when your mind is far away.

- When you feel you are losing concentration, review what you have been studying. If your task is part of a large piece of work, reflect on where the part fits into the whole and which part you will tackle next.
- Decide when you will study again—in an hour's time, the next morning, a day later.
- Then stop studying and relax. Reward yourself—enjoy that special reward you promised yourself earlier.

I do not happen to be a believer in the cliché that 'Virtue is its own reward.' As far as I am concerned, the reward for virtue should be at least a chocolate sundae, and preferably a cruise to the Bahamas. *(Barbara Sher)*

■ ■ ■ ■ ■

It takes time and practice to plan when to study and to learn how to concentrate fully so that you enjoy your formal learning and accomplish what you set out to do. It takes time and practice to become aware of and create your own study patterns and to discover the concentration techniques that you find most helpful. The alternative to spending this time planning when and how to study is to study when others expect you to or just to bumble along as you always have. Being in control of when and how you study is crucial to learning independently.

Further reading

Covey, S.R., 1990, *The 7 habits of highly effective people*, Simon and Schuster, New York.

Haynes, M.E., 1987, *Personal time management*, Crisp Publications, California.

Horn, Sam, 1991, *Concentration! How to focus for success*, Crisp Publications, California.

Pollar, O., 1992, *Organising your work space: A guide to personal productivity*, Crisp Publications, California.

CHAPTER 3

BECOMING AN INDEPENDENT STUDENT

It is in the first year that students are most likely to form lasting outlooks, values and patterns of behaviour with respect to higher education and lifelong learning. *(Craig McInnis)*

Starting university or college can be bewildering as well as stimulating. In whatever discipline you are studying and whether your study is full-time or part-time, internal or at a distance, face-to-face or online, the adjustments you have to make are considerable; and you will be faced with the challenge of becoming part of a new culture and of learning independently. You are likely to spend the first couple of weeks mostly in organising your timetable and in finding your way round campus and through administrative requirements. Hopefully you can do most of these things during an orientation period before classes start. You also begin to recognise faces among staff and students, and may discover some of the social activities that can be part of a tertiary student's life.

> This chapter begins by examining some features of tertiary institutions and looks at adapting to independent study within formal institutions—thinking about why you are studying, deciding what to study, handling difficult situations, making contact with teachers and other students, and combining study with other work.

Tertiary institutions and you

The modern university has at least six distinct functions. It conserves knowledge, through library holdings and scholarship. It transmits knowledge by guiding the learning of students through community education programs. It advances knowledge through basic research. It applies knowledge by applied research and consultancy. It refines knowledge through critical review and scholarship. It also fulfils the role of certifying standards of entry to a range of professions having different levels of commitment to intellectual endeavour. *(Ian Lowe)*

Universities and colleges have a mystique which shapes your expectations of them. *One* common image is that these institutions have little to do with the 'real' world, that they are full of professors who expound esoteric theories and young students who seem to spend more time playing than working. A *second* and somewhat contradictory image is that of superior training institutions where doctors, lawyers, architects, engineers, teachers and the like are prepared for their professions. A *third* image is of a community of scholars who dwell in the hallowed halls of higher learning, of professors who pursue ultimate truths and new scientific revelations and impart their insights to highly intelligent students. A *fourth* image which some staff and students come to hold is that:

> ... universities have become huge bureaucracies with an academic mind and no heart, careless and ignorant about students and their intellectual needs, organised by managers and managerial professors absorbed in their own pursuits, giving service to the existing social order and dispensing its conventional wisdom, bereft of a philosophy and the social imagination to create a new and compelling conception of their own future. *(Harold Taylor)*

If you enter university or college with high expectations, this fourth image may be disillusioning. On the other hand, it can help dispel the 'awesome' mystique embodied in the second and third images, and can help you realise that sometimes when you are having study problems the causes may not lie solely with you.

There is an ongoing debate about the role tertiary institutions should have in the modern world. For example, there are those who argue for an intellectual role which has intrinsic value; and there are arguments that higher education should 'sell' knowledge and respond to the market economy and consumer demands. At various times there are attempts to 'streamline' and 'rationalise' higher education and the level of funding varies accordingly. Recently, government funding for higher education has been reduced significantly and a user-pays approach has become increasingly prevalent. These changes will have a direct impact on your studies, for example, if you have fees to pay, if severe budget cuts mean that your teachers are not so readily available to give you individual help, or if there are fewer tutorials and lectures and you are thus left more on your own to learn.

It is virtually impossible to predict the future of universities but they will be very different from universities today. Already universities and colleges have lost their traditional monopoly on post-compulsory education. An increasing number of partnerships are being formed between universities and private providers, on both a national and global scale. With globalisation and the spread of electronic technology, a new and *fifth* image of the university is fast emerging in which learning is more flexible. Students can enrol at more than one institution, and students with Internet access take their courses online at places and times that are most suitable for them, while teachers work from their office (or home) with students.

Universities and colleges can be intellectually exciting places, but are also bureaucratic institutions like any other large workplace. Academics are people with a variety of concerns which can include highly specialised research, a lively curiosity about things of the mind and the world in general, and an involvement with teaching; but like other people, they have their share of human bias and ignorance. Students usually manifest interest in learning, but otherwise are impossible to categorise. Students of higher education are culturally diverse, at least on larger campuses, with a wide range of ages, places of living, ethnic and socio-economic backgrounds. Within this diversity you are likely to find others who share your background, world view, values, attitudes, and expectations. Interacting with students from these diverse cultural backgrounds can be a learning process both within and outside the classroom, if you remain open and flexible.

> Age, sex, socio-economic background and ethnicity contribute to and shape students' expectations of university, their adjustment to being university students, and ultimately their overall teaching and learning experience and satisfaction with it. *(Craig McInnis)*

Learning in different disciplines

At a local level, tertiary institutions at present are usually divided into faculties, departments or schools, each representing a body or closely related bodies of knowledge called 'disciplines'. Some of these disciplines provide professional training and some do not. Some institutions separate—and it seems at times even segregate—the disciplines into departments which teach what are considered to be 'subjects' in their own right. Each apparently discrete area of knowledge has an institutional hierarchy with professors, senior and junior academics, and senior (postgraduate) and junior (undergraduate) students. What constitutes these disciplines is always open to question and change, and new disciplines are always struggling for a foothold.

Each discipline or body of knowledge is a culture in its own right with its own discourse—its own language and vocabulary and its own methodologies for choosing, analysing, critiquing, interpreting, presenting and using this knowledge. In some institutions there are opportunities for interdisciplinary or multidisciplinary study, but this has been the exception rather than the rule. Thus, when you start tertiary study you enter not only the overall culture of the institution but the culture of the discipline in which you will study. As you progress through your studies you learn the current culture of your discipline through instruction in the content—through immersion in it. Sometimes you get explicit instruction in the nature of the discourse— its language and methodology. Within disciplines where there is conflict about what constitutes 'knowledge', there may be more than one appropriate methodology or language. And at times it may be confusing if you find that the approach to knowledge in one discipline is different from the approach in another. Some students, for example, do very well when asked to write in one discipline but not so well when they use the same approach in another.

In your first year you are not expected to be highly knowledgeable in your chosen field or to be familiar with the language or method of the field; this is part of what you are at college or university to learn. The way you approached a discipline area in secondary school or elsewhere may no longer be applicable at tertiary level. Take nothing for granted and be prepared to ask. If you are studying entirely at a distance or online these divisions between disciplines may not be so apparent to you. You will need to be especially vigilant in identifying what is expected in different disciplines.

> ... my time is exclusively occupied with study. It's a very bewildering matter to get educated in five branches at once.

> 'The test of true scholarship,' says Chemistry Professor, 'is painstaking passion for detail.'

> 'Be careful not to keep your eyes glued to detail,' says History Professor. 'Stand far enough away to get a perspective of the whole.'

> You can see with what nicety we have to trim our sails between chemistry and history. (*Jean Webster*)

You may find your cultural and social background at odds with the expectations of your discipline (see 'Your cultural and social self', Chapter 1). Understanding what is expected in learning and displaying your knowledge is an aspect of becoming familiar with the field in which you have chosen to study, for example, whether or not there is a strong emphasis on problem solving or critical thinking.

Thinking critically

Critical thinking is a lived activity, not an abstract academic pastime. It is something we do, though its frequency, and the credibility we grant it, vary from person to person ... the ability to think critically is crucial to understanding our personal relationships, envisioning alternative and more productive ways of organising the workplace, and becoming politically literate. *(Stephen Brookfield)*

Critical thinking, with its debates and arguments, is central to university culture. You may be unaccustomed outside university to participating in debates about ideas, or may associate 'argument' with unpleasant conflict. If so, it can be exciting to be in a milieu where debates about ideas are always on the agenda somewhere and where people can disagree strongly yet remain friendly. The topics or questions you discuss in your formal learning may be presented to you from only one world view, or you may be confronted with readings and ideas on a topic from many different views. When you enter into a debate on a topic you too become part of this ongoing dialogue—even if you are a student who is a novice in the content and method of debate, you are still part of that dialogue. When you enter the discussion you do so with your particular view of the world and your particular position on the topic. And our world views contain inherent contradictions, even though we may think they are coherent. A university education that focuses on critical thinking is designed to encourage you to identify and question your world view with its values and assumptions and contradictions, to be open to other views, to develop a position on topics under discussion and to construct cogent arguments in both your writing and your discussions.

When anyone presents an argument, in fact when anyone communicates or even thinks at all, he/she does so from within a world view. This world view is a set of assumptions about the world, along with values, attitudes, standards and so on. Some of these world views are rigid and closed. ... Other world views are open and flexible, valuing tolerance of other people's positions, though still striving for coherence. *(Paul Jewell)*

Many of your teachers at university will use terms such as 'criticism', 'argument', 'logic', and you may be told to 'be more critical in your approach' or to 'argue your case'. The definition of critical thinking used in this book is 'reasonable, reflective thinking that is focused on what to believe or do'.[1] Some of the fundamental elements of critical thinking that are pertinent to your studies are outlined below.

- Critical thinking involves the presentation of *arguments* to persuade or influence others. Academic arguments have two parts: a thesis, and reasons or premises to support the thesis. In your reading and listening it is important that you learn to identify the thesis and supporting parts of an argument, and that when you write persuasive essays you present an argument.
- Critical thinking involves *debate* and negotiating positions, resolving conflict and dealing with difference and oppositions.
- Critical thinking involves *reflection*. Thus, every time you reflect on and question what you do or think in your life and studies you are thinking critically. The questions you ask in your reflection are crucial to critical thinking.
- Although critical thinking is partly something we all do privately, it is also a *communicative* activity. In a sense, every time we are involved with others in a debate or discussion with differing opinions we are involved in critical thinking if we are prepared to question what we believe or are told. Similarly, every time we read and question material that presents us with different arguments on a topic we are involved in critical thinking.
- Critical thinking has as its outcome making a decision and *acting* on what you have come to think and believe.
- Critical thinking involves *emotion* as well as reason and rationality.

Asking critical questions about our previously accepted values, ideas and behaviours is anxiety-producing. We may feel fearful of the consequences that might arise from contemplating alternatives to our current ways of thinking and living; resistance, resentment, and confusion are evident at various stages in the critical thinking process. But we also feel joy, release, relief, and exhilaration as we break through to new ways of looking at our personal, work, and political worlds. *(Stephen Brookfield)*

The ability to think critically is a generic skill that you are expected to acquire in your undergraduate education and transfer to your everyday life and your future or current work. Although critical thinking is highly valued by most academics, few of your teachers will systematically and explicitly help you develop critical thinking skills and attitudes. Indeed, definitions of what it means to think critically will vary from discipline to discipline and in some cases from teacher to teacher within a discipline. You might usefully undertake one of the self-contained critical reasoning courses which are usually offered through the discipline of philosophy. However, you also need to develop your critical thinking skills in conjunction with your other learning skills—particularly your reading, listening, writing and discussion—and within the disciplinary context you are studying.

Developing skills and attitudes

In the wake of discussions in higher education on the quality of teaching and learning, universities have recently begun anew to clarify their purposes and the strategies by which they achieve these. An important component of this has been to describe the disciplinary knowledge and skills, job related skills (in vocational courses) and the generic skills, attributes and attitudes students are expected to acquire during their studies. Many universities, in their handbooks or on their home page on the Internet, have published lists of the desired qualities they wish their graduates to have acquired. You may find it useful to check if your university has such a list, and to use it as a checklist or benchmark for your own skill development throughout your studies.

The generic skills may include some or all of the following: learning independently, thinking critically, planning and organising, problem solving, communicating effectively in writing and orally, working with others and in teams, computer literacy, numeracy, and collecting, analysing and organising ideas and information. Some of the skills are higher order intellectual skills, while others are more technical skills. The skills are considered 'generic' because it is argued that in higher education they should be developed in all students in all disciplines, and that they can be transferred to a wide range of contexts in students' current or future work and learning. While there is debate about whether such skills are generic or context-specific, it is intended that you should develop these skills throughout your formal study and continue to develop and use them throughout your life.

Choices and decisions

'Would you tell me, please, which way I ought to go from here?'
'That depends a good deal on where you want to get to,' said the Cat.
'I don't much care where —' said Alice.
'Then it doesn't matter which way you go,' said the Cat.
'—so long as I get somewhere,' Alice added as an explanation.
'Oh, you're sure to do that,' said the Cat, 'if you only walk long enough.' *(Lewis Carroll)*

Your main experience of formal education may have been recent or in an education system of one or more decades ago. It might have been in the structured environment of compulsory schooling where from your first day at school the Education department and the teachers were responsible for directing what, when, how and where you learnt, and where the emphasis was on remembering and reproducing information correctly. You may have attended a private school such as a single-sex denominational school, or a boarding school which structured your study and daily life; or you may have gone to an alternative school where ostensibly you were free to learn what and when you liked. Your early learning may have been in a country where questioning a teacher's authority or thinking critically was not acceptable.

In tertiary education you make many decisions about why, what, when, how and where you learn. Unless you were lucky enough to have teachers and schools that allowed you to develop your abilities for learning independently, this may be your first experience of making such decisions about your formal education.

As mentioned earlier, your choice of when and where to study is becoming increasingly flexible. Universities are becoming more 'mobile' with multiple sites (satellite campuses), flexible courses, summer semesters and new teaching technologies. The rapid expansion of courses online now makes it possible for students with Internet access to study from an institution overseas, interstate or outside their immediate neighbourhood. In some cases, to study in a discipline of your choice you may decide to study at a university outside your locale. It will become increasingly important for students to examine their purposes for studying and to evaluate the appropriateness of the institution in meeting these purposes.

> Imagine learning with peers, expertise, and resources that are available whenever you want or need them. These 'class mates' are from Moscow and Mexico City, New York and Hong Kong, Vancouver and Sydney—from urban centers and rural and remote areas. And they, like you, never need to leave home. You are all learning together not in a place in the ordinary sense but in a shared space, a 'cyberspace', using network systems that connect people all over the globe. Your learning network 'classroom' is anywhere that you have a personal computer, a modem, and a telephone line, satellite dish or radio link. Dialing into the network turns your computer screen into a window on the world of learning. (*Linda Harasim*)

Why are you studying?

> Even the raven started out in human form, and he fumbled blindly, and his actions were haphazard until it was revealed to him who he was and what his purpose was. *(Peter Hoeg)*

You make your first choice when you decide whether or not to go to university or college. After secondary school, it should be your purposes which determine whether part of your learning takes place within the formal education system. Often there are pressures which seem to give you little choice, but the choice is frequently there if you are aware of it. Why have you chosen to further your education? Because your parents want you to, you can't find a job, you want to become an engineer, you like discovering new ideas, or you think campus life will be fun? If you are returning to study after some years away from it, why?

Research on motivations for studying has identified four broad clusters of reasons which are categorised as orientations to study: vocational, or concern about future employment; academic, or a desire for continuing education; personal, or developing as a person; and social, or enjoying the freedom of university life. Within these four categories some students had an 'intrinsic' interest in study, that is, in learning for its own sake, and some an 'extrinsic' interest, that is, in education as a means to an end.[2]

Why you are studying will directly influence how you learn. Thinking about and identifying your reasons for studying overall and for taking individual courses can give you useful insights into how you approach your work. It can also help you cope with the pressures that you face from peers or family who think that as a student you are working too hard or not hard enough. You have your own reasons for studying and as an adult you can make your own choices, but at times you will have to justify these choices to others. Your reasons for studying one course may be different from your reasons for studying another—one may be a prerequisite in an area you don't like and your aim may be just to pass at the required level, while another course may be so intrinsically interesting to you at a personal level that you give it a lot of time and do very well in it.

> Most people let themselves be pushed by chance or other people's expectations into environments of which they make the best, rather than into those which meet their inner needs. *(Michael Deakin)*

What and how will you study?

When you apply for tertiary study you indicate in which discipline areas you wish to study. And your choices are directed by your interests, your previous studies, and by the availability of places in your chosen area. Many students enter tertiary study with a clear idea of what they want to study, many start out on one track and then change to another. Some institutions are flexible and allow for these changes and others do not. If you have not been admitted to your first choice of discipline, it is up to you to accept this or to find out what you need to do in order to study your first choice at a later time. It may not be possible for you to study in your preferred discipline, either because of educational factors external to you such as quotas or the need to have a high grade point average, or because of personal factors beyond your control, such as where you live or the lack of childcare. In such cases you need to decide how important it is to you to pursue that area and to plan and make changes accordingly.

With the increasing flexibility now available you also decide whether to study full-time or part-time, internally and/or at a distance, face-to-face and/or online. For example, you may have the choice of mixing internal and distance or online courses, and you may be able to take some courses from another institution. You might include a semester of part-time study if you find yourself short of money and need to work for a while.

If it is more convenient or enjoyable for you and if you can afford it, consider your options for more flexible learning by studying part-time or taking some or all of your courses off-campus or online. You can benefit from being a part-time student taking only one or two courses at a time, especially if you have a lot of other demands on your time or have been away from study for a while. And if you are a metropolitan student, taking one or two external courses in a mostly on-campus program can give you flexibility in combining study and work. If you are a wholly external student, your choice of courses may be more restricted than for internal students. Seek information on courses as early as possible, so you can enrol in time for course material to be sent to you.

Choosing courses

Deciding which courses to take depends on why you are studying. Your choice is likely to be influenced by administrative and academic requirements such as prerequisite subjects or quotas on course intakes. In some situations you will have little choice, such as in a highly structured discipline with many required courses, or when confronted with yet another set of rules and regulations. Even so, you should be the one to decide whether to take that particular area, or whether complying with a particular rule or regulation helps you towards your long-term aims.

To help decide on your courses, consult as many sources as possible. Look through the official handbooks and read any student surveys or guides to courses and teachers. Remember that most printed handbooks and guides go to press six to nine months before a course starts, so any information they give may be out of date. Check to see if the university has informative Web pages for its courses and programs, but make sure that you check when this material was last updated. For recent information on courses, talk with (or e-mail) staff such as departmental heads, deans, academic advisers and counsellors.

If the institution in which you are enrolled does not offer a course on a subject you would like to study, ask a staff member in a related subject area if there is some other way you can undertake this study. For example, can you pursue it through an independent study contract (see 'Pursuing your questions', Chapter 4) or through another institution, perhaps online? For courses which interest you, find out who organises and teaches in them, and look for students who have taken them. Talk to (or e-mail) these staff and students to find up-to-date and detailed information on the aims and content of courses, on the likely workload for preparation and assignments, on assessment methods, and on books or materials you are expected to buy. Students who have previously studied the course will also have opinions about the teachers in the course. For online courses, check to see if there is a sample module of the course you can work through or a discussion list you can access to ask your questions. Make contact with the coordinator by e-mail, and check to see if the unit provides opportunities for interaction with the tutor and other students. For some courses materials are freely available so that you can audit the course and only need enrol formally if you want to be assessed to gain credit. Attend any pre-course orientation activities and do any recommended preliminary work. If you can, find out what is expected of you in the first couple of weeks of a course and start on this.

If you are taking several courses, try to calculate your total workload and plan a weekly timetable based on any requirements such as attending lectures or seminars (see 'Planning a semester's study', Chapter 2). See if the unit materials indicate how much time an 'average' student should spend each week in both formal and private study. If you have a choice of times and teachers, decide which classes to attend. The combination of courses you planned may be impossible because of timetable clashes or difficult because of a high combined workload. These difficulties can occur even for popular or required combinations of courses, so if you still want to take all these courses, check with the organisers if alternative arrangements can be made.

Unless your selection of courses is very clear, if possible delay your final choices until the end of the first or second week of teaching. This gives you a chance to find first-hand information on the courses which attract you, and to meet some of the teaching staff and students. You can't know all there is to know about a course at this stage, but you can check preliminary information against your own experience in the course.

Choosing teachers

Learning grows and develops by the dialogue of teacher and student, becoming sometimes greater than anything an individual, however brilliant, could produce. *(F.R. Leavis)*

Where you have a choice of teachers, sit in on their classes, read any handouts they write, and contact them personally. If a good student guide to courses is available consult this as well as talking to other students about the courses. Look for a course organiser who clearly sets out objectives, organisation, content, workload and assessment for a course and who is open to your comments and questions. Select teachers who know their subject, stimulate your enthusiasm, encourage you to follow your own interests and are willing to help you improve and extend your skills in studying. A good teacher whose subject areas are only broadly related to your interests can help you follow these interests better than a poor teacher whose interests coincide closely with yours. A skilled teacher whose ideology differs significantly from your own may challenge you to suspend your customary world view. How well you learn with a particular teacher also depends on how your personalities interact. The lecturer you listen to for several weeks or the teacher with whom you work for a whole course is important to your learning. If possible be prepared to change courses or teachers if, after a fair trial, you find you are not learning as much as you would like.

Choosing technology

No two people mean the same thing by computer literacy. Ten years ago computer literacy meant teaching kids BASIC to do their own programming. Then it meant desktop publishing. Then it meant multimedia. Now it means cruising around in cyberspace. Next year it will mean something else that requires updates and enhancements, faster chips, new programs and for sure spending more money. Computer literacy is a commercial fashion, not a specific skill, let alone a subject matter. If computer literacy does not include material on what computers can't do and shouldn't do, it is advertising, not education. *(Theodore Roszak)*

Students are increasingly using a range of technology such as facsimile machines, voicemail, graphics calculators and computers for presenting work and communicating with their tutors and other students.

Computers are becoming essential tools for study, at the very least for word processing assignments. There is a wide range of word processing packages available and you need to determine which is most appropriate given the computer system you use. The most limited use of a word processing package is to use it as you would a typewriter, to input the final draft of an assignment before you hand it in. In some instances students give the final draft of an assignment to a typist who does the final typing and spell check for them.

Some universities require that students own their own personal computer, while others provide extensive computer labs for students who cannot afford the latest technology or whose system is not compatible with what is required. Most universities have a computing centre where students can go for advice on the options, and some provide interest-free loans to enable students to buy their own computers. Most universities provide support classes to upgrade student computer literacy and some have computer literacy as a prerequisite for graduation. As secondary schools increasingly provide opportunities and facilities for students to become computer literate, there will be less demand for basic computing skills courses at university level. Indeed, it is mostly the younger high school leaver students who are familiar and comfortable with the new technologies, and often they are the ones teaching their teachers and peers to operate the new medium.

You might have to buy or lease a computer if you don't have one already, and if you want to establish an electronic connection to a campus you will usually have to pay for any online costs. Because computers are so rapidly outdated, carry out some consumer research to work out exactly what you want. Avoid believing that you must have the very latest bells and whistles, but be aware that you need sufficient speed and power to access services without frustrating delays. Seriously consider buying secondhand after seeking appropriate advice, especially if you have limited financial resources.

How you spend your time

The work pattern was one of alternate bouts of intense labour and of idleness, wherever men [*sic*] were in control of their own working lives … The pattern exists among some self employed—artists, writers, small farmers, and perhaps also with students—today and provokes the question whether it is not a 'natural' human work rhythm. *(E.P. Thompson)*

You largely decide on your study timetable—and you may be surprised at how much work is involved in being a serious tertiary student. The time you are expected to spend in formal class contact, face-to-face or online, varies as does the amount of time you will need to spend on a course overall. For example, fine arts or architecture students usually spend much more time in classes than humanities or social science students, while courses without a large component of practical work usually require more time outside class for research, writing and preparation. Whether or not you attend a class, read a book or hand in an assignment early depends on your enthusiasm for a subject, your desire to pass a course at a particular standard and your response to teachers and courses. Some teachers and courses are more flexible about these matters than others.

Except for formal class time such as lectures, discussion groups and laboratory sessions, you usually decide whether to access library services during the day or at home in the evening, to sit in the cafeteria or the local student pub talking to friends, to work at a job or be with your family. Hopefully you will have time to explore both social and academic student life, although this can be difficult if you are studying part-time or at a distance. Universities or colleges are more than institutions with collections of courses, and being a part of campus life can be a lot of fun (see Chapter 2, 'Planning when and how you study').

If you are studying online or at a distance you have more flexibility in combining study with the rest of your life. In such cases you need to be particularly careful in setting priorities and making certain that you give study the priority in your life that you wish it to have. (See Chapter 2 for ideas on how to go about this.)

If you are a student with a learning disability, your studies may be more time-consuming than those of other students. It is helpful if well in advance of semester you can get to know the campus and any equity support staff. If necessary, find out about parking arrangements; about any technical equipment such as voice-activated word processors or text-enlarged computers; and about services such as library assistance (with online searches and photocopying) or such as notetaking in lectures for students with writing difficulties. Check if there are alternative means of assessment which might be helpful, and if flexible modes of taking exams are an option.

Adjusting to independent study

You may enter the tertiary system after completing secondary school, from a workplace, or from an overseas educational institution. If you find your university or college strange and alien, remember that you are not alone in having to adjust to new organisational cultures and to a rapidly changing educational system. To become informed about how your university is organised and about your studies in general, attend orientation days, seek advice from the staff in the areas in which you plan to study, consult a counsellor or study adviser, or read the relevant sections of this book. If studying online or at a distance, work through any orientation material available to you.

Becoming a student in a new culture entails practical and emotional adjustments in your life. (Some aspects of your self and your surroundings which influence study are presented in Chapter 1.) If the people you are close to support you as a student, the changes are easier and you can relax and explore what your new life has to offer. If studying at a distance you may be able to contact other students in your area or join an online discussion group. If you don't have support from others, be prepared to spend time and energy in establishing a new lifestyle as a student as well as on study itself; but you need to be certain that you do want to be a tertiary student.

Coping with personal change

> I don't feel it is necessary to know exactly what I am. The main interest in life and work is to become someone else that you were not in the beginning. If you knew when you began a book what you would say at the end, do you think that you would have the courage to write it? What is true of writing and for a love relationship is true also for life. The game is worthwhile insofar as we don't know what will be the end. *(Michel Foucault)*

For some students the changes wrought by higher education are secondary to the other events in their lives. For others the educational process stimulates ideas which force them to question their life and view of the world. This in turn can lead to the desire (frequently accompanied by many difficulties and fears) for a life that is more in keeping with a changing world view and changing values. Many mature age students enter university at a time when they already perceive the need for changes. For a woman living in a nuclear family relationship with husband and children who expect her to fulfil the role of 'housewife' and 'mum', a course in Women's Studies can create exciting and confusing questions about her role. A student from overseas faces educational challenges as well as the possibilities inherent in adjusting to living in a new culture away from many supports and expectations at home. For some students changes occur that are independent of their studies, such as moving house, starting a new relationship, or a sudden bereavement in the family. If you are a school leaver starting tertiary study at 18 or 19 you are probably facing a time of intense personal growth; this can be a time of leaving home and finding your own social niche. These changes impinge on studies and there is a two-way interchange between learning and the rest of your life.

It may help to ask the following questions:

Is your education stimulating you to think about issues that make you want to change the way you live?

When the changes in your life create stress, how do you cope with your studies?

Where do you go for help when you are stressed by such changes?

How do you usually deal with change in your life?

Do you have a friend or acquaintance who will help you explore new possibilities and listen to your problems?

Do you think you need to seek professional help to deal with these changes in the most positive way?

How are these changes affecting the people close to you?

Foucault aptly points to the uncertainty of where life can lead and reminds us that changes can be seen as opening new possibilities rather than primarily as something of which to be afraid. However, too many major changes all at once can be unsettling. But if you are seeking certainty in your life and do not want to change your views and values, then many of the courses offered in higher education may not be the best place for you.

> He believed to the end exactly the same things he started with. It seems to me that a man who can think straight along for forty-seven years without changing a single idea ought to be kept in a cabinet as a curiosity. *(Jean Webster)*

One of the fundamental approaches to coping with change concerns focusing in depth on why you want to study. When you are confronted with confusing changes and the decisions which go with them, it helps to be clear about the essence of why you are studying and what you hope to achieve; then to stay open to ideas on how to achieve this.

Imagine, for example, that you are studying because you want to work with people, so you have enrolled for a psychology degree. However, you find that the way that psychology is taught at your institution does not seem to coincide with your vision of how you would work with people. You then need to define as clearly as possible what are the essential characteristics of your vision. Do you want to work with people with severe problems or people who are having temporary difficulties? Do you want to work on your own, in a small team or in an institutional setting? Is your orientation towards a particular school of psychological thought because of its views of human nature? With these essential characteristics in mind you can then brainstorm to see firstly, what your current psychology degree program offers you, and secondly, what other avenues might be open to help you achieve your vision. Of course your vision itself may well change with time and with changes in you. It is important to keep refining the essence of what you want, and not to mistake the means of achieving this for the vision itself.

One way to clarify the essence of what you want and to deal with change is to talk with other people. While other people can't live the changes for you, you don't have to deal with the situation completely on your own.

Even if you feel alone now, talk with:

- other people who are going through similar changes or have done so in the past
- possible new friends who care about you achieving your goals, or
- counsellors or sympathetic teachers who have seen other students going through similar experiences and can pass on some handy hints and provide a listening ear to help you sort out how you want to handle the changes.

You may find that you look to one person to discuss your changing views of society, to another person to help deal with the repercussions at home of your changed lifestyle and to a third person for moral support when you have to write your first tertiary-level essay. Think creatively and stay open to all sorts of possibilities for help—words of wisdom and warm support can often come from unexpected sources.

Dealing with difficult situations

As a student you will inevitably find yourself in situations that are difficult. One technique which many students have found useful and which can be used to cope with difficult situations such as exams, is the 'imagine the worst' approach.

> When things are really bad ... I picture a black tunnel in front of me. I go up to it ... I know a train is coming ... I go to meet it ... I know that inside the tunnel, underneath the wheels, down between the sleepers, there is a little spot of light. *(Peter Hoeg)*

Imagine you find yourself in an exam room, and are faced with a question which requires an essay answer. You have the sinking feeling that all you know on the topic could be put down in half-a-dozen sentences. What do you do? Panic instantly? Start scribbling furiously in the hope of inspiration? Leave the exam room? Most students worry about not being able to answer exam questions and imagine themselves in this situation. But their imagination stops there. You can help yourself cope with this problem ahead of time by also imagining what you will do about it.

Now continue imagining that you put down your pen, sit back, stretch a bit, and take several deep breaths. You read the question again, slowly and carefully. You pick up your pen and start to jot down anything which comes to your mind on the topic. You don't try to order this knowledge, but concentrate instead on recalling as much of it as you can. If you start feeling rushed, you deliberately pause for a few moments, and then continue. When you feel you have all your knowledge before you, you check that each item is relevant to the question. You then organise your information into one or two main points. When this is done, you start writing, concentrating on saying what you want to, as clearly as you can. You avoid the temptation to pad your answer with irrelevant facts or long-winded language. If at any stage you find yourself feeling rushed, you stop for a minute and concentrate on relaxing. You may just sit and look out of the window as a way of relaxing. When you have finished saying what you want to, you sit back and feel pleased at knowing more about the question than you thought you did. Then you check your essay over carefully to make sure it answers the question and is clearly expressed. Finish.

Imagining the worst and imagining how you will handle it cannot guarantee you will answer the question successfully. Nothing can. However, it does make that outcome a lot more likely. (See 'Exams' in Chapter 5 for some help, and 'Writing Essays', Chapter 13, for ideas on essay-type answers.)

A part of the 'imagine the worst' approach is to think beforehand about why you are worried about an exam. Is it because you might fail a course, of which the exam is part? Imagine yourself failing the course, and then go on to imagine other possibilities once you have failed. Can you sit for a supplementary exam, or repeat the subject? Think about why you want to pass the course. Can you realise these aims in other ways? It can be invaluable to realise that there are often alternatives to some of the difficulties you face. If you know that you always panic in exam situations, despite knowing your subject well, it may be possible to arrange with your teacher for alternative forms of assessment. You may be able to select a course where exams don't count for all or most of your final assessment.

'Imagining the worst' can be used to help you cope with other difficult situations apart from exams. Are you anxious that you will make a fool of yourself in a discussion group? Imagine this happening—then go on to imagine yourself handling the situation. Think about why you are anxious, and what you can do about the causes of your anxieties. Do you need to prepare more thoroughly for the group so that you feel more confident about contributing to the discussion? Getting to know a couple of other group members outside the discussion time might make you feel that you have sympathetic listeners for anything you say during a discussion. Getting to know other students also enables you to share your feelings and experiences in collaborative learning groups and other learning situations. Such sharing will probably lead you to discover that you are not alone in your anxieties. Other students may have helpful advice on how to cope with a situation which is worrying you. If you are all worried, try 'imagining the worst' together and see what alternatives you come up with. (See Chapter 11, 'Participating in discussion groups'.)

Now stop, and think of a situation which is worrying you at present.

Imagine the worst that could happen—then imagine yourself coping with it. What are your alternatives after the worst has happened? Which ones seem most viable? Think about why you are worried, and what you can do to deal with the causes of your worry. Share your anxieties with others and see what they have to suggest. And perhaps most important of all—don't accept that you have to be worried. Is it really a matter of life or death?

Contacting people

It is anything but easy to enter a classroom full of people whom you feel must be more intelligent than you, and quite demoralising when your worst fears are realised, you think. Still you must persevere. *(Brian's Wife Jenny's Mum)*

Adjusting to tertiary study takes time and practice and often courage. Many of the adjustments involve approaching other people—asking questions of a remote professor, seeking help from a teacher you see only once a week, putting forward your own thoughts in a discussion group, or making contact with a stranger sitting next to you in a class. To deal with these anxieties, you often need to take the initiative in contacting people.

As a part-time, distance or online student, you may have particular difficulty contacting teachers and other students. Perhaps you enjoy the pleasures of being a solitary scholar and your opportunities to learn independently, and your isolation can partly free you from the pressures of competing with other students. But you may miss sharing the pleasures and problems of study with other students, and if no one in your community sees tertiary study as valuable, you may feel particularly isolated.

Maximising your access to other people's ideas and to learning facilities is one aspect of part-time and distance study which takes time and energy. Personal contacts with a teacher and students can make a big difference to the depth and enjoyment of your formal learning, particularly if you start your studies with high expectations or are worried about your academic abilities.

Approaching teachers

Only an unrealistic teacher would expect you to be an authority on a subject you have just begun studying or expect you to write a perfect first essay. You are expected to ask for the help and information you need. Teachers usually appreciate students whose questions and comments show genuine thought and enthusiasm for learning, and like most people, teachers take pleasure in discussing their special interest and explaining what they know to others. Often the students that a teacher comes to know best are those who ask questions, seek advice or are keen to discuss ideas—and it is more satisfying to teach people you know than to impart information to a collection of names and half-remembered faces.

What is the worst that can happen when you approach a teacher for help? Perhaps you persistently have trouble finding them. If so, try to arrange an appointment or leave a message. Perhaps you won't receive a helpful answer to your question. If the teacher is busy at the time, remember that tertiary teachers have responsibilities for research and administration as well as for students, so make an appointment for another time. If he or she isn't skilled at clear explanations, look to another teacher, a student, or a book for your information. Perhaps the teacher you approach is cursory or condescending. If so, maybe he or she is having a trying day, so ask if you can come back another time. Maybe the teacher is inadequate as a teacher. Nevertheless teachers are paid to help you learn, so if you want to, persist with your request. If you don't want to persist, look elsewhere for help. There are always one or two friendly, helpful teachers or advisers on campus who can help with your contacts with other teachers, with your study, and in some cases with your personal problems.

If you study at a distance and/or online, many teachers like to receive communication from you other than the assignments you are required to submit. Send a letter or an e-mail or make a 'phone call to tell your teacher a little about yourself. Ask about comments on an assignment or thank your teacher for help. Send an informal tape to talk about ideas not covered in lectures or to discuss your concerns about your work or about course requirements. If you can arrange to visit your teachers on campus, you will be able to visualise the place and person to whom you are sending your work, rather than simply delivering it up to the postal service, fax, or e-mail and to a red marking pen with a person at the other end.

These contacts help your teachers come to know you as an individual, and enable them to make comments on your work which are directed to your individual strengths and difficulties. Your teachers may also be encouraged to make more detailed comments and to return your assignments more promptly—important factors for all students, but particularly so when you have to wait anxiously for an evaluation of your work to arrive in your letter box, fax, or mail bag.

Getting to know other students

... the social nature of the university experience has the potential for contributing positively to academic performance, and more generally should influence the individual's sense of competence ... The nature and extent of social involvement is meaningful in its own right as part of the process of personal development and identity formation. *(Craig McInnis)*

Having at least one or two fellow students with whom you can toss around ideas and share study problems is an invaluable part of a student's life. Sitting by yourself in the cafeteria, not knowing anyone in the first weeks of class, not being part of student social life or being an isolated student, can make you feel very alone. If you are a new student from the country or overseas, you may feel disoriented without your usual contact with family and friends. For overseas students, this feeling can be compounded by language problems but can be lessened by special orientation programs. Rural and isolated students are unlikely to have such programs, but may find it easier to maintain 'home' contact in the first few weeks so that they can share their experiences.

If you find university or college strange, if you have difficulties with your work, or if you feel shy with other students, you can be certain that other students feel this way too. Help someone else as well as yourself by talking to the person you sit next to in class, or by contacting another student and not always expecting them to contact you first. Take part in some of the social or academic activities on campus if you can and take advantage of the multicultural campus community. (See 'Social groupings', Chapter 1.) If you have trouble with work or with a teacher, mention it to a couple of students in your class. They may have ideas on what you can do, and if they share your problem you can tackle it together. One of the most valuable learning experiences can be to find another student or a group of students studying the same subjects with whom you can regularly share ideas and read and comment on each other's written work. (See 'Collaborative learning groups', Chapter 11 and 'Share your writing', Chapter 12.) This sharing is particularly important in the current educational climate where teachers are becoming less accessible because of large classes and increased workloads.

What is the worst that could happen when you try to make contact with other students? They don't seem interested? Perhaps they are shy, or preoccupied with other things—try another time or approach someone else. Perhaps they don't seem interested in your particular study problems—find other people you can ask for help. If you continue to have difficulty getting to know a few other students, talk this over with a friend or counsellor. However, most students are willing to talk about courses or teachers, the test next week or the essay you are supposed to finish in two days' time. You won't become close friends with everyone you meet, but you will find some people with whom you enjoy spending time.

If you are a distance education or open learning student, check with the appropriate campus office to see if there are other students in your area. Try to make contact with someone who has taken or is taking the same course as you, but realise that even talking to somebody studying different courses can provide you both with invaluable moral support. Take part in e-mail discussion groups in online courses. If you can sit in on the occasional class on campus you will have a chance to meet other students and share your learning with them. If you are nervous at the thought of attending special on-campus sessions, you will usually find that some other students feel the same way. Once you actually meet each other, you are likely to have plenty to say.

Contacting the people around you and on campus helps you come to know them as individuals, to learn about the real people behind your images and expectations of what teachers and students are like. It is one of the most important parts of your learning.

> Open learning may be carried out at a distance but it is not conventional distance learning. Neither is it contingent on IT [information technology]. Learners could stay in contact through computer, 'phone, letter or face-to-face meetings. However, IT does address the key problem of quick and easy contact between learners and between learner and tutors through electronic mail and electronic delivery of resources. Indeed electronic communication can be so effective that it may prove valuable even where learners are studying fulltime on the same campus. *(JITOL [Online])*

Combining study with other work

Your job may be directly related to the subjects you are studying and so provide opportunities for you to transfer skills and knowledge from one context to another. For example, you may be a veterinary student working part-time in an animal clinic or a parent studying children's literature. Even if your work isn't directly connected with the content of the subjects you study, it may require you to use your mind imaginatively to solve problems and to grapple with new ideas. In this case, your brain won't feel rusty when you tackle formal study. Useful connections between your employment and your study can be particularly important if you are a distance or part-time student with little opportunity to discuss your learning with teachers or other students. However, close connections between your work and study can sometimes create problems if, for example, as a teacher you read a book which criticises teaching methods you use, or if courses you take for further job qualifications seem irrelevant.

The amount of energy you put into your job affects your energy for studying. The high level of energy and creativity which you devote to a satisfying job can carry over to your studies. If your studies are less stimulating than your work, you may rapidly lose interest in them. A job which isn't satisfying but is financially necessary may demand a lot of your energy. If you do heavy outdoors physical work or spend your day looking after children, sometimes you will be too tired to study but at other times you will welcome the change to mental exercise.

If you work in a high speed job, you can find yourself impatient with the leisurely pace of some courses, especially if you have only limited time off work for classes. If a course doesn't regularly require work to be handed in, the apparent aimlessness of your study may be frustrating. However,

study can provide you with a relaxing change from a high pressure job—
and the workloads in most courses become demanding soon enough.

The overall time that your work requires, the particular hours that
you work and the travelling time from home to work to campus all
influence your study. They affect your choice of courses, how much time
you can spend on private study, and sometimes make distance or online
study the only possibility.

Financial decisions may affect your study. If, for example, you have
to find a part-time job to finance your education, you will have less time
for study itself. If you have been a secondary school student or housewife
without an independent income, you may have to justify your desire to
study to the person whose income will now support you. You may feel
under pressure to 'succeed' or to choose vocational courses, particularly
if your study calls for extra money to pay for books or travel or childcare.

■ ■ ■ ■ ■

Allow yourself time to discover what university or college is like for you.
Expect to feel both confused and excited in the first six to twelve months
while you settle in, while you begin to understand what is expected of
you and to define some of your own objectives. During this time, as well
as trying to pass courses, put some energy into learning how to learn
and into making contact with staff and students. Remember that outside
school you have acquired knowledge and skills that you can transfer
into your formal learning. Have confidence that you do know how to
learn when you want to.

Think about what you want from higher education, and how you can
reach your objectives. After a while it may make sense for you to defer
your study for a short period or to leave university or college because of
other interests, because your studies aren't sufficiently stimulating, or for
pragmatic reasons. (If you are thinking of withdrawing from study, find
out what you need to do in case you later want to return.) If you continue
to study, your objectives in your formal learning will probably change.
Any serious attempt to come to grips with new concepts, especially those
which raise questions about yourself, your world and your beliefs, always
engenders confusion and suggests new directions to consider. Learning
what is important to you changes you, often in unexpected ways. Universities or colleges can offer you real learning if you explore what is offered
and if you are able to make your own independent decisions about learning.

Have a broad picture of the place of further study in your education
rather than automatically thinking of it as the be-all and end-all. 'Lifelong
learning' has become something of a catch-cry and is a term with a
multiplicity of meanings covering formal and informal learning. But just

as some decades ago relatively few people went on to tertiary study and secondary school to the age of fourteen was seen as the end of formal education, now there is an increasing likelihood that you will need and be expected to continue your formal education and training beyond a degree or diploma. You may, for example, be required to update or broaden your professional knowledge or to acquire knowledge to enable you to move into a new field or to specialise in a particular area. You may have to acquire new skills for accessing and selecting up to date information in your field.

As well as any further formal education you undertake, your informal learning will continue for the rest of your life. Hopefully your formal study will enhance your ability to learn and to discover future directions you want to pursue both informally and in further education. Whatever directions your learning takes, remember to ask yourself 'What is my purpose in wanting to learn this?' just as you did during your initial education at university or college.

Further reading

Ballard, Brigid & Clanchy, John, 1988, *Studying in Australia*, Longman Cheshire, Melbourne.

Barry, V.E. & Rudinow, J., 1989, *Invitation to critical thinking*, 2nd edn, Holt, Rhinehart and Winston, Sydney.

Brookfield, Stephen D, 1989, *Developing critical thinkers: Challenging adults to explore alternative ways of thinking and acting*, Jossey Bass, San Francisco.

Clanchy, John, (ed.), 1994, *Making the most of your arts degree: A guide for students in the humanities and social sciences*, Longman Australia, Melbourne.

McEvedy, M. Rosanna & Jordan, Mike, 1986, *Succeeding at university and college*, Nelson, Melbourne.

Percy, Diana, 1989, *Adult study tactics: A springboard to learning*, Macmillan, South Melbourne.

McInnis, Craig, James, Richard & McNaughton, Carmel, 1995, 'First year on campus: Diversity in the initial experience of Australian undergraduates', A commissioned project of the Committee for the Advancement of University Teaching. Centre for the Study of Higher Education, Melbourne University.

Marshall, Lorraine, 1997, *Critical thinking in context*, A Gripping Films Production, Murdoch University, Murdoch, Western Australia.

Morgan, Alistair, 1993, *Improving your students' learning: Reflections on the experience of study*, Kogan Page, London.

Taylor, Gordon, Ballard, Brigid, Beasley, Vic, Bock, Hanne, Clanchy, John & Nightingale, Peggy, 1988, *Literacy by degrees*, The Society for Research into Higher Education and the Open University Press, Milton Keynes, Bucks.

Notes

1 Robert H. Ennis, 1981, 'Rational thinking and education practice', in J.F. Soltis (ed.), *Philosophy of education*, (80th yearbook of the National Society for the Study of Education), Chicago, National Society for the Study of Education.

2 Elizabeth Taylor, et al., 1980, 'The orientations of students studying the Social Science Foundation Course', *Study Methods Group Report no. 7*, Institute of Educational Technology, The Open University, Walton Hall, Milton Keynes, Bucks.

CHAPTER 4

ASKING YOUR OWN QUESTIONS

Knowledge is a process in the minds of living people. It is what we do as we try to find out who and where we are, and what is going on about us. (*John Holt*)

You ask questions all the time, both consciously and unconsciously. When you walk, as you take each step your foot is seeking out information to relay to your brain. When you pause at an intersection and glance both ways, you are checking the traffic. You learn when you have a question in your mind—whether as a small child continually asking 'Why?', or later as you learn about dinosaurs, gardening, jet aeroplanes, philosophy or toxicology. You learn when you are curious, when you want or need to know. Sometimes you may express your curiosity as interest in a field of study such as ancient history, modern music or marsupial reproduction. Turning your interest into a series of questions focuses your explorations in the field.

In formal education, usually teachers ask the questions and you provide the answers. Much of your primary and secondary education would have asked questions that began with 'What ... ?' and you would then have been expected to give correct answers which showed an ability to remember and reproduce information. In tertiary education, while 'What ... ?' is a valid question, you are expected to ask questions that lead you to be more analytical and critical. These questions begin with 'Why ... ?' 'How ... ?' 'How important ... ?' or 'How valid ... ?' Asking 'What if ... ?' or 'What might happen if ... ?' are higher order speculative questions intended to lead you to reconsider your assumptions and beliefs.

> Knowledge, like nature, is revealed not in itself but through our methods of questioning. Those methods have, over time, become more and more highly differentiated, more and more specialised. Within the university these different ways of questioning can be identified with the disciplinary foundations of knowledge. The disciplines are marked off from one another less by the uniqueness of the area of reality or experience they set out to investigate than by their distinctive methods of investigation— their distinctive modes of analysis. (*Brigid Ballard & John Clanchy*)

In tertiary education, it is usually the teacher who formulates the questions that you discuss in tutorials or write about in your essays, reports and examinations. Some will help you to formulate your own questions when you lead a discussion group, write on a topic of your own choice or undertake some form of independent study. Throughout your education many of your teachers will be committed to teaching you to think critically and try to lead you to an understanding that there are no correct and definitive answers.

Some questions you ask constrain you and stop the learning process. Other questions enable you to ask other further questions, perhaps by generating initial answers that lead on to questions that enable you to critically evaluate and analyse. As a higher education student you need to ask questions that explore your relationship to learning, questions that help you understand, criticise, evaluate and analyse what you learn, and questions that help you to integrate what you learn with your previous knowledge and ideas.

This chapter looks briefly at a few types of questions and suggests some fundamental questions you can ask when thinking about or researching a topic which interests you. It is designed to stimulate you to ask your own questions and to pursue them in your formal education.

What questions might you ask?

Just before she died she asked 'What is the answer?' No answer came. She laughed aloud and said: 'In that case what is the question?' Then she died. (*Last words of Gertrude Stein, quoted by Donald Sutherland*)

What questions do you have on your mind right now? Questions about your work, your personal relationships, your ideas, who you are?

A simple question such as 'Should I cook spaghetti or a stew for dinner?', 'Did I leave my glasses behind?' can be answered without much imagination, perhaps with a 'Yes' or a 'No'. Questions such as these close off other possibilities and leave you with the option of only a limited answer. This may be all you need when checking if you know a fact, such as 'How many grams in an ounce?', 'Where is my clavicle?'

If you are looking for information on a topic such as basic human needs, to ask 'Do humans need food to survive?' is asking a closed question, while the more complex question 'What types of food do humans need to survive?' opens many possibilities. **Complex questions** demand time and careful thought when you attempt to answer them. Some complex questions you can never answer. 'Am I making the right choice?' 'What would have happened if I hadn't gone to university?' Perhaps you check your horoscope or consult the I Ching in an attempt to find answers to such questions. It is tempting to believe that there are absolute or 'yes/no' answers to questions which can't be answered so simply and for which there is no one correct answer.

What men [*sic*] really want is not knowledge but certainty. (*Bertrand Russell*)

Often an answer which is right today may be wrong tomorrow, or an answer which makes sense in one culture may be a mistake in another. Are there any answers which are always right? Much of what you are told is true later turns out to be not quite the whole truth; and many so-called 'objective facts' are actually the results of a consensus of the subjective opinions of the people concerned. The same question can generate many different answers depending on the position that you take, and the positions available to you will depend on your culture and world view (see 'Thinking critically', Chapter 3).

The way in which you ask questions shapes your answers. If you ask 'Is intelligence determined by genes or environment?' you have precluded the possibility that both of these or other factors might be important, as well as making assumptions about what intelligence is. Such 'either ... or ...' questions are examples of how language limits your exploration of a topic and encloses what you can learn.

Every language conceals within its structure a vast array of unconscious assumptions about life and the universe, all that you take for granted and everything that seems to make common sense ... (*N.J. Berill*)

When you are curious about a subject, there are some basic questions you can usefully ask. As you read the questions suggested here, apply them to a topic which interests you and make notes on the answers and further questions that arise. (See 'Developing and analysing a question', Chapter 6.)

Why do I want to know?

> Tiger got to hunt,
> Bird got to fly;
> Man got to sit and wonder, 'Why, why, why?'
> Tiger got to sleep,
> Bird got to land;
> Man got to tell himself he understand. (*Kurt Vonnegut Jr.*)

Asking why you want to know about a topic can clarify what you want to find out and how to go about your search. How did you become curious about the topic in the first place? What is *your purpose* for seeking the information? Perhaps you want to share it with others, use it to pass an exam, complete an assignment or progress through a sequence of practical skills. If you need to remember information for a short while, such as for a seminar paper next week, how you go about learning it will differ from your approach if you need the information for long-term use (see Chapter 5, 'Learning and remembering').

What do I want to know?

What do I want to know? What interests me about this topic? What seem to be the most important aspects? These are some of the *first questions* to ask yourself when you want to find information on a topic. For example, if you are interested in convicts in eighteenth-century Australia, ask yourself 'What do I want to know about this subject?' You might have questions about who the convicts were, why they were transported, how many were women, their living conditions, the number of convicts who were political prisoners, how they were organised and used in the colonies, and their role in the economy of the new colonies.

How do I know that ... ?

> Artists can colour the sky red because they know it's blue. Those of us who aren't artists must colour things the way they really are or people might think we're stupid. (*Jules Feiffer*)

Perhaps you 'know' that the sun will rise tomorrow because in your experience it always has. Perhaps you 'know' that the grass is green because your eyes and the labels available in your culture tell you so. Perhaps you 'know' that Marie Curie discovered radium because you read that she did.

What are *the sources of your knowledge*? The first-hand evidence of your senses is one source which can be deceptive—for example, if you believe that the world is flat (see 'Gathering information from primary sources', Chapter 8). Much of what you know is not from first-hand experience. Much of your knowledge comes from your cultural and personal biases, many of which you may be unaware of, such as the belief that technological progress is always desirable or that a woman's primary role is to be a wife and mother. Much that is believed to be 'common sense' in your culture is not thought about or questioned (see 'Your cultural and social self', Chapter 1). It is thus crucial to question the nature and reliability of your sources of knowledge. Can you prove that Marie Curie discovered radium or that the sun will rise tomorrow? If you can't prove it, it may still be true, but you need to be careful to draw on supporting evidence before you assert its truth.

On the topic of convicts in eighteenth-century Australia, ask yourself 'What do I already know about this topic, and where does my knowledge come from?' Do you 'know' that most convicts were petty thieves or that women convicts were prostitutes or have you assumed this? Asking yourself how you know these 'facts' should lead you to examine whether or not they really are facts.

> People who are reflectively sceptical do not take things as read. Simply because a practice or structure has existed for a long time does not mean that it is the most appropriate for *all* time, or even for this moment. Just because an idea is accepted by everyone else does not mean that we have to believe its innate truth without first checking its correspondence with reality as we experience it. (*Stephen Brookfield*)

Why?

> ... and books that told me everything about wasps except why.
> (*Dylan Thomas*)

'Why?' is one of the most important questions you can ask, especially if it enables you to *identify assumptions* which may be hidden. As an example of this, debates about education frequently ask 'How can we do this particular thing better?' while the question 'Why are we doing it in the first place?' is not dealt with. It might be more useful to start by asking 'Why are teachers trained?' instead of 'How can teachers be trained better?', or to ask 'Why am I going to write this report?' before you ask 'How can I best go about writing it?'

If you have a problem to solve, you might ask only how to solve it, for example, which methods you should use to remember material for exams. If you also ask why the methods are effective, you can decide if they suit you and will find it easier to remember how to repeat them and to use them in different exam situations. On the topic of convicts in Australia, asking why convicts were transported will uncover further questions about the social, political and economic conditions in England in the eighteenth century.

When? Where? How? Who? Why? What?

Asking these questions one after another is a *brainstorming* exercise to let your mind generate ideas without having to justify their immediate relevance. It is a useful way to stimulate your initial thinking about a subject and to provide new directions if you are stuck while researching. For example, if given the adage 'Know thyself', you could ask:

- who said this?
- when?
- where was it first used?
- what was its original context?
- how has it been interpreted?
- why has it been important?

What happens if ... ?

'What happens if ... ?' is the *cause-and-effect* question that experimenters ask, whether the experimenter is a 3-year-old child pulling a cat's tail or a professional researcher testing a hypothesis or solving a problem. Experimenting involves manipulating your environment to see what happens, sometimes predicting what is likely to happen, and then describing what happened. Here are some examples.

- What happens if you drop a piece of paper and a heavy lead weight from the top of a high tower?
- What happens if you write an assignment as a dialogue instead of in prose?
- What happens if you stop drinking coffee?

What if ... ? What might happen if ... ?

> Why, sometimes I've believed as many as six impossible things before breakfast. (*Lewis Carroll*)

Imagine living in the sixteenth century and asking yourself, 'What if the sun rather than the earth is the centre of our universe?' What answers might you arrive at if you ask 'What if our traditional energy sources are no longer available by the end of this century?', 'What if Robert Ardrey's theory that human animals are predatory killers is true?,' 'What if most of the convicts transported to Australia were political prisoners?' or 'What might have happened if men were the sex that had babies?' These *speculative questions* require that you transcend your customary frameworks for viewing the world. Using your creative imagination and suspending disbelief enables you to look at the world through new eyes which is essential for critical thinking and problem solving.

> Critical thought ... has an epistemological edge. It places its object. It sets it in a framework. Critique asserts that no framework has priority, even if we cannot but place our observations in a framework of some kind. Critique, and a higher education founded on critique, obliges us to take the responsibility for the frameworks we employ. Critique points up the epistemological insecurity of any truth claim. It denies the pretentiousness of knowledge represented as Knowledge. (*Ronald Barnett*)

■ ■ ■ ■ ■

You don't need to ask the above questions in a particular sequence, but you are likely to move backwards and forwards among them. What you want to know and the questions you ask will be influenced by how much you already know about a topic. For example, when confronted with a new topic you can immerse yourself in it by asking *basic questions* that uncover fundamental information about your topic, such as 'What is evolution?' 'What is Freud's concept of the unconscious?' 'What is carbon bonding?' 'What is Wall Street?' or 'What are marsupials?'

In contrast, when familiar with a subject you can ask *higher order questions* which lead you to evaluate this information. For instance, 'How has Freud's theory of the unconscious been applied in late twentieth century psychoanalysis?' If you already know something about marsupial reproduction you might then ask if the reproductive process in kangaroos is an adaptation to the Australian environment. (Chapter 6, 'Choosing and analysing a topic', suggests a systematic way of analysing a question or topic.)

Pursuing your questions in formal education

> The teacher's work, therefore, begins when that other person asks a question ... If you ask me a question all I can do in my reply is try to put into words a part of my experience. But you get only the words, not the experience. To make meaning out of my words, you must use your own experience. (*John Holt*)

Without curiosity, learning is dull and mechanical if it occurs at all. Wanting to know, enjoying stretching your mind, feeling wonder or delight at a new experience or idea—all these need a mind which is receptive and questioning.

Unfortunately, the crucial part your curiosity and questions play in learning is often forgotten or disregarded. Formal learning is frequently based on a model which assumes that there is a body of knowledge to master, and a particular way to master it; and the proof of your mastery lies in correctly answering set questions. This model of learning is most evident in the exam process but can also underlie work such as essays, tutorial papers and laboratory reports. If you are given a question for a tutorial paper, do you approach it by asking your own questions, or by doing what you think your teachers expect? If you read a lot for an assignment, but feel uncertain about what to write on the topic, perhaps you are trying to guess what you are expected to write, rather than reading and writing about what seems most relevant and interesting to you. In a discussion group, are you hesitant to take an active part because you fear you might say the 'wrong' thing, or give the 'wrong' answer?

> We kill, not only their curiosity, but their feeling that it is a good and admirable thing to be curious, so that by the age of ten most of them will not ask questions, and will show a good deal of scorn for the few who do ... (*John Holt*)

No teacher can tell you what you want to learn, but he or she can help you discover this. Teachers with an active curiosity who are interested in you as a learner can stimulate your curiosity in new ways; they can help you articulate your questions and help you ask more sophisticated questions. Such teachers also help you rediscover the confidence and skills needed to pursue your own questions in formal education. Obviously some teachers and assignments allow you more scope than others for asking the questions which interest you. If your learning is to be satisfying and mean something to you, you need to ask your own questions, even with teachers who prefer you to answer theirs.

Independent study

> Students are partners in learning and they have a responsibility to contribute to their university experience. Most realise this and want to take charge of their learning. In some instances, however, they are denied the opportunity by the structures of courses, restrictive assessment schemes and the 'firehose' approach to teaching taken in some courses—which seems to operate on the principle that teaching involves the transmission of vast amounts of information. The overloaded curriculum is a particularly insidious obstacle to independent learning. (*Craig McInnis*)

The basic questions of why, what, how and when you learn apply to any independent learning, and can be applied to an individual assignment or to your formal tertiary education as a whole. If you want to be a more self-directed learner, think about who is determining the direction of these objectives. Studying independently requires thinking about and formulating your objectives. It involves studying a subject of your own choosing, on your own initiative, and making your own decisions about how and when you study it and with whom. Independent study which is fully self-directed differs from 'individualised' learning, self-paced methods and studying formal courses online. In the latter, you study alone but are supervised and have limited choice as to what and how you study, and your learning objectives are a subset of the course or teacher's objectives.

Studying independently entails asking yourself the following questions.

- What do I want to study, and in what depth and breadth?
- Why do I want to study this particular topic? You might explore an interest more fully, acquire specific skills, or examine previous work in a new context.
- How will I study the topic? Perhaps you want to conduct library research, interviews, or laboratory experiments, or to undertake field work, or to read extensively.
- How do I want my work to be evaluated? You need to decide what work to produce specifically for recorded assessment, and who will evaluate your work and by what criteria (see Chapter 16, 'Learning from evaluation').
- How much time will I spend on this study?
- With whom will I discuss my work?

If you usually rely on material from your teachers for the 'right' answers without questioning their information or assumptions, you may find it frightening to consider asking your own questions. Perhaps you have become so accustomed to teachers asking you questions that you have largely forgotten how to ask your own, or have lost the confidence to ask them. Even if a teacher encourages you to approach a topic in your own way, you might be so unaccustomed to this that you prefer to retreat into the safety of looking to the 'experts' for the answers. In this case you are probably assuming that your task at university or college is to meet the requirements of courses and teachers, rather than seeing them as resources enabling you to move towards your objectives and to think about your questions. So perhaps the first question you should ask yourself is 'Why am I at university or college?', 'What are my objectives?' and 'What are my questions?'

A few universities and colleges allow you to complete part or all of your study program independently. Sometimes you can obtain credit for exploring a topic in depth through a study contract. If independent study appeals to you, explore the possibilities for this method of learning within your institution or through cross-crediting from another institution, perhaps online. If you develop a serious academic interest which you want to explore further, you may decide to go on to study as an honours or postgraduate student.

Within a course, the extent to which you are allowed to work on your interests varies. In some courses you can spend most of the time exploring your interests without close supervision. Other courses allow you little scope for independent study; the work you do is assigned by teachers and you are told what to read, what experiments to conduct, and how to present your written work. When you do have the opportunity for independent study within a course, this often takes the form of an individual or group project for which you choose the topic and the methods of research.

> Asking questions is a constant taking apart, putting back together, and reshuffling into new creations. At their highest level, questions probe, discover, explore and manipulate information. They constantly seek new and stable ways to understand information. (*Crawford Lindsey*)

Often your learning becomes largely a matter of asking more exact or more intricate questions, rather than finding answers. Despite a formal education system which talks of having 'done maths' or 'done history', it is impossible to learn all there is to know about any subject. When pursuing your own questions, you may realise that the more you know, the more there is to learn, which leads you on to further questions.

What questions would you like to pursue in your formal learning?

Further reading

Boud, David (ed.), 1981, *Developing student autonomy in learning*, Kogan Page, London.

Gibbs, Graham, 1992, *Independent learning with more students*, The teaching more students project, The Polytechnics and Colleges Funding Council.

Lindsey, Crawford W., 1988, *Teaching students to teach themselves*, Kogan Page, London.

Percy, Keith & Ramsden, Paul, 1980, *Independent study: Two examples from English higher education*, The Society for Research into Higher Education, University of Surrey, Guildford, England.

Robbins, Derek, 1988, *The rise of independent study*, The Society for Research into Higher Education, University of Surrey, Guildford, England.

CHAPTER 5

LEARNING AND REMEMBERING

Oft in the stilly night,
When the mind is fumbling fuzzily,
I brood about how little I know.
And know that little so muzzily. (*Ogden Nash*)

Why do you remember the things you do?

Why do you forget?

If you want to know how to ride a bicycle, you practise with great concentration, and persist with your riding despite the occasional spill. Once you can ride with skill, even if you sell your bicycle you always remember how to ride one.

A small child who wants to learn how to build a tower of blocks concentrates intensely while trying various ways to make the blocks stay put one on top of the other. After repeated attempts, she comes to understand the most effective way to build a tower of blocks. This skill is later remembered and transferred to a new context to build other towers of toys, of books, of cushions.

If you concentrate while learning what you want to know, you are more likely to understand and be able to use it. Remembering what you learn well enough to use it depends on why and how you learn. If you learn to ride a bicycle because you want to, and if you learn at your own pace, you easily recall the skill. You are less likely to remember it if you learn because someone else decides you should and teaches you in the way they think best. Whether or not you want to learn depends on you—what you already know, how you learn, your current interests and how you feel at the time.

This chapter begins by looking at how you filter what you learn and remember, and at why you might want to remember. It discusses how you learn in order to remember—by learning what suits you, when and how you wish, and by using methods which help you learn material thoughtfully. Deliberately learning in these ways makes it more likely that you will be able to use what you learn later and recall it in situations such as exams.

Filters on what you learn and remember

The past which we remember is partial and distorted; it has been edited by the censors to exclude events which are disturbingly painful or disturbingly pleasurable ... The history we recall tends to be propaganda which preserves the status quo of personal identity. (*Sam Keen*)

Your mind and body unconsciously select and interpret what you learn and remember from your daily life, and what you remember changes with time. Five people who witness the same car accident have five different versions even if asked soon afterwards to describe what happened, and a year later each person will have yet another version of the episode. They may even 'recall' things which didn't actually happen, such as events which could have been expected to occur but didn't or details of a 'long argument' between the drivers which was in fact only a couple of remarks. What each of the five recollects is their personal experience of the accident, modified by their experiences in the meantime.

What do you remember about today?

What immediately comes to mind?

Try recalling in order everything that has happened since you woke up.

What do you remember from yesterday?

What do you remember from last week? Why?

What memories do you have of your last birthday?

Do you remember your first day at school?

What is your earliest memory?

Spend about half an hour answering these questions. If you finish in less time, go back and see how much more detail you can recall. Can you work out why you recalled what you did?

Share the questions with someone else. How do your memories differ from theirs? How are they the same? Why?

> 'I could tell you my adventures—beginning from this morning,' said Alice a little timidly; 'but it's no use going back to yesterday, because I was a different person then.' (*Lewis Carroll*)

Now stop for a moment, and let yourself become aware of everything your senses are telling you. Of what are you most aware? Smells? Sights? Sounds? Tastes? Touch? After your first sense impressions, what else do you begin to notice? What thoughts are running through your mind?

Trying to be fully aware of even one fleeting moment makes you realise how much you forget—perhaps for a short time, or perhaps for all of your life. Some things you need to 'forget', in the sense of taking them for granted. Imagine if you wanted to be fully aware and decided to consciously breathe every breath. You would soon give up because you wouldn't have time for anything else. Other things you 'forget' by pushing them below the surface of your mind—items that have little interest for you, that have unpleasant associations, or that don't fit with your view of the world.

> A world view is a paradigm. It is all of the assumptions that you hold that all build up, and it is like a framework that we have in our heads, and then whatever we see out there we filter through that framework. (*Julia Hobson*)

Sometimes you forget things you would like to remember. Have you ever read a childhood autobiography and marvelled at the amount of detail the writer recollects? Few people remember such detail without making a conscious effort to do so. Keeping a diary or taking photographs can make you more aware of your surroundings and help you remember them. Photos or diaries also help you realise how much you forget. Have you ever read back over a diary entry from several weeks or years ago and been amazed at how your memory of that time has changed and how much you have forgotten?

Try it now. See if you can find a letter, a poem, or a diary you wrote, or a photograph you took. Look at it and conjure up your memories of that time.

Remembering isn't just something you set your mind to do—**your senses** are involved too. Do you have a good memory for faces? For 'phone numbers? Or for jokes? Some people remember mostly what they see, and can see a word once and remember how to spell it; others remember what they hear, and can repeat verbatim snatches of dialogue from a movie (see 'Senses', Chapter 1).

Your background, experiences and world view lead you to knowledge and beliefs about yourself and your world which influence what you are aware of at any moment. If you have been a keen surfer or sailor for several years, you are more likely to know and remember how the wind and waves have changed from one season to another than will someone who plays cards for their recreation. If you have worked as a carpenter, you can pick up and remember new information about the craft because of your previous knowledge.

Your active interest in a subject increases what you remember about it. A football fan can tell you in detail about the previous wins of her club, but if she is not interested in horse racing she may have no idea who won the Melbourne Cup. If you are concerned about the role of women in Australian society, you will remember facts from a history of Australia which others without your concern wouldn't notice. Interest in a topic can be kindled by another person's enthusiasm. Skilled teachers who care about their subjects can hold your attention so that you remember far more than expected. You may remember a conversation with someone you met at a party because you were entertained by them.

How you feel emotionally and physically also influences what you learn and how vividly you remember it. If you are alert, perhaps because you are feeling exuberant or slightly uncomfortable, your chances of remembering that particular time more fully increase. Your surroundings influence how you feel and are part of what you remember. Have you ever picked up a book you have read and been reminded of when and where you read it? And items you can recall in one situation you can't remember at all in another.

Reflection is a vital component of learning and remembering. If following an experience you take the time and create personal space to reflect on that experience—to let your impressions, feelings and ideas about it gel in your mind—you are more likely to remember the experience and to be able to draw on it in a new situation. If we are busy we often fail to make sense of our learning or we lose much of it because we don't take the time to reflect.

Your background and experiences, your interests and world view, your senses and current state of being act as filters on your life, both past and present. They affect what you are most aware of and what you will reflect on and learn, and so influence what you remember from the information you are offered.

Why remember?

Memory is the mother of imagination, reason and skill ... This is the companion, this is the tutor, the poet, the library with which you travel. (*Mark van Doren*)

Remembering enables you to learn more about yourself and your world. Newborn human babies seem to operate mostly by reflexes rather than by consciously knowing and remembering. But toddlers in their second year are able to call on what they have learned, and can form a concept such as 'dog-ness' by remembering the characteristics of dogs which aren't present and comparing them with a dog which is. As an adult, the more you can remember, the less you have to relearn. The more you can remember concepts, the more you can solve problems and cope with new situations and ideas. If you can recall the fundamentals of Darwin's theory of evolution, you can move on to further related knowledge instead of relearning the theory repeatedly.

When you find **pleasure** in what you learn, you probably want to remember it. Perhaps you do this unconsciously because your senses and curiosity are more active, or perhaps you deliberately heighten your sense of awareness. You may relive the experiences in your mind, in a diary or through photographs. You may learn by heart the words of a song which please you. Maybe you want to remember an intriguing idea, so you can contemplate it further.

If you **apply what you learn**, you are more likely to remember it. To cross the road and live, you learn and use an array of skills which become habits, or unconsciously recollected knowledge. If you need to prune fruit trees, you have a reason for using and remembering what you learn about pruning. If you want to use an idea in a discussion paper, you try to understand the idea and its links to your topic so that you remember it fully enough to explain it to others.

Some things you are required to remember for **reasons not directly your own**. You might enjoy learning the manual skills of flying an aeroplane but not want to study the navigation theory required for a pilot's licence. In your formal education you are expected to remember material so that your progress towards course objectives can be evaluated and recorded according to tangible criteria. For example, you may be required:

- in an exam, to show that you remember and understand the rudiments of a particular subject
- in an essay, to recall information well enough to argue your position
- in a report, to remember and describe a sequence of steps in an experiment
- in a tutorial, to review and present a summary of your reading on a topic
- for a seminar paper, to remember material in the short-term, such as dates or data, and
- to remember information and skills for long periods so you can take a final exam, or transfer them to a subsequent course or a future job.

These requirements are based on the assumptions that in formal education there is certain knowledge worth having, certain learning skills and abilities worth acquiring, and a specific sequence and time limit in which this learning should be acquired. These assumptions shape why and what and how you learn and remember. Those assumptions with which you disagree can still influence your learning and remembering if you decide to accept them as a means to your own ends. For example, even if some course material doesn't interest you, you may study it for an exam, because you accept the exam as necessary to acquire a qualification you want.

> 'But what did the Dormouse say?' one of the jury asked.
> 'That I can't remember,' said the Hatter.
> 'You must remember,' remarked the King, 'or I'll have you executed.'
> (*Lewis Carroll*)

How you learn to remember

There are times when your assumptions about and objectives for learning and remembering differ from those of your teachers. At such times, what you learn may be difficult to recall. However, you are likely to remember what you learn if your curiosity about a subject remains alive. To sustain your curiosity, there are certain prerequisites for learning.

1 What is important to you

You need to learn according to who you are—your purposes, your background and experiences, your interests, your world view, your questions (see 'Beliefs and values', Chapter 1).

2 When you are ready

You need to learn at a place and time and in a way that makes sense to you, at 'the moment of readiness'. You are not always ready to learn during specified hours each week in a lecture theatre or when you have free time after a busy day. If you are not ready, it is more difficult to concentrate on and to understand what you are supposed to learn, and you are more likely to forget what you do learn unless you use memory techniques such as those mentioned in this chapter (see also 'Concentrating while you study', Chapter 2). One advantage of learning online is that you can learn at times and places that suit you.

3 A way that suits you

> I never was from boyhood one of those for whom skill came easily. The throwing of a stone at a mark was a conscious effort of concentration rather than an instinctive fling. It was the same with fishing. Every cast was the result of drill, theory and earnest business. (*Patrick O'Brian*)

If you have some insight into how you learn informally, your formal learning can be enhanced. Some people have strong visual memories, some learn by doing, others learn by discussion, others by reading and making notes. Which ways suit you best? If you want to find out about kangaroos, do you go to look at them in the zoo or try to study them in their natural habitats? Do you ask other people about them? Do you read books on the subject? Do you take a course in marsupial physiology? Do you search the Internet for information? Learning in a way that suits you enhances your ability to remember.

4 Building on what you already know

I can give you nothing that has not already its being within yourself. I can throw open to you no picture-gallery but your own soul ... I help you to make your own world visible. That is all. (*Hermann Hesse*)

You need to learn by building on your skills and experience, on the patterns and beliefs which shape your world and your language. Even if you know only a little about a new area, having a context in which to understand this new field helps you remember it more clearly. Have you ever attempted to read a book you don't understand and then some time later read it more easily and remembered it? By the second reading you have acquired new knowledge to which you can relate the book's contents.

If you are required to reproduce ideas or information that you can't relate to something familiar, you may have to resort to rote learning and mnemonics, acrostics and rhymes such as '30 days hath September'. One of the most powerful tools to help you remember unfamiliar material is linking it to familiar information and concepts. Here are some examples.

- Learn the principles which underlie a good book review before reviewing a book on a new topic, and your recall of the book will be more thorough.
- To help you remember the intricacies of Darwin's theory of evolution, test it against species differences with which you are familiar.
- Use analogies, similes and metaphors based on comparisons with familiar ideas and information when learning and remembering new material. (For example, the metaphor 'the body politic' helps you think about a political system in new ways by comparing it to your own body, and what you learn from such a metaphor is likely to stay in your mind.)

5 Suspending previous knowledge and beliefs

Unless you are self reflective, you don't recognise that no matter who you are, you're operating within a particular conceptual framework, a particular way of seeing and way of doing. (*Patsy Hallen*)

There may be times when you are required to suspend your previous understanding, and to think about and reassemble information in an entirely different way. This can be disorienting and it can be difficult to learn and remember the information. For example, if you are concerned about drug addiction, you may have first learned about it in a psychology course based on a paradigm which centred on changing the individual addict. If you then take a course in sociology which examines the social construction of individuality and looks to change individuals through changes in society, you will need to try re-ordering your information and ideas within this new framework. Making shifts such as this requires that you reflect on and question your world view. It is important to recognise that you are operating within a particular world view, a particular conceptual framework with its values and assumptions. Although it is tempting and comforting to hold on to your entrenched view of the world, making an effort to understand, accept and remember different or at times conflicting world views is very challenging but can be rewarding. Being aware of the influence of your personal world view on questions in your studies, and being willing to accommodate different world views, is crucial to thinking critically.

> Frameworks are not given; they are not uncontroversial. We can always step outside the framework in which a position has its natural home and we can try looking at the phenomenon from a different point of view. Our understanding can be challenged; and radically so.

> This is a characteristic of genuinely *higher* education. Are students encouraged to recognise that what counts as truth can be viewed and evaluated from a number of perspectives? (*Ronald Barnett*)

When you come to learn about a new topic in a class, study session or assignment, spend some time considering what you already know about it. Think about what you want to learn on the topic and, if you have a choice, how you want to learn. This preparation provides reference points or a framework for your learning and enhances your ability to remember.

Selecting what to learn

Even if you are able to learn what, when and how you want to, you can't possibly remember everything. Every minute you 'learn' a great deal of information, but most of it you remember only if prompted. To retain some things, you need to 'forget' others, focusing your conscious awareness to select what you take in and learn. To remember what a teacher is saying, focus on just that and ignore other thoughts which impinge on your awareness, such as what the teacher is wearing.

It is essential that you consciously select what you want to remember. As a student you are confronted with large amounts of information, and your research in libraries or the Internet might yield more information than you can possibly use or absorb. You quickly discover there is little point in trying to remember it all and that some time needs to be spent:

- clarifying why you need the information
- selecting what you need to remember, and
- deciding how to record and retrieve it (see 'Selecting, recording and filing information', Chapter 7).

In your written work and discussions, for example, your time should be spent selecting important points that you need to remember; and you might choose to remember and discuss a particularly striking example to illustrate a point when several other examples would have been just as valid.

How much material you need to concentrate on and remember for tests and examinations varies according to the course objectives and the preferences of individual teachers. Be aware of course objectives and find out from your course coordinators and teachers how much detail you need to learn and remember. Generally, you will need to remember the arguments and frameworks presented and the concepts, theories and ideas developed in your course, and be able to recall sufficient detail to explain them. In a biology course, for example, if the greenhouse effect has featured in discussion, in essay topics and readings you would be well advised to learn and remember the basic principles underlying the effect. Similarly, in a social science course if the concept of 'power' has featured prominently it is wise to study and remember the different meanings of this concept and to concentrate on the way the concept is used in the course. In an exam you may need to write an essay showing you understand the concept or you may need to apply it to a real life situation.

Learning thoroughly

Our memories have been impaired by print; we know we need not 'burden our memories' with matter which we can find merely by taking a book from the shelf. When a large proportion of the population is illiterate and books are scarce, memories are often tenacious to a degree outside modern western experience. (*J. Chaytor*)

Once you have selected what you want or have to learn, you need to learn that material thoroughly. Even material you thought would be dull or difficult can be unexpectedly interesting when you set out to learn it thoroughly, if you make a game or challenge of learning it well.

Different ways for the same material

Take in the same information in as many ways as possible. In your learning utilise as many of your senses as possible, especially your strongest sense. If a friend explains to you the difference between a ketch and a schooner, you are more likely to remember these if you also see a diagram of each and then sail on them. If you read about a topic as well as discuss it and listen to a lecture on it, your recall of what you have learned will be greater. This approach is particularly important if you are trying to remember complex material like the elements of existentialist philosophy or the intricacies and implications of Einstein's theory of relativity. For some people, such material can only be understood and remembered after different and repeated encounters.

Patterns and principles

Previously we learned more and more about less and less. In future people will need to know in a very real sense less and less about more and more. The basic required skills will be to understand patterns quickly and to make sense of their meaning in specific times and places, rather than to solve problems within previously understood approaches. (*Robert Theobald*)

If you learn by comprehending the patterns and principles, the structures and relationships which link individual ideas and information, it is easier to remember these items than trying to do so one by one. Learning in patterns also makes it easier to recall information you thought you wouldn't need, since you can search for it by reconstructing the patterns in which you learned it. Use patterned notes, concept maps, flow diagrams or charts with different colours to summarise information from a lecture, a chapter of a book, a section of a course or a topic. Convert numerical information embedded in text to sketch graphs or tables, and vice versa. Depending on the way you remember information, colourful graphic summaries can make it easier to recall information because they show at a glance central concepts and the links between ideas. The form of argument used in critical thinking, with its thesis and supporting reasons, provides a pattern or structure into which you can organise much of the material you need to learn (see 'Genres', Chapter 6). Patterned notes can also be used to clearly separate a thesis from supporting premises, a controlling focus from supporting material or main points from details (see 'Notemaking and/or underlining', Chapter 9).

Before, during and after classes and study

'—but there's one great advantage in it, that one's memory works both ways.'
'I'm sure mine only works one way', Alice remarked. 'I can't remember things before they happen.'
'It's a poor sort of memory that only works backwards', the Queen remarked.' (*Lewis Carroll*)

Thorough learning from a class or study session partly depends on what you do before, during and afterwards. Many of the chapters in this book use this principle as their framework, and you will remember more of what you learn if you use the approaches they describe. 'Concentrating while you study' in Chapter 2, for example, describes warming up, concentrating fully, and concluding a study session. The chapter on lectures discusses how to make the most of a lecture by preparing, questioning as you listen, and reviewing and using the material soon afterwards.

Study session techniques

There are techniques which you can use in a study session to enhance your ability to remember what you learn.

- Vary the length of your study sessions according to the material. Your mind can only take in so many statistics at once, while in contrast you need time to understand a philosophical argument well enough to remember it.
- Learn from the general to the specific. Take in the big picture by previewing for the thesis or main idea, and then focus on the supporting reasons or specific details.
- When learning details from two similar subjects, study a contrasting subject in between so you don't confuse information. This applies, for example, if you are trying to remember dates from two similar history courses, or studying verb tenses in Spanish and Italian. Avoiding interference between subjects is especially important in the early stages of learning and for long-term recall.
- When trying to remember concepts, studying related subjects creates associations, because the differences and similarities between them enhance your understanding of each. For example, this approach can help when studying concepts of human nature in Rousseau's philosophy and in humanistic psychology.
- Use your body as you study. Get up and move around. Gesticulate. Read aloud. Talk to yourself. Pretend you are debating with someone. Explain the information to a fictitious person.

Memory keys

One way of consciously remembering is to précis the essential parts of what you have selected to learn, and then to find memory keys for each of these parts. These keys can then be used to unlock your memory of each part and its associated details. You unconsciously use such keys when an unexpected memory is evoked because you hear a particular piece of music, walk past a certain street, or drink a once-favourite drink. In your formal learning you can use memory keys consciously, for example to recall the discussion in a seminar. Summarise the argument and structure of the discussion, represent these by key words or phrases, and use these keys to review and recall the discussion.

What would you choose as memory keys to help you remember each paragraph in this section 'Learning thoroughly'?

Transferring and using what you learn

If you think back over an event from your day, what you remember depends on what has happened to you in the meantime, even if that time has been very brief. When you use your knowledge in a new context, you don't reproduce it exactly unless it has absolutely no meaning for you. Your knowledge and skills are extended and changed by the new context. For example, if you describe an event in your journal, your description of the event is influenced by the surroundings in which you write and these too become part of your memory.

> ... Funes not only remembered every leaf on every tree of every wood, but even every one of the times he had perceived or imagined it. He determined to reduce all of his past experience to some seventy thousand recollections, which he would later define numerically. Two considerations dissuaded him: the thought that the task was interminable and the thought that it was useless. (*Jorge Luis Borges*)

Unless you continue your learning by recalling it, you forget even things you wanted to learn. Going over your day helps fix it in your memory, and recording the day in a journal makes it available for you to relive, to 'use' again. Discussing the ideas from a lecture with other people who have shared it has a similar effect, with the added dimension of the others' perceptions now becoming part of yours.

Use what you learn as soon, as often and as widely as possible if you want to remember it. You recall the alphabet easily because you have used it over and over again in different situations. When you first learn to ride a bike, if you practise every day and in many different conditions you are likely to remember the skill more quickly than if you practise once a week and have to spend some of that weekly time in re-learning. Unless you have an exceptional memory for figures, you are unlikely to remember statistics such as the population of Singapore unless you use them frequently. If you want to remember an important idea, write it down and try it out on various people. You will come to a new understanding of it each time and remember the original idea more fully. To remember material for long-term use (for instance, for exams or future employment), use it by revising it periodically and relating it to new knowledge you have acquired.

> What is ... central to a properly educative endeavour is the identification of what is involved in transferring ... knowledge, learning, understanding or skill gained in one cognitive domain and/or social context to adapt, modify or extend it in such a way as to be able to apply it in another. (*David Bridges*)

You will rarely use information in the same context as you learned it. You need to assess a situation and adapt your prior learning to the new context. When you begin higher education you will bring knowledge and skills from your previous studies, work and life that are transferable to your learning. For example, if you worked in an office you will have developed organisational skills that you will be able to use in your studies. As you progress with your studies you will acquire knowledge and skills that you will transfer and use in future courses. Similarly, the skills and knowledge that you learn during your degree studies are designed to be used and transferred into other contexts and into your life generally.

Exams

You are likely to need to remember material in exams and tests. Your memory in exams depends as much on being prepared for the exam situation as it does on learning material well. Even if you know material, you may be unable to recall it effectively if you become very anxious in an exam room or if you have a learning disability which means that you tire easily. 'Dealing with difficult situations' in Chapter 3 suggests how to handle the exam situation.

Table 5.1 looks at techniques to help you remember what you have learned when you read the questions in a limited-time, 'closed' book exam. And whatever else you do, make the most of what you remember by reading and analysing each question very carefully.

Table 5.1 Exam techniques

1 If you are uptight before an exam, try to relax (see 'Tension and relaxation', Chapter 1).

2 When you are given the exam paper, and before you start writing, take the following steps.
- Carefully read the instructions which should tell you how you are expected to answer the paper, how many questions you should answer and the value of each.
- Read through all of the questions.
- If you have a choice, decide which questions you will answer or at least which questions you will do first.
- Decide how much time you will need to spend on each question because of its value and according to how thoroughly you can answer it.
- Decide on the order in which you will answer the questions. Answer first the questions you know most about and which are easiest. If you run out of time, you do so on a subject which will earn you fewer marks.

3 When you are allowed to start writing, jot down any thoughts or ideas you have about each of the questions you will answer. These jottings can be useful memory triggers when you actually come to answer the question.

4 For essay-type questions, analyse the wording of the question (see 'Developing and analysing a question', Chapter 6) and plan your essay (see 'Writing to a plan', Chapter 13). Include your plan in your exam booklet.

5 Write as quickly and as clearly as you can.

6 For multiple-choice questions, don't waste time over questions you can't answer. Be careful about guessing answers if points are deducted for incorrect responses.

7 When answering mathematical problems, include all of your calculations. Even if your answer is incorrect, the examiner can see where you went wrong and you may gain some points for your method.

8 If you have a memory lapse in the middle of a question, leave a few pages, go to another question, and later return to the first question.

9 In an essay-type exam, answer the required number of questions. Answer fully the questions you know well and write as much as you can on the others. Make sure you write on the set question.

10 If you run out of time, jot down the main points you were going to make.
11 Try to leave time at the end of the exam to read back over your answers. Correcting poor expression or spelling or checking your calculations can make an important difference.

I never told you about examinations. I passed everything with the utmost ease—I know the secret now, and am never going to fail again. I shan't be able to graduate with honours though, because of that beastly Latin prose and geometry ... But I don't care. Wot's the hodds so long as you're 'appy? (That's a quotation. I've been reading the English classics.) (*Jean Webster*)

■ ■ ■ ■ ■

Look back at the section on 'Why Remember?'. What do you remember from this section?

Why do you recall this material?

How could you remember this section more effectively?

Without remembering, each day, each event, each moment would be a totally new experience. How fully you remember depends largely on how thoroughly you learned in the first place, and the material you recall is as unique to you as is why, what and how you learn. As you learn in your formal education, think about how you can learn in order to remember more effectively.

Further reading

Bolles, E.B., 1988, *Remembering and forgetting: An inquiry into the nature of memory*, Walker and Co., New York.

Buzan, Tony, 1989, *Use your head*, BBC Books, London (revised edition).

—— 1993, *The mind map book*, BBC Books, London.

Galica, G.S., 1991, *The blue book: A student's guide to essay exams*, Harcourt Brace Jovanovich, San Diego.

Highbee, K.L., 1988, *Your memory. How it works and how to improve it*, 2nd edn, Prentice Hall, Eaglewood Cliffs, New Jersey.

Orr, F., 1984, *How to pass exams*, George Allen & Unwin, Sydney.

CHAPTER 6

CHOOSING AND ANALYSING A TOPIC

As a student in a tertiary institution, most of the work that you are expected to submit for assessment is in the form of assignments in which you communicate your ideas and knowledge to others. These assignments are usually written (essays, seminar or tutorial presentations, reviews, exams, projects and reports) or oral discussion papers, and occasionally audiovisual. In addition to assignments, you are expected to gather information for lectures, discussion groups, practical sessions, field trips and for exams. Most of this work you undertake on your own, but it is also worth seeking opportunities to work collaboratively.

This chapter looks at purposes for an assignment, at expectations of academic writing, and at choosing and analysing a topic or question. This approach is applied to essays, but many of the suggestions also apply to other written work. The chapter is intended for students who need to choose and analyse a topic or question and to find their way through reference lists, rather than for those undertaking advanced research. It is the first of several chapters directly relevant to work on written assignments.

Purposes for assignments

'Why, if a fish came to me and told me he was going on a journey, I should say 'With what porpoise'?'
'Don't you mean 'purpose'?' said Alice. (*Lewis Carroll*)

Your purposes

Your purposes for a particular assignment ideally should reflect your reasons for enrolling in the course, and on a broader level, your reasons for being at university. You might enrol in a course to complete a prerequisite or to follow up an interest or to work with a particular teacher. When you are given a particular assignment, you might decide that the work you do for the assignment would enable you to obtain background information for your main area of study, to complete a required section of course work, to increase your knowledge in a new area, to read more in an area of interest, or so that you can practise communicating your ideas and receive feedback on them. It is useful to write down these purposes and refer to them as you do your research. If you have trouble articulating your purposes, ask yourself the following questions:

What knowledge do you want to acquire?

What do you hope to accomplish by producing this piece of work?

What skills do you want to improve?

What new skills do you hope to learn?

What aspect of your learning and writing do you most need to improve?

There are times when your purposes for an assignment conflict with what is expected of you by the course or teacher. You may be expected to give a seminar paper on a topic which doesn't interest you, or to present a written report when you feel that an audiovisual presentation would be more effective. When such conflicts arise, ask your teacher if you can choose an alternative. Many teachers welcome such initiative and allow you to pursue your own topic and form of presentation. If no alternative is possible, your discussions with the teacher should at least give you a clearer idea of the purposes of the assignment. It is then up to you to decide whether you agree with these purposes. If you can't use the assignment to pursue your own long- or short-term purposes and questions, you may need to find an alternative way of pursuing these (see 'Independent study', Chapter 4).

If you are working collaboratively with other students on a group project, it is necessary in the initial stages to clarify what each of you sees as the purpose of the assignment, and what each of you want to learn during work on the project. Making your expectations explicit is a vital ingredient for a harmonious working relationship and for achieving a satisfying end result.

Your teachers' purposes

When we mean to build
We first survey the plot, then draw the model. (*Shakespeare*)

Teachers who design and teach courses usually do so with particular purposes in mind, and each assignment should have a place within an overall plan to instruct you in the disciplinary subject area and to develop certain skills (see 'Developing skills and attitudes', Chapter 3). These purposes may or may not be explicitly stated—at times your teachers may not have clearly articulated their purposes and underlying expectations of your work. Some of the purposes may be to acquaint you with an issue central to a subject area, to stimulate you to think critically or to question your attitudes, to give you practice in the methodologies of the discipline, to diagnose your ability to write clearly and logically, or to give your teacher some tangible work by which to evaluate your progress. Most assignments are designed with several purposes in mind.

Expectations of assignments

Expectations is the place you must always go to before you get to where you're going. Of course, some people never go beyond expectations ... (*Norton Juster*)

Before you begin writing an academic assignment, as well as being clear about purposes, it is important to clarify what is expected of you in your work. These expectations are at different levels.

Tertiary study

At a macro level, there are the overall expectations of tertiary study, and the skills and attitudes you are expected to develop as part of your university education (see 'Developing skills and attitudes', Chapter 3). The generic skills pertinent to your written assignments include:

- researching information
- planning and organising
- summarising and paraphrasing
- analysing and critiquing information
- presenting a reasoned argument
- writing clearly and concisely, and
- using formal writing conventions and appropriate referencing conventions.

Most importantly, your teacher will expect you to answer the set question or address the set topic, and to do this in the genre required.

Disciplines and courses

You need to be aware of the expectations or conventions of the discipline and courses that you are studying. The essays you write in one discipline in a tertiary institution will differ in significant ways from those in another discipline. Thus, the essays you write in history (or economics or philosophy) will be different in some ways from what is expected in politics (or law or media studies). Similarly, the expectations of a written report in psychology are different from those in the physical sciences, and scientific report writing in chemistry differs from report writing in biology.

> ... discourse ... means that knowledge in any domain, in any social domain, is organised from the point of view of a particular institution ... like law for instance. The knowledge of law is organised by the institution of law so that when particular forms of social practice come into the domain of the law, it talks about them in certain kinds of ways and not other kinds of ways. For example, if my neighbour and I have an argument over the back fence which has deteriorated in a particular way then this is talked about by my wife and I in a certain kind of way, but when we go to see the lawyer it gets talked about in a different kind of way. And this is what I mean by discourse. Now discourses are important in schools, particularly in secondary and tertiary education, because the organisation of knowledge becomes more and more specific to the disciplines which a ... student enters into. Thus you have particular ways of writing which correspond to the ways of organising knowledge within particular disciplines. (*Gunter Kress*)

Genres

You will be required to write in certain genres, and you are expected to use the conventions of that genre. The predominant genres include essays, reports, reviews and discussion papers, and each conforms to certain rules (see Chapter 13, 'Writing essays, Table 9.4 'Writing reviews', Chapter 14, 'Writing scientific reports').

Many students coming from secondary school believe that what is expected of their writing at university is similar to what was expected in secondary school. This is not the case. For example, university or college essays are different in important ways from essays written in English courses in school and require a different approach. The defining feature of a university essay (and an academic discussion), even if not explicitly stated, is that it should have an argument or a controlling focus. Essays should not consist purely of description. In tertiary studies usually only students in creative writing and other highly specialised courses have the opportunity to experiment with purely descriptive writing or with fiction. Writing a narrative story or dialogue or a poem is not something many students do as part of their tertiary education.

You are expected to build on your abilities in organising and expressing ideas and information. However, unless your secondary education has encouraged you to be critical in your thinking rather than to simply reproduce and select from given information, some of the advice you were given at secondary school is not applicable once you reach tertiary study. Similarly, much that you are told in one discipline arises from the conventions and methodologies of that particular discipline and does not apply to another. It is important to read carefully any course instructions on written work which should outline the aims of assignments and how to present them. If in doubt, ask your teacher before you choose your topic.

What is expected from an essay that is intended to persuade will differ from one that is are primarily intended to be informative. This difference influences how you organise the main points in your essay.

In an **informative or expository essay**, you choose material according to a *controlling focus* which frames and limits your choice of ideas and information.[1] You then choose main points which explain, describe, define or illustrate significant aspects of your particular topic or question. For example, if your topic is to explain the different treatments of capital and income under income tax law, you choose the three main points which seem to you to be the most significant in explaining these differences. In your introduction you justify why you have chosen these main points and not others. Your controlling focus is your view of the aspects that are most significant.

In a **persuasive or argumentative essay**, you must have an argument that consists of a *thesis* which is supported by a number of *reasons* (or premises) and each of these reasons will form a main point in the essay. The thesis you choose to develop will depend on your position, your interests and world views. It is the thesis, and the reasons you choose to support this thesis, that help to make the essay distinctively yours. For example, you choose a question on deep sea fishing and you hold a conservationist position on the question. Your argument consists of the thesis that fishing quotas should be implemented; and your reasons are the declining fish stocks and the impact on the food chain. (Note how your argument can be expressed in a full grammatical sentence.) You support your reasons with evidence and examples (see 'The body of your essay', Chapter 13). The way that you sequence your reasons and the weighting you give each are central to developing your argument.

Sometimes you may find it difficult to identify your position on a topic. Usually this is because the position seems so self evident to you that you are unable to recognise it as a position. In such a situation, remember that there is always more than one possible stance on a topic and you are expected to make yours explicit and argue for it.

Individual teachers

Your written academic assignments are normally produced for only one person and for the purpose of assessment. What does your individual lecturer or tutor expect of you? How do you find this out? You should be told the aims of an assignment and how you are expected to present it. Beyond these explicit requirements you cannot be expected to second guess your teacher's mind, and if you try to do so your assignments are likely to be cautious and dull. It is of course difficult to imagine exactly what this person wants from you and impossible to understand fully what this person knows. You are not an expert in your field and as yet you are not expected to be. However, it is your purposes, interests and views which make the assignments distinctively yours, so spend your time researching and presenting these interests and views as effectively as possible. Most teachers prefer a well-researched and well-argued original piece of work which expresses your position and addresses a precise question, rather than a rehashing of familiar textbooks or their own lectures.

Topics and questions

Before you choose and research a topic or question you should define your purposes and clarify what is expected of you in the assignment. Sometimes you will be given a topic or question, and sometimes you are free to devise your own.

At times you will be given a *general* topic, such as 'The ecology of euca-lypt forests', 'Romantic literature', 'British Journalism', 'The French Revolu-tion', or 'Scientific method'. Other topics are more *specific,* for example, 'Discuss the Hindu ideas of forgiveness and tolerance', 'Analyse the distin-guishing characteristics of university culture', 'Critically examine the likely effects on the local flora and fauna of the freeway proposed for your capital city', or 'How should Piaget's theory of stages in children's development be applied to teaching mathematics in our primary schools?' Specific topics may be worded as a question or as a directive sentence or sentences.

In this chapter the term 'topic' is used for a general content area, while the term 'question' refers to a research question which is more specific and focused. If you are given a general topic, it is important to re-word it yourself into a specific, more focused question. Your specific question may consist of one or more sentences. Remember, however, that your teachers may use either the term 'topic' or 'question' when referring to essays and other assignments.

Choosing a topic or question

Deciding on a topic or question can seem deceptively simple—a matter of choosing from a list of suggested or set questions, or selecting a topic from within the subject matter of a course. However, your decision also involves analysing possible questions. Start making your choice by thinking about the possibilities of each. Explore a couple of options and choose between them as you analyse them in some detail, or decide on one at the start and change your mind if your initial exploration suggests that it has limited possibilities. Often a question which at first doesn't seem very interesting may become attractive as you explore it.

- Your choice of topic is affected by what you already know. If you are given a list of topics and are uncertain which to choose because some of them are unfamiliar, find out more about these options from someone who knows about them and/or from a reference such as a specialist encyclopedia or a course text. If you have limited time to gather information, choose a familiar topic. If you have ample time, decide whether to explore a previous interest further or to learn about a unfamiliar topic.
- Your enthusiasm for a topic also affects your choice. For example, if you are interested in women's history you might choose a topic such as the suffragette movement. If you are an athlete, you might write on the physiology of marathon runners.
- Your choice of topic is often influenced by the information sources available. Being aware of sources other than libraries, lectures and your teachers can increase your choice of questions (see Chapter 8, 'Using libraries and other information sources').

Unless your choice of topic is quite clear from the start or unless you have little time in which to choose, keep several options in mind. Allow yourself time to analyse their possibilities further, and to find out if the resources you need are available.

A subjective approach

The trouble is that essays always have to sound like God talking for eternity, and that isn't the way it ever is. People should see that it's never anything other than just one person talking from one place in time and space and circumstance. (*Robert M. Pirsig*)

Your approach to a question is always subjective to some degree. Even a set specific question can be tackled in a variety of ways, and your particular approach is reflected in what you include and omit from the possible material. Even if you are presenting a report in which you try to eliminate as much subjectivity as possible, the words you use carry with them personal associations for you and your audience. So the most useful question to ask is not 'Shall I take an objective or subjective approach?' but rather 'What is the most effective way of dealing with my subjectivity?' Examine your biases and preconceptions so that they distort your research as little as possible. Be prepared in your writing to let your audience know your beliefs and biases on the subject. (See the Appendix 'Discrimination' for examples of bias.)

In an assignment such as a laboratory report you are required to report only what you see as 'facts' and to make personal input only in your critical interpretation of raw data. In other assignments such as a philosophy essay you will be required to present your argument based on your ideas and research. However, remember that in reporting facts, no two people will choose to do so in the same way or in exactly the same language. Your scope for presenting personal opinions or theories often depends on the conventions of a particular discipline and the personal preferences of your teacher. If you feel unsure about including your opinions, even when asked to, remember that practice in communicating your ideas and arguing from a position is a vital part of learning—and given practice and some encouraging response, it does become easier. Usually it also makes your assignments more interesting to read. But remember that an outpouring of unexamined assertions and prejudices is not acceptable.

> ... my purpose is to employ facts as tentative probes, as a means of insight, of pattern recognition, rather than to use them in the traditional and sterile sense of classified data, categories, containers. (*Marshall McLuhan*)

Developing and analysing a question

If you are given a *general topic* you need to develop it into a specific question that will give you a research direction. In a persuasive essay, this will enable you to decide on an argument and in an expository essay, your controlling focus (see 'Genres'). For example, in the general topic 'The French Revolution' you might narrow the topic down to the causes of the revolution. You might then argue from a Marxist position the thesis that the economic situation in France caused the revolution and give reasons to support this.

If you are given a *specific topic*, the wording will help define how to develop it as a question. For example, in the specific topic 'Analyse the distinguishing features of university culture' your question might be 'What are the main distinguishing features of a university culture and how do they differ from the features of another culture?'

When devising your own specific question, it can be useful to devise a clear and accurate working title. As you are still at the stage of analysing your question, you are unlikely to be ready to choose the final wording of a title. As you proceed with your analysis, revise the wording as necessary.

The following section applies both to specific questions your teachers have set for an assignment or in an exam, and to questions you have devised yourself.

The points listed below are designed to help you with the process of analysing an essay question. They should lead you to a written statement which conceptualises a possible argument or focus and defines a structure for the essay. When writing an assignment or exam answer, it is important to answer the set question. Rigorously analysing a set question is a fundamental prerequisite to answering it, and failure to do this is one of the main reasons capable students do not produce work which reflects their abilities.

Apply each of the suggestions below to your essay question before you begin your research and writing, although it is not necessary to apply the questions in the order given here. It will help if you make notes as you go, and you will be surprised how much you already know.

Items 1 and 2 will lead you to information on the content of the essay, items 3 to 5 will help you articulate your position on the question, develop an argument or controlling focus that reflects this position, item 6 will help you structure your essay, and item 7 will help you articulate your assumptions and views on the question. You need not move though these items in a linear fashion.

1 What is the question about?

- Think about the wording of the question so that you understand more clearly what you are expected to write about and the possibilities that the question offers.
- List terms and concepts in the question and their possible meanings. Does the question contain terms and concepts you don't understand? For example, the possible uses of the word 'culture' in the question 'Analyse the distinguishing features of university culture' may not be clear. Consult an appropriate concept dictionary such as *The Fontana Dictionary of Modern Thought*. Ask your teacher to explain terms you don't understand or, if a question isn't clearly worded, ask your teacher to explain it more fully.
- Ask yourself 'What assumptions seem to underpin the question?' For example, the question 'How should Piaget's theory of stages in children's development be applied to teaching mathematics in our primary schools?' assumes that Piaget's theory should be applied to maths teaching in our primary schools.

2 What do I already know about the question?

- Jot down any ideas or knowledge which comes to mind.
- Use any available lists of study questions on the content area to start your mind ticking over.
- Brainstorm the question by asking, 'Why?' 'Who?' 'What?' 'When?'

'How?' 'Where?' about it, or ask 'How do I know that ... ?' to check
the validity of your existing knowledge. (See 'What questions might
you ask?' in Chapter 4 for more questions to start you thinking.)

3 What might my thesis or controlling focus be?
• What is my position on the question?
• For an argumentative essay, how would you complete the sentence
  'In answer to this question I will argue that ...'?
• At this stage keep in mind that the reasons to support your chosen
  thesis constitute the main points in your essay. At this stage your thesis
  may be only tentative and you may have to revise it several times.

4 How much breadth or depth can this essay have?
Given any requirements of the essay (such as length or format) ask
yourself the following questions.

• Should I concentrate on presenting a broad overview of the question,
  or on exploring one or two facets of it in depth?
• How many main ideas can I convey?
• How many questions can I answer?
• How much information can I present?

For example, in the topic 'Scientific Method' you may focus on the
question 'Is there a scientific method?', arguing that scientific method
is dependent on time and place. You might do this by contrasting the
ideas of Paul Feyerabend (who argues that there is no single scientific
method) with the views of John Kemeny (who posits that there is one
basic method common to all scientific activity). You argue your case
using only these 'experts' because the length and time set for the essay
don't permit you to look at many writers in detail, and because you want
to contrast two theories on the question.

5 What are the possible main points?
• Ask yourself the following questions as a starting point:
  – What interests me most about the question?
  – What aspect of it do I most want to explore?
  – What seems most important about the question?
• Compile a list of points which seem to be central to the question, in
  preparation for finding information.

  In a set specific topic, you may be given an indication of some main
  points. For example, briefly describing your understanding of central
  terms or concepts might form an early part of the assignment; so in
  the Piaget topic you would need (a) to describe Piaget's theory of child
  developmental stages before (b) discussing its possible applications
  to maths teaching in primary schools. Otherwise possible main points
  are likely to come from your background knowledge, from course

materials or lectures, from recommended reading or from tutorial discussions on the topic.

- For an argumentative essay ask: What key reasons might I use to support my thesis?
  For an expository essay, ask: What main points seem to be central to the controlling focus? (See 'Genres')
- Make an initial list of alternative or related terms for each point. A library catalogue or reference works can help you revise your list so that your information search is as effective as possible. For example, to find information on migrants in a catalogue look at the entries before and after 'Migrants', and in particular look at associated headings which suggest alternatives such as 'Emigrants', 'Immigration', 'Multicultural', or the nationality of a migrant group. To find references to the changing composition of the workforce, you may need to look up 'Unemployment', 'Trade Unions', 'Women, working', as well as the obvious heading 'Workforce'.
- Use reference works such as subject dictionaries to look up your initial list of subject headings and to find any related terms which are associated with each heading. Consult a general thesaurus, or a specialised work such as the *APAIS Thesaurus*, as a way of coming up with alternative or related headings for your points.

6 How might I structure my answer to the question?

Most questions include 'directive' or 'process' words such as 'criticise', 'discuss' or 'evaluate' which help to shape the type of essay you write and its structure (see Table 6.1).

- Decide which words are 'directive' or 'process' words.
- Find how many parts there are to the topic.
- From the directive words (or the instructions on the essay) decide if the essay is to be argumentative or expository.
- Analyse the directive or process words to work out how they will direct the structure of your essay. Using the words decide, for example:
  - whether the question involves description and/or analysis of this description
  - whether to compare two different aspects of a question , or instead to clearly define all of its components
  - whether to argue a case for or against a particular controversy relating to the question, or to review the range of opinions on it.

7 How will I acknowledge and examine my subjectivity?

- Check any available guidelines, and note how much personal opinion you are able to include.
- Think critically about any preconceived ideas or biases you may have in relation to the question. How might you minimise the effect of these and remain open minded as you develop a possible thesis or focus?

Table 6.1   Directive words

'When I use a word', Humpty Dumpty said, in a rather scornful tone, 'it means just what I choose it to mean—neither more nor less.'
(Lewis Carroll)

Terms indicating an argumentative essay

Analyse	Show the essence of something, by breaking it down into its component parts and examining each part in detail
Argue	Present the case for and/or against a particular proposition
Criticise	Give your judgement about the merit of theories or opinions about the truth of facts, and back your judgement by a discussion of the evidence
Critique	See 'criticise'
Discuss	Investigate or examine by argument, sift and debate, giving reasons for and against
Evaluate	Make an appraisal of the worth of something, in the light of its apparent truth or utility; include your personal opinion
Interpret	Bring out the meaning of, and make clear and explicit; usually also giving your own judgement
Justify	Show adequate grounds for decisions or conclusions
Prove	Demonstrate truth or falsity by presenting evidence
Review	Make a survey of, examining the subject critically

Terms indicating an expository essay

Compare	Look for similarities and differences between propositions
Contrast	Explain differences
Define	Set down the precise meaning of a word or phrase. Show that the distinctions implied in the definition are necessary.
Describe	Give a detailed or graphic account of
Enumerate	List or specify and describe
Examine	Present in depth and investigate the implications
Explain	Make plain, interpret, and account for in detail
Illustrate	Explain and make clear by the use of concrete examples, or by the use of a figure or diagram
Outline	Give the main features or general principles of a subject, omitting minor details, and emphasising structure and relationship
Relate	Narrate/show how things are connected to each other, and to what extent they are alike or affect each other
State	Specify fully and clearly
Summarise	Give a concise account of the chief points or substance of a matter, omitting details and examples
Trace	Identify and describe the development or history of a topic from some point or origin.

Source: Adapted from Harry Maddox, 1967, *How to Study*, 2nd edn, Pan Books, London, pp. 119–20.

Group writing projects

A written assignment which is to be part of a group project involves firstly agreeing on a question which the whole group will explore; deciding which specific aspects of the question each person or sub-group, will research; and clarifying how each person's work contributes to the overall question and to the total project (see 'Collaborative learning groups', Chapter 11). Once the group has agreed on a question, the steps outlined in steps 1 to 7 can be applied to it, so that the group can collectively prepare a written definition of the question before they begin research.

Your initial working definition

Before you begin full-scale research for an essay, write down:

- a brief statement of your purposes and the aims stated in your course materials and by your teacher
- the exact question you will research
- your responses to your analysis of the question under the headings:
  (i)   Possible thesis or controlling focus
  (ii)   Possible supporting reasons or main points
  (iii) Proposed structure (sequence of reasons or main points)
  (iv) Assumptions or views
- the position underlying the argument.

This working definition may be reasonably clear at this stage if the essay is short and straightforward. But it is more likely that you will not have a clear statement of your thesis or focus, or a complete list of likely points as supporting evidence from which you can choose. As yet you may not be able to determine a structure.

If you have trouble analysing a question, write down any ideas you have on it and discuss them with other people. Expressing your thoughts accurately in writing or verbally to others will help you clarify them (see 'The process of writing', Chapter 12).

It can be useful to return to this initial definition of the question as you go about your research. When you have completed your research, repeat the process of defining your question by writing out your thesis or focus, supporting evidence and structure (see 'Your revised definition', Chapter 7).

■ ■ ■ ■ ■

These initial steps in analysing a question will largely determine the material you select for research and how you finally present your essay. However, as you proceed with your research the information you gather reshapes your original definition or conception of the question, and may even lead you to change to another question. Analysing your question and researching it are interdependent processes, rather than two separate activities.

Further reading

See 'Further reading' at the end of Chapter 13.

Notes

1 The notion of a controlling focus has been adapted from Martin L. Arnaudet & Mary Allen Barrett, 1984, *Approaches to academic reading and writing*, Prentice Hall Regents, Englewood Cliffs, NJ.

CHAPTER 7

RESEARCHING A TOPIC

Once you are clear about what is expected of you in your assignment and you have analysed your topic or question and written down an initial definition of it, you are then ready to begin full-scale research. The next step is to think about where and how you will find material. You will be given information in lectures and tutorials, supplied with reference lists for courses, tutorials, lectures and assignments, and perhaps directed to sources such as the Internet, the media and individual people. At times you may have to search out and know how to use less obvious sources so that you don't overlook significant material.

This plethora of material can be overwhelming, particularly as the information on most subjects is increasing rapidly all the time, and the array of information on the Internet compounds this. You may feel bewildered because you want or are apparently expected to absorb so much. You may feel under an obligation to use the Internet. When researching a topic it is easy to become sidetracked by fascinating but irrelevant information, locked into a Net search, held up by little or no information, or bewitched by mystifying technical language. You can avoid these pitfalls by keeping in mind your purpose, the scope of your assignment, how much material you need, how much you can absorb and how much time you have. Obviously you can't use or absorb everything, so as well as being aware of potential material, you need to decide which material is most useful to you.

> People who think education equals information have no idea what either education or information is. Always ask computer enthusiasts to define what they mean by information. If they tell you everything is information and information is everything: beware. That's a sales pitch, not a sensible idea. A good working definition of information might be: it is an answer to a question that purports to be a fact. At least a definition like that reminds us that the quality of the question is more important than the quantity of data that appears as an answer. (*Theodore Roszak*)

This chapter prepares you to use research material, and gives some hints on selecting and evaluating material for your purpose, and for its relevance and complexity. It looks at the practical aspects of making your selection—buying, copying and borrowing. It also suggests how to make the most effective use of the research material as you work towards a more considered definition of your question. The chapter focuses on research for essays but can also be applied to reports or discussion papers.

Preparing for your research

Selecting relevant material

If you are not given a list of references from which to choose, check the available information sources and make up a list of material relevant to your question (see 'Topics and questions', Chapter 6). Consult your teacher and any course guides, handouts or reference lists for suggestions. Ask for guidance on which material is essential and which material to read first. Look for both primary and secondary sources on your question (see 'Identifying primary and secondary sources', Chapter 8). The length of your list should depend on the time available for your research.

When analysing your question you should have drawn up a list of the main points and key search terms. Keep these firmly in mind and use them in your research. Browsing through material which is vaguely connected with your question can be highly enjoyable, and while it does not constitute seriously selecting material for full-scale research on the topic, it can lead to serendipitous insights. Keep in mind your time constraints. For example, following a trail of web sites can be haphazard, and waiting to access them can be slow, especially if you do not have a powerful computer setup.

When browsing you may come across material which isn't precisely on your topic but deals with the general principles underlying it. An article on scientific methods, for example, can spark off ideas about an individual question on physics. Other material may provide valuable background. For example, a conversation with a person who lived through the Depression years in Australia may help you understand a specific aspect of this era more fully. Occasionally an idea can be illuminated by juxtaposing it with material from an unexpected source; for instance, astronomy with Alice in Wonderland, semiotics with Sufi philosophy, poetry with popular music.

If using the World Wide Web, you need to be prepared to do a certain amount of browsing through hypertext links. But in an area you will probably want to revisit, short circuit this process for future visits by 'bookmarking' sites to which you will want to return. Don't, however, randomly bookmark sites as you only have to go back and re-check each one for its usefulness, and this will be very time consuming.

Look for material on your topic which is not obvious or recommended. One of your own books, for example, may contain suggestions for further reading, or an organisation you contact for information may refer you to another source.

> Like any kind of exploratory activity, library research benefits from good planning and proficient technique (e.g., subject searches, catalogues, indexes) ... but it also profits from unplanned encounters with the unknown. Contrast the tunnel vision effect produced by a data base that only reports what you ask it. Try wandering down the stacks; let yourself get distracted by what's in the vicinity of the item you're hunting. Who knows what exciting or inspiring adventures in knowledge lurk there? (*Zoe Sofoulis*)

Consider the practical steps for selecting information from the research material you will use. For example, you gain more from a book if you are aware of what is involved in the process of reading and how you might improve your skills as a reader. However, the skills needed for reading a printed book or article differ from the skills needed to read material online, so it is important to reflect on these differences. You learn more from a lecture or radio program if you have thought about how these media convey information and what you need to do in order to listen more effectively. (See 'Using sources effectively' in Chapter 8, the introduction to Chapter 9 on reading, and Chapter 10 'Listening to lectures'.)

Evaluating your selection

Once you have selected relevant material, evaluate it according to the purpose for which you need it and its complexity for you.

According to your purpose

Why do you want to use the material you are evaluating? Is it preliminary reading for a lecture or for a discussion paper, follow-up reading to a field trip or study material for an exam? ('Your purposes' in Chapter 9 looks at why you might want to read a book, and Table 9.1 on previewing suggests questions which help clarify how useful a book is for your purpose.)

Some material, such as a course text, you use for more than one purpose. Sometimes different materials may complement each other, such as two books each with information on a different aspect of your topic, or a lecture and a course text which present the same information from different perspectives. Sometimes you have to choose between materials because they are repetitious, such as two video documentaries which cover essentially the same ground.

Complexity of material

> You can only understand a textbook when you are at the point where you almost don't need to read it, where it helps you comprehend (if it is any good) some higher-order connections among things which you separately have already worked your way through or around. (*David Hawkins*)

Previewing material can help you discover the complexity of the text or material for you and hence the background knowledge you require to use it.

- The topic may or may not be interesting or familiar to you and may or may not accord with your beliefs and biases. If a topic or perspective is new to you, you won't understand all the material in it, but its very newness can be exciting. Don't automatically reject apparently difficult material—even as a beginning it may provide you with one or two important ideas, and later you may find it easier to understand and very stimulating.
- The structure, format and writing style of material can make it easy or difficult for you to follow.
- Perhaps you are more comfortable using some media than others. For example, perhaps you usually take in more from printed journal articles or online course materials than from lectures because you can revisit difficult sections in the former. Any medium becomes familiar if you use it often enough, but if there is no time for this before selecting material, opt for media which usually yield you the most information (and learn how to use the others later).

If material you are required to use seems too advanced or too basic for you, discuss this with your teacher and with other students. There may be other material you can use, or if you need the material for an assignment you might need to choose another topic.

Buy, copy or borrow material?

I do the yoga exercises I managed to learn before I received the eightieth reminder from the library, and they sent a messenger, and I had to pay such a big fine that I might just as well have bought the book. (*Peter Hoeg*)

Your choice of material depends on its availability. Sometimes you will encounter problems with material you want to use because you can't buy it or borrow it through a library. Often you can avoid these problems by doing your research well in advance, arranging to borrow material from friends, seeking out electronic sources of similar items and asking your teacher if an alternative reference is possible. When researching for an assignment, you may need to reconsider your choice of a topic or question in the light of available resources.

Some material you are likely to want to refer to again, such as a course text or a reference book you need for a final exam or for a seminar paper. If you do need to consult material more than once, you may want to obtain your own copy—to buy a book, to tape a lecture or an interview, to download an article located through a CD-ROM database or to photocopy an article (subject to copyright laws). If the information is on the Net, bookmark it so that you can easily find it again. If you can't have your own copy, try to borrow the material, or if your information comes from a person or a place, arrange to visit them again. If you need to use borrowed material heavily, take full notes on the content and note source details such as page numbers.

When deciding which books to buy, be wary of relying on course booklists given in handbooks. Such lists are usually drawn up six months or more before a course starts and may change substantially, or a different edition or translation of a book may be recommended. Before you buy books or start your reading, check to find out if there have been changes with a teacher or with up-to-date course lists which may be online.

Whether you buy, copy or borrow material depends on:

- your finances
- whether the materials are easily available through a library, online, from another student, or from a teacher
- how heavily you will use the material
- how much you rely on course materials and references for stimulation, for instance, if you have little opportunity to discuss your work with other students

- whether you remember more if you underline the books or articles you read, and
- whether or not the material will be useful in other courses or in your future or current occupation.

Previewing research material

Once you have decided which material to use in your research, previewing the material, that is, surveying it as a whole before you work with it, acquaints you with its general structure, content and presentation. This previewing enables you to consider how you could best use the material for your purpose. For example, you can plan how detailed your reading of a book should be, or whether to take notes on a television program, or which parts of online course material seem most immediately relevant for an essay (see 'Previewing', Chapter 9).

If you are using material from Web sites, previewing critically is particularly important. Except for items such as refereed electronic journals, there are few indicators to inform a novice in a subject area which information is more reliable and reputable. Your teachers are unlikely to be impressed by information which turns out to be from a strongly biased sources, such as apparently scientific writing on evolution which comes from a fundamentalist Bible college. So while the Net potentially offers rich and diverse material, use this information carefully. Acquire some basic previewing techniques, such as checking when a site was last updated and information about the authors. Check to see if the information is associated with an official home page or has been refereed by academics. Unless you know your subject area well or have guidance from someone who does, acquire some basic familiarity with the area through reliable sources such as encyclopaedias, key texts and knowledgeable academics. Then as part of your preview begin to undertake a preliminary evaluation of Net material to decide if it is worth working with in depth.

> On the Internet, there is no quality control as there would be in any school library. If a bibliography on the real, historical Aztecs surfaces amid the gleanings it may very well be out to date and unattributed. It might be the work of an amateur Aztec enthusiast in Peoria who never read basic materials in the field. If there is an essay on the Aztecs it may have been written by a fellow in Moose Jaw who has rather unusual theories about pre-Columbian peoples and space aliens. The Internet is a free-for-all, as enjoyable as any conversation one might strike up in a saloon or coffee house. But it is hardly governed by the critical safeguards and intellectual structures that have been developed across the centuries to discriminate between honest thought and rampant eccentricity. (*Theodore Roszak*)

You have to record, store and retrieve useful information, so give some thought to how you will do this (see 'Selecting, recording and filing information'). A filing system evolves as you use it, but have a basis for your filing before you start researching. When writing an assignment, if you have thought about your purpose and analysed your question, this should form the basis of your system. You will then need to consider which medium is the most appropriate, for example, a computer database or portable index cards.

Thinking about your audience

In the preliminary stages of your research, give some thought to how and to whom you will communicate your ideas and information. A written essay or report isn't automatically the most appropriate means for expressing ideas. If, for example, you are researching children's poetry, a taped essay which includes live poetry readings may be most effective. If your topic is animal behaviour, you may decide to include photographs or a videotape to convey your findings. Asking yourself, 'To whom do I want to communicate the information I find?' can help you decide how to convey your information. Writing just for your teacher differs from preparing a paper for a group discussion.

> 'Don't grunt,' said Alice, 'that's not at all a proper way of expressing yourself.' (*Lewis Carroll*)

As you work with material

Questioning and evaluating

> Where there is much desire to learn, there of necessity will be much arguing, much writing, many opinions; for opinion in good men [*sic*] is but knowledge in the making. (*John Milton*)

You should have already previewed your material for its overall relevance to your purpose and the topic. As you work with a book, listen to a lecture, explore a Web site or watch a film, question and evaluate the information offered. This involves examining the purpose, argument, content, structure and presentation of the material for its general quality and for its specific relevance to your purpose and topic. (See Chapters 9 and 10 for details on how to criticise information from reading and lectures.) Be prepared to discover that some of the material you have selected may not be as useful as you hoped, and don't expect that set or suggested references will automatically suit your definition of a question. If you feel material is of limited use to you, abandon it as a source or try to incorporate a criticism of it into your assignment.

As part of evaluating information in your research, hopefully you will learn to interpret primary sources confidently. In some assignments you are expected to use both your interpretation of primary source material and opinion from secondary sources (see 'Identifying primary and secondary sources', Chapter 8). For example, when you conduct an experiment, you may be expected to interpret the data yourself and to refer to other people's interpretation of data from a similar experiment. In an essay you may be expected to criticise a well-known author's works (a primary source) and use other critics' evaluations (a secondary source) of these. You might feel uncertain about presenting your argument and your own ideas, and think that you should play it safe and rely mostly on secondary sources, or you might come from an intellectual culture where what you write is expected to rely heavily on presenting ideas from authorities. To develop your confidence in presenting your own ideas on primary sources, practise the following:

- get to know the primary source material thoroughly, and see what ideas and interests this sparks off in you
- refer to secondary sources to help clarify points you don't understand in the primary source material
- read selectively among secondary sources and critically examine other people's interpretations of the primary ideas or data you are studying, and
- use secondary sources for occasional new insights and for any unexpected connections they may make.

Above all, trust your own intelligence and common sense in questioning and evaluating research material.

In a private debate the scholar Salih Awami said to Sufi Rahimi: 'What you have just said lacks references and proofs through quotations from ancient authority.' 'Not at all,' said Rahimi, 'for I have them all here, chapter and verse.' The scholar went away, saying, 'That was what I wanted to know.' The next day he made his famous speech on Rahimi which began: 'The lecture which you are about to hear from Sheikh Rahimi lacks conviction. Why, he is so unsure of himself that he actually adducted written proofs and authorities to what he says.' (*Idries Shah*)

Selecting, recording and filing information

As you evaluate material, select information and record it in an easily accessible form. For example, photocopy the abstract of an article, download a valuable reference list to disk, tape parts of an interview, or take photographs. You will probably record most of your information in note form even if preparing an oral or audiovisual assignment. (See Chapters 9 and 10 for more on selecting information and making notes from reading and lectures.)

Some information you don't need to record and keep because it is relatively accessible or because it is unlikely that you will need it in future. However, some information which you may want again is available to you only once (such as material in an interview or radio program) or is difficult to find again (such as information from a person awkward to contact or a book which isn't readily available). In these instances, as you select the information you want, think how you can best record and store it.

The basic reasons for systematically filing information are so that you can easily find it again, can add to or subtract from it, and can re-arrange it when useful. You might prefer stationery such as looseleaf paper and a ring binder, a box of file cards, a concertina file or several filing trays to make it easier to arrange and re-arrange material as necessary. Alternatively, compare the usefulness of various software tools designed for creating a database or a filing system. Be selective about what you print out in hard copy, and make sure you always back up your research material to disk.

Methods for filing information depend on the specific purposes for which you need it. Often it is convenient to organise and file material according to its content or its source, as in the following examples.

- To follow the development of themes within a course, keep your lecture notes in sequence in a looseleaf folder. You can then interleave notes from discussion groups, fieldwork and research wherever their content is related to a theme.
- When preparing to write an essay in which you are expected to base your ideas on a careful examination of primary source material, keep your notes taken from the reading of primary sources separate from those from secondary sources.

You might choose instead to organise and file your material in chronological order (such as dates on lecture notes), alphabetical order (such as Web addresses or authors of books read) and/or numerical order (with each item or each page of notes numbered). Record the source of your information in detail, including page numbers, in case you want to find it again or cite the reference.

Read material and edit notes before you consider filing them. Ask yourself if you are likely to use the material again. A growing pile of 'to-be-read-or-edited-material' indicates that you need to be more realistic about the amount of information you think that you can take in and use. An efficient system is of little use if all it yields is an impressive collection of file card boxes whose contents you have mostly forgotten, a stack of folders full of photocopied articles you intend to read one day, or an elaborate database which has been of more interest to you than its contents.

> Knowledge is of two kinds. We know a subject ourselves, or we know where we can find information upon it. (*Samuel Johnson*)

Organising and integrating ideas and information

When preparing for an assignment, as you research and think about your topic or question you need to organise and integrate your ideas and the information you find, for example, so that it supports your thesis in a persuasive essay or your controlling focus in an expository essay (see 'Genres', Chapter 6). The following method is one way of doing this for an essay.

- In a persuasive essay write out a tentative statement of your thesis. Capture the essence of your argument in a sentence. For an expository essay, clarify the controlling focus. Keep this in front of you as you work.
- Write each of the possible main points as a heading on separate sheets of paper or cards. If you have a computer and the appropriate software you might prefer to use the outlining facility to help order these points. At this stage many people who go to a library to carry out their research find a portable system such as cards more convenient, but this is not so important if you often work at home and access library resources online.
- Enter relevant information and ideas (and references to any graphic or audiovisual material) under the appropriate heading.
- As you build your research notes, add a new heading if you decide on another major point, such as another main reason supporting your thesis. Alternatively, you may decide to delete a point which comes to appear less significant. If you have much more information for one heading than for others and if that main point is central to the question and clearly supports your thesis, consider if you should base your whole assignment on this point or perhaps rethink your thesis. In this case develop new main points under that heading. If necessary, reorganise and delete material.
- Check the number of major points you want to make against the possible assignment length and the time available. It is better to err on the side of making a few points clearly, with plenty of evidence and examples and explanation, rather than trying to cover a large number of possible major points superficially.
- Check that each of the main points clearly supports your thesis or focus and is clearly relevant to your topic or question (see 'Developing and analysing a question, Chapter 6).

Organising your information and ideas in this way helps you see the main points more clearly. You begin to understand how they could effectively be part of your argument and connect to one another, and the order in which to develop them. Your researching, thinking and organising should extend and clarify your original analysis of the question. As you continue your research, you probably revise your original working definition of the question and begin to structure the content.

Expressing your ideas

Talking to others about your ideas and the information you find helps you begin to sort out your thoughts and become accustomed to putting them into words. For example, in an online course you may have the chance through a discussion list to work collaboratively with other students in researching and drafting an essay.

As you carry out your research, it is often valuable to write individual paragraphs or sentences (or to make part of a tape) so that you capture an idea you may use later. Put these ideas down when you think of them in case they vanish; and if you have a half-formed idea in your head, try expressing it without editing and see how it takes shape. If you can use a word processor for this, it is easier at a later stage to refine what you want to say. Trying to express your current thoughts accurately can lead you to other useful ideas (see 'Free writing', Chapters 12 and 13).

Towards the end of your research

When your research is almost complete and you are ready to begin to make use of the material, allow yourself time to sort out your ideas, for your thoughts to sift and settle. Do this rather than read another article or conduct another interview, especially if you are finding it difficult to work out what you want to say. Look at your notes as a whole. This will refresh your mind about your ideas on the topic and will allow you to review the information you have selected from your material.

Talk again about your ideas and information with others, perhaps in a discussion or writing group, so that you begin to express your thoughts orally or in writing. New ideas and relationships will emerge, and any difficulties you might have in deciding and articulating what you want to say often resolve themselves. To clarify your thesis or focus, look at the connections between your main points, and ask yourself again what strikes you as most important and interesting about the question.

Your revised definition

Before you began your research you wrote down some thoughts on the purposes, a probable thesis or focus and main supporting points, and outlined a likely structure.

After your research, review your written statement about the essay's purposes and produce a revised definition or conception of your question. Look again at the question and using the items in the 'Analysing your question' section of the previous chapter, make notes again outlining your thesis or focus, the main points you have chosen, and the way in which you will structure them. Indicate how your world view has influenced your position on the question. Compare the initial and revised definitions. Have you omitted anything important? Does your revised definition still reflect your purposes for the essay?

Make sure, especially in the case of specific questions, that you are answering the set question or sticking to the topic set. With topics of your own choice, re-read any guidelines to ensure that you have incorporated all of the requirements when developing your question. Remember that focusing your written work around a thesis is a fundamental expectation for argumentative essays.

■ ■ ■ ■ ■

Now that your research is more or less completed, your thesis or focus and the main points which you will cover should be reasonably definite. If you find that you have omitted any important content you may need to do some further research. The way in which you structure your assignment—how you will show the relationship between the main points and organise them so that they support your thesis or focus—may be quite clear now or may still be tentative. In either case, leave some flexibility so that if necessary you can revise your definition further when expressing your thoughts and information in writing your assignment (see 'Before you begin your writing', Chapter 13).

An assignment is designed for a specific, limited purpose, rather than to find out all you are ever likely to know on a topic. Analysing a question and researching a topic should enable you to select from your current knowledge of that topic, even if your knowledge continues to grow and expand in areas far beyond the focus of your assignment.

Further reading

Bell, Judith, 1993, *Doing your research project: A guide for first time researchers in education and social science*, 2nd edn, Open University Press, Milton Keynes, Bucks.

Burns, Robert B., 1997, *Introduction to research methods*, 3rd edn, Addison Wesley Longman Australia, Melbourne.

Lane, Nancy D., 1996, *Techniques for student research: A practical guide*, 2nd edn, Longman Cheshire, Melbourne.

Rottenberg, Annette J., 1986, *Elements of argument: a text and reader*, St Martin's Press, New York.

Zimmerman, D. & Rodrigues, D., 1992, *Research and writing in the disciplines*, Harcourt Brace Jovanovich, Sydney.

CHAPTER 8

USING LIBRARIES AND OTHER INFORMATION SOURCES

We live in the midst of information networks. In both the face-to-face and virtual world, you are a point in many networks, sometimes giving information and sometimes seeking it. No one can possibly learn all there is to know about a subject, so you can be both a learner and a teacher in subjects which interest you. Even as an interested beginner, you probably know enough about an area to teach someone else a little about it. If you can't answer someone's queries on a subject, you can probably direct them to another part of a network where they are likely to find what they want to know. Which network you plug into when seeking information depends on what you want to know, why you want to know it, and whether you know how to use available information sources.

This chapter centres on the processes involved in making effective use of libraries and other information sources, while emphasising the need to be aware of the diversity of possible sources including the Internet. The chapter looks at identifying primary and secondary sources and at using sources effectively. We begin by looking at library services, since tertiary institutions rely heavily on these as an information source.

Libraries

If you have physical access to more than one library, explore each one to find out what it offers you. Look at each as a place to work. Consider the facilities and services, material in your areas of interest, and staff expertise and helpfulness. A large library may have most of the material you need, but you may prefer a small library where the staff are familiar with your interests and you feel more at home. On the other hand, the small library nearby may be frustrating because it never seems to have the books you want, and you may prefer a large library with a more sophisticated range of collections.

There are various types of libraries which have many different functions. These include:

- large state libraries, with special sections such as archives
- university libraries, often with individual subject libraries attached
- government departmental libraries
- specialist collections, such as a historical society library, a photographic collection, a substantial private collection
- public libraries serving a local community, and
- school and college libraries.

Online libraries

Traditionally, students have used on-campus libraries most heavily, and occasionally visited or made use of services available from other libraries in the same city or region. Today, through inter-library loans and electronic information services you also have access to material in libraries other than the one or two which you can visit most easily, or from which you usually receive materials. In addition, students with home computers and electronic connections to a library can access catalogues online.

When using the library once meant hunting through physical collections, it is now more appropriate to think in terms of accessing library services and library networks. Many materials from the core collections of academic libraries are now online, and for computer-literate students this has the advantage of 24-hour access to materials which can't be misfiled or defaced and whose text, for a fee, can be downloaded. Once an article is found, it can be e-mailed or faxed to a student. When it comes to searching for material, most university libraries now only mediate searches for newer users who are not yet familiar with using CD-ROM networks. Also they may conduct information searches where needed by students with specific learning disabilities. Higher education students now need the skills to access information electronically, and most university libraries provide courses and support to help students develop these skills.

> The technology will deliver anything you want to your door if you're able to pay for it. (*Grant Stone*)

Making full use of libraries

It takes time to become familiar with the contents and organisation of a library, and practice to learn how to access library facilities and services. This familiarisation is a means to learning more about subjects which interest you, and the exercise at the end of this chapter can help you with this. To update, extend and diversify your knowledge of the information that any library has to offer, explore its resources when new topics stimulate your curiosity.

1 Knowing what materials libraries contain

Explore the libraries to which you have access to find out what materials they contain. Print material such as books and journals are familiar sources of information to most of us. The following list may include materials which are unfamiliar to you or which you have not considered for academic research:

- graphic material, such as maps, prints, illustrations, paintings and models
- audiovisual material, such as slides and photographs, audio cassettes, videotapes, films, and overhead transparencies
- microfilm, for example, of back issues of newspapers
- microfiche, such as the *Human Relations Area File*, and
- collections of ephemeral material, such as newsletters, posters, advertisements and lapel buttons.

There may also be materials, such as a collection of taped versions of print materials, which are available for students with particular learning disabilities.

As well as holding such diverse types of material, libraries have printed and electronic information sources available to student researchers.

a Books and other printed material

Twenty-two acknowledged concubines, and a library of sixty-two thousand volumes, attested the variety of his inclination ... (*Edward Gibbon*)

Apart from books, some libraries contain:

- periodicals, journals, newspapers, bulletins and other serials, with current issues usually on display and back issues shelved or available on microfilm
- government publications, such as reports, yearbooks, and manuals, and
- pamphlets on a wide range of subjects.

Chapter 8 suggests ways of reading such printed material effectively.

One important group of books in any library is **the reference collection**. You probably are aware of standard references such as *The Encyclopaedia Britannica* and *The Oxford Dictionary*, but reference collections can also contain works such as:

- specialist encyclopaedias or dictionaries, such as *The Encyclopaedia of Philosophy, Dictionary of Film Makers*
- atlases, gazetteers, guidebooks, such as the *Archaeological Atlas of the World, Bartholomew Gazetteer of Britain*
- yearbooks and almanacs which give relatively up-to-date statistical information and which are often government publications, such as *The West Australian Yearbook*
- handbooks which contain useful and detailed information for people in specific fields, such as teaching, writing, surveying, skin diving, and
- resource directories which are catalogues of useful material, people and places, such as a directory for a particular city or small interest group.

To find works on a topic, it can be extremely useful to consult some bibliographies, indexes and abstracts in the reference collection as well as using the subject catalogue.

- Bibliographies list books by a particular subject, author, printer or country, for example, *The Current Bibliographies on African Affairs, The International Bibliography of Economics, A Bibliography of Sex Rites and Customs. The Australian National Bibliography* lists recent Australian books and official reports, and *Books in Print* lists non-fiction books printed in the USA.
- Indexes are usually:
  - indexes to multi-volume reference works such as an encyclopaedia
  - indexes to government publications, for example, *Australian Government Publications*
  - indexes issued by publishers of a periodical, for example, the *Scientific American Cumulative Index*

- indexes issued by an independent publisher for a number of general periodicals, for example, *APAIS* (the Australian Public Affairs Information Service), a major indexing journal for the humanities and social sciences which is issued by the National Library, Canberra, and
- indexes to periodicals in special fields, for example, *Index Medicus* in the medical field.
- Abstracts include a précis of books and articles in a field, and also index them, for example *Psychological Abstracts*. The CD-ROM database *Psychlit* contains the same material as Psychological Abstracts and the search software enables you to do in seconds what would take hours by hand in the print version of *Psychological Abstracts*.

To make efficient use of bibliographies, indexes and abstracts—especially in an online catalogue—you need to develop a list of search terms central to a topic (see 'Developing and analysing a topic', Chapter 7).

b Electronic reference material
Most research libraries now have CD-ROM disks which hold bibliographical and statistical databases and other reference sources including some dictionaries and encyclopaedias. These disks can hold the equivalent of 1500 floppy discs or over 200 000 pages of text. CD-ROM databases such as *MLA* and *ERIC* will give you references to five years of journal articles in literature and education respectively, and *CDATA* contains recent census data from the Australian Bureau of Statistics. To access these databases you need search terms to browse headings, hypertext links and alphabetical menus; and you can view the references on a workstation screen, print them out or capture them to disk. CD-ROM materials may also come in a multimedia form and include visuals (such as photographs or drawings), sound (such as music and foreign language phrases) or both (as in videos and film clips).

Another form of technology which may be useful, particularly later in a degree or in postgraduate work, is online data retrieval. This connects you to a distant database via telephone and is usually expensive to use.

2 Learning how to find items
- Ask the *library staff*—they are usually helpful with anything from the most basic to the most esoteric of queries.
- Learn about the *operation* of a library, for example, how the borrowing system operates or how to request an interlibrary loan. Through the academic library electronic catalogue network, you can gain access to a wide range of material (such as journal holdings), although this service can be expensive. Conversely, in times of restricted funding the collections in libraries often do not increase in proportion to the increase in students, so more print material may be placed in limited-

access reserve collections. This is done to try and make material available to a greater number of students, and you need to learn how to make the most of these collections.

- *If you are not able to visit the campus* library easily, perhaps because you are a student who is part-time, external or disabled, be particularly well-informed about the facilities you need to use most often, such as online access, photocopying services and special loan arrangements.

  When you send in a request for help, or if you do manage to visit the library, be very clear about the sort of information you are seeking. Explore any other library facilities near you, work out which books you will use most heavily, and be prepared to buy them (see 'Buy, copy, or borrow material?' Chapter 8). The cost of mailing books or making special trips to a library can soon add up to the price of several books, and libraries don't regard provision of textbooks as one of their functions.

- Find out which *system* the library uses for cataloguing, classifying, indexing and shelving the material it contains. For example:
  - some libraries use a classification system other than the familiar Dewey system
  - methods of shelving materials such as large books, pamphlets and audiovisual material vary from one library to another
  - the alphabetical order of catalogue entries may vary, for example in how entries for authors with hyphenated names are filed.

- Learn how to use *the catalogue system*. Ask the library staff to help or take a course on how to use the library. Taking time to do this can save you many hours later on and gives you access to a much greater depth of information. Some libraries (such as some local ones) still use catalogue cards, but most libraries now use online catalogues. You may be able to access the catalogue online via Telnet.

To find items using online catalogues, you choose from a menu on the screen which is accompanied by instructions directing you how to search for an item by author, by subject or by title. In this initial search you will usually find information on:
- the call number, which gives you the exact shelf location and also appears on the item itself
- the classification number, which arranges material by subject
- the author's symbol, which is used to sub-arrange material on the same subject
- a location symbol, which indicates the sequence of materials with which the item is shelved—with oversize books, for example, or with journals, pamphlets, or general books (Your next step is to find where such material is shelved and how each of these categories of material is organised.)

- publication details for an item, which include the publisher, place, publication date and edition (Note that the date of first publication may differ from the publication date of the particular edition or reprint which the library holds.)
- the loan status, which indicates if an item is on the shelf, on loan, or waiting to be recalled or reshelved.

To look up an item using the author's name or the title, you need the correct spelling of the name and the correct wording of the title. If you know the title of a book you are seeking, then search for that first. There may be several authors with the same name and each one may have written several books. Most titles are unique so a title search is the most direct way to find the book in the catalogue. If you can't find an item in the catalogue, check that you have been given an accurate reference.

Once you have located the item and the relevant information from your initial search using author, title or subject, you can carefully follow the instructions in online catalogues to find further information such as other books by the same author or the titles of items shelved nearby. In some catalogues you will also come across reference entries which direct you to alternative headings for a topic (such as 'Motor cars ... see Automobiles'), or to related headings (such as 'Naturalists ... see also Ecologists'), or to more specific headings (such as 'Biology ... see also Marine Biology').

- Become familiar with *the layout* of a campus library—find out where the different types of materials are located, and where facilities such as photocopiers and audio visual equipment can be found. Most libraries have maps and publications describing their layout and operation, but it is easy to fall into the habit of only using one section of a library and being unaware of what other areas have to offer.
- Find out what extra *guides* the information or reference desk holds to enable you to locate material. There may be a print out of material currently on reserve, a list of journal issues, information about material in special subject libraries elsewhere on campus, or information about branch library holdings. A large tertiary institution with more than one campus or with long-established departments may well have branch libraries in addition to the main one, and if so it is useful to have some idea of what each branch holds, both in the way of general collections and in specialist subject material which could be relevant to your interests.
- If t*he item isn't on the shelf* in its exact location, check if it is on the same shelf but slightly out of order, and double check the call number, location and loan status of the item. If none of these steps help you find the item, it is probably in use in the library by another reader or waiting to be re-shelved. Try the shelves later on. If the item is already borrowed, enter a recall request if you need it.

A Harvard Librarian of last century was notorious for his unsmiling countenance. One day a professor saw the librarian coming across the quad, beaming. 'You seem particularly jovial today' he said. 'Yes,' replied the bookman, 'all the books are in except two, and I'm going to get them now.' (*A Librarian*)

3 Accessing facilities and services

It is helpful to find out when the library you use most often is busy and when it is quiet. Then if you possibly can, visit or access the library's services at the quiet times (such as Sunday morning) when staff are more available to help, when reserve collections are less in demand, and when easier access to online catalogues enables you to save time by searching for a batch of items all at once.

To be able to use the materials a library offers means learning to use catalogues and equipment such as photocopiers, tape recorders, and video cassette players. When you need this equipment ask one of the library staff to show you how to use it, as most students who are not initially confident with equipment rapidly become so once it is familiar.

Some convenient forms of storing information—such as microfilm and microfiche—can be demanding to use, so request help if you run into difficulties or if you want to make copies of the material in the least expensive way. If you find that using these information sources is tiring to your eyes, to obtain the information you may need to plan several short work sessions rather than one long one.

Using electronic library services

Whether you are a school leaver familiar with computers from school or home, a mature age student who uses computers at work, or someone still in a state of computerphobia, you will need to acquire specific skills and equipment to make the most of electronic academic library networks.

- If you are unfamiliar with online catalogues or information technologies such as CD-ROM disks, take part in a library tutorial on these or ask the staff for help.
- Acquire at least basic computer skills, including touch typing if possible.
- Compare the pros and cons of electronic and manual searches, for example:
  - how quickly they enable you to locate specific information
  - ways of limiting or broadening searches
  - whether you can browse nearby items, and
  - potential pitfalls and useful techniques.
- Acquire skills relevant to online searching (see 'Previewing research material', Chapter 7).
- Put into practice some time management skills (see 'Planning your week', Chapter 2) so that you decide how much time you are prepared

to spend on a particular search, and so that you avoid 'over-searching' for a minor assignment (see 'Preparing for your research', Chapter 7).

If you want to access library services and catalogues from home, invest in a home computer and an electronic connection to the library (See 'Choosing technology', Chapter 3).

With an electronic connection, you will gain 24-hour access to the library; be able to conduct quick subject searches with no postal costs and delays; and obtain high quality copies of articles; and exchange e-mails with library staff as part of your information searches. You can download information and save time-consuming visits to a library and photocopiers. For students who are isolated in the long term (due to limited mobility or being in prison, for example) or in the short term (due to illness or one-off commitments), online access to library services can be particularly valuable. For distance students, electronic connection costs are currently cheaper than an STD call. Within a course, once many students are connected to a campus information network, library staff can send multiple copies of the one article direct to each of them. And apart from library services, with an electronic connection you can also gain access to online courses and discussion groups (see Chapter 11, 'Participating in discussion groups').

As an alternative to home access, you might be able to gain access via a local public library or, in remote areas or small country towns, via private vendors, your employer, or organisations such as a mining company.

To make the most of current information technology as a student, stay informed about available electronic services from your 'home' library and others, and be alert for alternative ways of accessing these and a range of other information sources.

A diversity of sources

Not even the largest 'multiversity' can offer all the resources needed by students today. (*University Without Walls*)

An initial step in choosing information sources on a topic is to become aware of the range of possible sources. As a student at the turn of the century, the mass media and the Internet form a large part of your information networks and a large part of the reality in which you live. As a student in an educational institution, you have some obvious sources such as:

- classes—including lectures, laboratory sessions and discussion groups
- people, including teachers and other students, and
- printed and audiovisual material, such as course guides, laboratory manuals, handouts, recommended books and library materials.

You limit your potential sources if you look only to educational institutions and libraries for your information and ignore the groups and individual people in your community. So before automatically consulting your lecture notes or going to a library for information, ask yourself 'How would I find what I want to know if I wasn't a student with access to these sources?' You can learn much in your formal education from people who are not considered experts or teachers. If you are studying local history, for example, you can gain a wealth of information from people who have lived in your community for a long time. If you are studying insect behaviour, the person next door who has kept bees for many years can be extremely helpful. But it is easy to overlook sources of information outside libraries unless specifically directed to them.

Being able to use a range of information sources requires:

- defining your purpose and analysing a question as clearly as you can
- locating a range of potential information sources
- choosing sources which suit your subject, and
- examining sources to find out how to use them most effectively.

Defining your purpose, analysing your question and researching your topic are discussed in Chapters 6 and 7. In this chapter, this section and the next one look at identifying primary and secondary sources in relation to your topic; and at the skills necessary for using a source. As examples of these processes, the section refers to several broadly different sources of information—organisations, people, the mass media and the Internet.

Identifying primary and secondary sources

The information sources available to you vary according to your subject. Sometimes you can go directly to your subject for first-hand information. For example, if your subject is the ideas of Mao Tse-Tung you may be able to obtain and read his writings, or if you are studying goldfish behaviour you might have facilities so you can conduct experiments on this. At other times, you will have to rely on other people's reports about your subject. For example, you may read a journal article about Mao Tse-Tung if you can't obtain his books, or you might ask an aquarium owner about the behaviour of goldfish. Often you will use both first-hand (or primary) and second-hand (or secondary) information.

If you are studying a local community group and you gather your information on them by attending several meetings, your source is also your subject and is described as a primary source. If you read a newspaper article on the group to obtain your information, the article is a secondary source: that is, the information doesn't come directly from your subject.

Similarly, if your subject is a scientific research organisation, a filmed interview with the head of the organisation is a primary source, whereas someone else's written report about the interview is a secondary source. If you are studying an historical event, the testimonies of participants and witnesses are primary sources, while a source of secondary information would be a book written by an historian using these testimonies.

Communities offer a wide variety of organisations which can be used as primary and secondary sources, depending on your topic. The following are just a few of the possibilities:

- public agencies and institutions, such as museums, government departments, art galleries, courts, scientific research organisations
- commercial businesses, such as mining companies, factories, insurance companies, shopping centres, and
- community groups, such as church organisations, business associations, environmental groups, women's health care houses, ethnic broadcasting groups.

Some organisations offer library and public information facilities. You also have access to services and organisations designed to provide information, such as Citizens' Advice Bureau, and local government information offices. Often a person or group can refer you to further sources.

Do some preliminary research and decide on some questions you want to ask before contacting people and organisations for information (see 'Developing and analysing a topic', Chapter 7). Make inquiries to find out who is most likely to be helpful for your purpose and don't hesitate to make an initial polite request for information. You may be surprised at the help people are willing to give, and this process of finding material is a valuable learning exercise in itself.

Gathering information from primary sources

Other chapters in this book look at tools for using sources such as books and lectures. As an example of information gathering, here we look briefly at the tools needed to gather primary information from various sources (see 'What questions might you ask?', Chapter 4).

When you are curious about a subject you can learn much by **observation**. Listen and look closely, and use your senses of taste, smell and touch if appropriate. If you can observe a subject consistently and intently over a period of days or weeks, you will come to see it with new eyes. You can observe the natural physical environment—phenomena such as a sunset, a bird, trees, rain and mountains. You can observe your manufactured and technological environment, with its aeroplanes and advertisements, its technology and toys. You can observe the people in your world such as parents, friends, work colleagues or strangers.

Observing people and seeking information from them are activities you engage in for many of your waking hours, and you consciously or unconsciously learn much of what you need to know from your interactions with others. Deliberately seeking information from and about people requires carefully directed observation if you are to obtain useful information on a specific topic. You need practice in the skills of observation, even if you are 'only watching' people to describe them, or 'just talking' to a person to find out very specific information.

However, observation alone can't tell you all you want to know. No matter how acute your observations, don't mistake them for a sophisticated analysis. Skilled researchers are very cautious about drawing conclusions from their research.

> Natural science does not simply describe and explain nature; it is part of the interplay between nature and ourselves; it describes nature as exposed to our methods of questioning. (*Werner Heisenberg*)

As well as careful observation you also need considerable familiarity with the **appropriate research techniques** if your observation is to be extended and directed towards specific ends. Research techniques are more of a hindrance than a help if used without sensitivity to the complexity of people and of environments, or if used in the belief that they provide 'objective' answers. But if used cautiously they can be appropriate tools in your search for information. For example:

> Anyone interested in human beings and why we act as we do won't want to limit their inquiry to reading books or listening to lectures. The raw material of all our understanding of human behaviour is observations of people—ourselves and others. These observations include study of how people act in certain situations and what they report about how they feel and why they do things. From these observations we infer their motives, their values, their attitudes, and their opinions. Social science has developed a whole array of tools to assist in these analyses. These tools include questionnaires, interviews, field studies, participant observation, laboratory studies, and unobtrusive measures.

> Each of these techniques is an entire skill area in itself and consists of a whole series of sub-techniques. For example, an interview may be open-ended or closed, structured or unstructured, in-depth or limited. The proper construction of a reliable and valid questionnaire is a skill requiring months or years of training and experience. Unobtrusive measures for observing people can range from activities such as measuring carpet wear patterns in an art gallery to find out which paintings are most popular, to gathering statistics from pharmaceutical companies about sales of oral contraceptives to Catholic and non-Catholic communities.

> Each technique has its own characteristic strengths and weaknesses. The nature of the question being asked, the population being studied, the resources available, and the preferences of the questioner, all influence the

choice of appropriate techniques. This area of 'research methodology' is one of the most complex and difficult in the social sciences and scholars spend entire lifetimes studying small aspects of it.

The interpretation of the results of these information-gathering techniques is equally complex and requires a sophisticated level of skill if it is to be properly done. The path which leads from initial formulation of a question in the mind through gathering data from observations of people to drawing valid conclusions from those observations, is a long and thorny path which is pitted with traps for the unwary. Expert guidance is essential. *(John Raser (1980), written for this book)*

Humans don't follow neat patterns of behaviour, don't act in totally predictable ways, and are distinctly prone to present a researcher with a mass of complex material to analyse. As you acquire information, your clear definition of what you wanted to know will hopefully remain the same in substance, but it will inevitably change in shape as you come to grips with the uniqueness of another human being. To acquire skill in using research techniques, practise them and learn from your successes and failures how each technique can best be applied.

Even when you have considerable skill with such tools you will continue to learn more about their use because of the unpredictable nature of your 'subjects'. This very unpredictability shows the limited use of even sophisticated research tools unless you seriously consider the nature of the relationship between yourself as a researcher and the people from whom you are seeking information. For example, if in a series of interviews you treat your interviewees only as information sources who should confine themselves to passively answering your questions, you are ignoring the input that these individual human beings can make to the substance and validity of your research.

Another aspect of the relationship concerns your respective cultural backgrounds, since these affect how you interpret the responses you receive from someone whose background differs from your own. Imagine, for example, how the responses of an older female factory worker might be interpreted differently by a young male student, by an older woman who works in a professional occupation, and by an older unemployed man whose mother worked in a factory. When you do not share the cultural background of the person you are interviewing, it is advisable to seek guidance from a cross-cultural specialist when planning and interpreting your research.

> ... the active voice of the subject should be heard in the account. Our interpretations should avoid transforming the acting and thinking human being solely into an object of study, while recognising that some objectification is inherent in the process of interpretation or reconstruction. Moreover ... the theoretical reconstruction must be able to account for the investigator as well as for those who are investigated. *(Joan Acker et al.)*

Using sources effectively

As well as choosing from a range of information sources, examine each source you decide to use so that you can understand and evaluate it more fully. If, for example, you are going to interview a person, think about the process of interviewing and about the skills you will need to obtain information on your topic. Other chapters in the book look at the processes involved in using books and lectures. Here we briefly discuss the Internet as an information source, and then look at the mass media as an example of analysing a source and planning how to use that source systematically.

The Internet

> Trained as a librarian, I find the Web untidy. Libraries are organised according to established principles, and if you understand them, you can find your way around any library. The Web has protocols for data transfer, but beyond that, there's inconsistency. (*Nancy Lane*)

To learn about the possibilities of the Internet for your purposes in learning, acquire a basic understanding of how it has been put together. Become familiar with the inevitable acronyms and jargon. (Up-to-date lists of these are widely available, in Internet magazines for example, and are not repeated in this book.) If you are a new user, take an introductory course and/or work your way systematically through a beginners' guide. If you have used the Net for other purposes before becoming a student, become familiar with aspects of it which could be particularly useful to you as a student. The advantages of using the Internet for research include accessibility to material without limits on time and place, access to worldwide experts in a field, and the ability to participate in discussion lists on an equal footing.

Information sources on the Net include:

- Web sites
- discussion mailing lists
- newsgroups
- e-mail exchange
- electronic publications such as journals and newsletters, and
- electronic videoconferencing, for example, via CU-SeeMe.

Search engines such as *AltaVista* and *Yahoo!* help you find Web sites and the home pages of these sites, and you locate the sites by using key words or a topic search. The information at the sites may be presented as text or visuals, and there are multiple pathways from one site to another through hypertext links. Since these pathways are part of webs rather than hierarchies, repetition is built in and during a search you may find yourself coming across the same site more than once. Such recurrences can be frustrating, as can the experience of putting in a search command and receiving large numbers of references to unrelated sites.

Search engines, with their half-baked algorithms, are closer to slot machines than to library catalogues. You throw a query to the wind and who knows what will come back to you? You may get 234 468 supposed references to whatever you want to know. Perhaps one in a 1000 might help you. But it's easy to be sidetracked or frustrated as you try to go through those web pages one by one. Unfortunately they're not arranged in order of importance. (*David Rothenburg*)

However, there are techniques you can use to minimise such frustration, such as learning which of the many search engines are most appropriate for your purposes or locating Web rings. And once a useful site is found, you can 'bookmark' it for easy re-visiting.

If you have a heavy workload, beware of the trap of spending too much time browsing; and unless directed to do so by a teacher, don't feel obliged to search the Net exhaustively simply because it's there. Other chapters in this book refer to principles which make your Internet searches more effective (see for example 'Preparing for your research', Chapter 7). And once you have located material, there are Net-specific skills to learn, such as previewing material on a screen (see 'Previewing', Chapter 9) and correctly referencing items from a Web site (see Table 15.2 'Reference list or bibliography entries').

However, once you begin to gain enough familiarity with the nature of the Internet to dispel any initial fears, the sense of exploring this vast virtual information source is exciting for all but the most convinced technophobes. Just as physically handling books and turning newly-printed journal pages can be one of the pleasures of being a student, so can voyaging through Web sites and discovering connections between ideas.

The mass media

The discoveries to be made from examining and using the information in the mass media are plentiful—if you accept them as a significant information source in your formal education. How can you observe and analyse the nature of the mass media?

The mass media are part of your daily life. When you read a daily paper or watch the TV news, you see your community, your society and your world as they are reflected, selected and shaped by the media. What you see, read and hear is happening now, and you expect the media to provide you with more up-to-date information than in books. But this simultaneity makes it difficult to stand back from the information the media convey. For example, it is difficult to evaluate and use a documentary shown on TV last night in the same way as you would a book. And because the media deal almost entirely with topical issues and events, they frequently select information which will make 'a good story' or has visual appeal rather than presenting a balanced view of a subject. In cases where the ownership of large sections of the media is concentrated in the hands of a few people, the information with which you are presented is likely to be limited in its scope. Use the media but keep their limitations in mind.

> How does television shape our views of the world? How do we use television to make sense of happenings outside the immediate sphere of our lives?... it is not what television does to us that is important; it is what we do to television. (*Stephen Brookfield*)

1 Comparing mass media with traditional sources

One way to learn about the nature of mass media is to compare them with information sources traditionally used in formal education. Listening to a ten-minute current affairs commentary or a radio book reading requires a different approach from listening to a fifty-minute lecture. To criticise the content of a radio program as though it were a lecture delivered by a person in front of you is to ignore the way the medium itself shapes the content and your perceptions in each instance. The same is true if you evaluate feature articles in a daily newspaper as though they were written with exactly the same aims as a chapter in a book which took a year to write and which you could take a year to read.

> The newspaper format ... offers short, discrete articles that give important facts first and then taper off to incidental details, which may be, and often are, eliminated by the make-up man. The fact that reporters cannot control the length of their articles means that, in writing them, emphasis can't be placed on structure, at least in the traditional linear sense, with climax or conclusion at the end. (*Edmund Carpenter*)

Like books and traditional lectures, radio programs and newspapers present you with information in a one-way process. Their messages come to you with little possibility of engaging in immediate dialogue with them. If you recognise this, you can see that you need to question and evaluate and use the information they convey if you are to understand and remember it. This entails discussing it, writing about it, or applying it to a problem you need to solve. In this way you think actively about the information, make it your own and construct your own meanings from it. As with listening to a lecture, it is easy to delude yourself that you have learned something from listening to and looking at a TV program, when in fact all you have done is passively receive words and images.

You may also realise that, unlike books and lectures, the media mix direct information with advertisements and trivia which convey information indirectly. When using the media as sources, look out for both types of information.

Some examples of indirect information include:

- examples of attitudes to sex in our society, as seen in a family comedy series or in films
- political attitudes and issues, as presented in the 'letters to the editor' columns and the cartoons in daily newspapers, or

- a mystification of science and technology, revealed in the way advertisements use the word 'scientific' and in the lack of informative and accessible technical reporting.

Much directly informative material that may be helpful in your studies is broadcast on television, including:

- regular programs in areas such as science, women's issues, current affairs, wildlife and music
- individual series or programs on the ideas of people such as Jung and Einstein and on issues such as nuclear power and racial discrimination, and
- performances of Shakespeare's plays and dramatisations of novels by modern authors.

2 Learning through practical experience

The most direct and powerful method to help people decode and deconstruct broadcasts is to involve them in making their own programs. (*Stephen Brookfield*)

'Hands on' experience is another way to learn about the nature of the mass media—making films or videotapes, writing or taking photographs for a student newspaper, preparing a broadcast for community radio, working in public access television. Learning about the media by only observing them is somewhat akin to expecting to learn how to conduct experimental scientific research only by observing experiments conducted by others.

3 Planning to use a source

Plan how to use the mass media systematically according to their particular demands. The media present you with masses of information, much of which you won't want to use in your formal learning. But be aware of the valuable information that is offered, and make the most of it when you do use it. If you see a TV program only once, how can you best take in and select the information it offers? If you buy a newspaper every day, how can you decide which items to re-read and keep?

Prepare, evaluate and review material as suggested in Chapter 9 on reading and Chapter 10 on lectures. Think about the nature of the media and how they influence your information. For example, if you have been listening to a radio program, ask yourself how the same material would have been presented in a lecture or on television.

Electronic media

TV, radio and film are essentially transient. Unless you record them for future use, you usually see a TV program or a film only once, you listen once to a radio program. There are several ways to take advantage of the information they offer.

- Use guides to films and to TV and radio programs. Don't overlook the less obvious alternatives in these areas such as community radio or a cinema screening of 16 mm films. Go through the guides and pick out programs which you know or expect will be useful. Note the times for these in a 'Things to do' list, a diary, or a weekly study plan.
- Make arrangements to record a radio or TV program (subject to copyright laws) if you can't listen or watch when it is broadcast or if you think you may want to replay it. Keep a couple of blank tapes on hand, and buy or borrow a tape or video recorder with a time switch. Some libraries videotape programs for you if you don't have access to facilities for this.
- Think about the topic of a program or film ahead of time, talk about it with others, and perhaps arrange to watch or listen to it together and discuss it afterwards.
- If you will hear or see a program only once, concentrate fully so that you can absorb and select information quickly and competently. Take notes if these would be useful, for example to remember certain facts or figures, or to record impressions (see 'Understanding as you listen', Chapter 10).
- If you haven't made notes during a radio or TV program or film but would find these useful, write notes immediately after while the material is still fresh in your mind.
- Review any notes you have made or replay a tape recording or videotape you have made as soon as possible after a program (preferably the next day).

'She reads at such a pace,' she complained, 'and when I asked her where she had learnt to read so quickly, she replied, 'On the screens at Cinemas.' (*Ronald Firbank*)

Print media

When you read newspapers, magazines and periodicals, you probably browse and skim, glancing through some items, reading a few others in detail, and passing over most. You can re-read newspapers and magazines, but except for a few items of special interest you are unlikely to do so. After all, there is the next day's paper and the next issue of a favourite magazine to be read, and today's news article loses much of its impact by tomorrow or next week or next month. What can you do to discover and select the information available in the print media?

- Regularly skim read a daily and weekly newspaper (perhaps in a library) to see if they often contain any information useful to your study interests.
- Survey several issues of the magazines, periodicals and newsletters in your areas of interest, and decide which ones you really find useful.

Subscribe to them for yourself or on a shared basis, or find out if your library will subscribe to them. Look through their contents regularly for useful material.

- Practise the skills of surveying material, selecting what to read and deciding how closely to read it when looking through newspapers, magazines and periodicals (see 'Approaches to reading', Chapter 9). Clip out useful items and note on each the page number, date and title of the paper or periodical.
- File clippings so they can easily be found again (see 'Selecting, recording and filing information', Chapter 7).

People don't actually read newspapers—they get into them every morning like a hot bath. (*Marshall McLuhan*)

■ ■ ■ ■ ■

As with any information source, using the mass media as learning sources requires that you think about their general nature and about their roles as information providers in both formal and informal learning. Theories about the nature of the mass media are many and complex, and such theories offer insights into the nature of knowledge and its social contexts, and into the effect of a particular medium on the forms of language used and on the distribution of knowledge.

Similarly, enthusiasm for the Internet and for electronic library services needs to be tempered by a critical theoretical awareness of the place of information in learning and of the social, economic and political underpinnings of electronic information webs.

The rhetoric of 'individualisation' with regard to computer applications in education and training has tended to blind enthusiasts to the social complexity of the real world in which the technologies actually have to function. The interaction taking place is all too often seen as occurring between 'the learner' and a computer: a sterile, sanitised world safely free from such unnecessary clutter as other people. It should be obvious that this is utter nonsense. Learning, even when 'individualised', is an intensely social activity. Even a prisoner in solitary confinement exists in a social context. (*Mike Cooley*)

As well as remembering such broad social contexts, at a time when vast amounts of seemingly disembodied information can potentially be accessed via the Internet it is worth remembering that people around you are still an invaluable information source. Learning with other humans, whether as fellow novices or as expert guides, whether individually or in groups, continues to present us with unique challenges and satisfactions.

One way to use this chapter

The aim of the following exercise is for you to become more aware of a wider range of information available to you on a particular topic. To do this, set aside a couple of days at the beginning of your academic year to do the exercise, or return to it at intervals over a longer period of time. Continue it until you decide that your knowledge of your topic has been usefully and noticeably increased.

1 Choose a topic which strongly interests you but which you have not systematically researched.
2 Turn the topic into a question which you define as clearly as possible by asking yourself what you want to know. List key search terms (see 'Developing and analysing a question', Chapter 6).
3 Write down as many possible information sources from your community as you can think of. Don't bother at this stage to evaluate how helpful they might be—simply list any people or organisations that might be useful.
4 Use a library catalogue to list a dozen references on your subject, and search a CD-ROM database to discover further references to your topics.
5 Locate one relevant Web site on your topic.
6 Choose four or five information sources from your community list which you think will be the most helpful for your purposes. Choose another four or five sources from your list of library references.
7 Follow up each of these information sources to find out more about your subject.

Further reading

Burdess, Neil, 1991, *The handbook of student skills for the social science and humanities*, Prentice-Hall, Sydney.

Eichler, Margrit, 1988, *Nonsexist research methods*, Allen & Unwin, Boston.

Goodacre, Phillip & Follers, Jennifer, 1987, 'Communicating across cultures' in Terry Lovat (ed.), *People, culture and change*, Social Science Press, Wentworth Falls.

Keats, Daphne M., 1988, *Skilled interviewing*, Australian Council of Educational Research, Hawthorn, Victoria.

Lane, Nancy D., 1996, *Techniques for student research: A practical guide*, 2nd edn, Addison Wesley Longman, Melbourne.

CHAPTER

READING

I would sooner read a time-table or a catalogue than nothing at all.
(*Somerset Maugham*)

As you silently read this paragraph, your eyes are moving from left to right in a series of quick jumps along the line of print. Each time your eyes stop, they focus on individual words or a cluster of words. The number of words you take in depends on your eye span and your word recognition skills.

You instantly perceive and recognise familiar words by their shape without needing to think consciously about their spelling, pronunciation or origin. However, sometimes you need a context to give a familiar word meaning. For example, how do you read 'read' in 'I have read six books' or in 'I'm about to read the paper'? At other times you need knowledge or experience to identify the intended meaning of a word. For example, do you interpret 'The East is red' to mean that the sun is rising or that China is a communist country?

When you come to a word you have never seen before, such as 'transmogrify' or 'simulacrum', your eyes focus on it for longer. You might re-read the sentence or paragraph to understand the meaning of the word from its context, or you might refer to a dictionary. Perhaps you recognise parts of the word ('trans-' in 'transmogrify'), or you attempt to divide the word into syllables (trans-mog-ri-fy, sim-u-la-crum) and pronounce it to see if you have ever heard the word spoken. Sometimes the word reminds you of another familiar word ('simulacrum' may remind you of 'similar', 'simulate', 'simultaneous' or 'fulcrum'). You might skip the word and move on.

There is much more to understanding what you read than the physical movement of your eyes and your ability to recognise words. When reading the paragraphs above, you gained an overall impression of what was written without needing to identify every word or literally reconstruct the printed message. You filtered the message through who you are as a reader and were influenced by your cultural background, experiences and world view. These in turn have influenced your knowledge of and interest in the subject, your reading purpose, your reading abilities, your feelings about reading and your understanding and interpretation of what you read.

> Recent theory ... argues that experience is not personal but cultural. That is, although you, as an individual, may have an experience—such as falling off a bike, loving someone or winning a prize—you can only think about those experiences in particular ways that are available to you. So, it is argued that texts are read and gaps filled by readers, not with ideas that they personally 'make up', but with meanings that are already available in their culture.
>
> The different ways readers can make meaning from texts—the range of reading positions they can take up—depends on their access to different ideas in their culture. (*Bronwyn Mellor, Annette Patterson & Marnie O'Neill*)

Stop for a few minutes to think about and answer the following questions about you as a reader.

Do you like to read? Why?

If you don't enjoy reading, why?

What genres do you like to read? Historical novels? Scientific journal articles? Biographies? Cookbooks? Newspapers?

When do you read? Before you go to sleep? Whenever you have a spare moment? While cleaning your teeth?

Where do you most enjoy reading? In the bath? On the bus or train?

Do you enjoy reading on a computer screen or do you prefer to print out the information and read it in hard copy? Why?

Do you have several books 'on the go' at the same time?

Do you talk to others about what and how you read?

What comes to mind when you stop and think about a book which has changed the way you thought or acted?

As a reader, you differ from other people in what you read, when and where you read, and how much you enjoy reading. You have your own reading 'personality' which was influenced by your cultural background and which began developing when you first made contact with words and books as a small child. This reading 'personality' influences the type of reading material or genres that you prefer, and your attitudes and approaches to reading as a student. If you like to read novels, you can sit absorbed in them for hours. If you prefer magazines, you may be accustomed to reading in short bursts. If you usually read the paper, you probably read some articles closely and glance through others.

When confronted with reading material for a higher education level course, only some of your previous reading habits are appropriate. The way in which academic materials are presented can differ from discipline to discipline, and the way in which you are expected to read them also varies. You shouldn't read medical texts as you would science fiction, and novels in a literature course require a different approach from magazines. However, if you enjoy reading and read a lot, you can build on this enjoyment and transfer the appropriate reading abilities to your academic reading.

Most of the academic material you read in papers, articles and books is organised in a linear form with the information beginning in the first sentence, paragraph or chapter and concluding in the final sentence, paragraph or chapter (see Table 10.1 'Notemaking'). This linear text is based on the idea that the reader begins at the beginning and reads (or listens to as in the case of lectures) a coherently and consistently organised argument or exposition to the end. The text uses guides provided by the writer to lead the reader through the material (for example, see Table 9.1 'The anatomy of a book'). Within this structure the reader has the freedom to move backwards and forwards or to dip into the text.

> To communicate ... experience through print means that it must first be broken down into parts and then mediated, eye dropper fashion, one thing at a time, in an abstract, linear, fragmented, sequential way. This is the essential structure of print. (*John M. Culkin*)

On the Internet some material within individual Web sites is presented in this linear fashion. However, much of the Net material is presented through hypertext whereby segments of information are linked conceptually by association or relationship. Hypermedia links text with a variety of other media and makes visual literacy important in 'reading' material. A wide range of pathways through the material is possible, as you can click on a highlighted word or graphic of your choice, thus opening up the information which then provides further choices, and so on. The information can be accessed via multiple pathways, thereby enabling you to follow the links which are most suitable for your reading purposes. When reading discrete pieces of information at Web sites, similar strategies and ideas apply as for reading hard copy.

> ... how does instant access to any piece of data, connected to any other piece of data by the slenderest of threads, how does this translate into knowledge, let alone understanding? And how will knowledge be imparted and how will children's brains be trained if the joys of hypertext make the concept of the linear argument redundant? We'll end up with soundbite education, just as we've got soundbite politics and soundbite journalism. (*John Neiwenhausen*)

It is important to learn to read actively as opposed to passively. A passive reader looks at and recognises the words on a page or a screen but doesn't actively engage with the material. Have you ever 'read' a passage or several pages and realised that you haven't taken any of it in? If when you read you sit looking at the printed text and your mind is elsewhere, if you cannot recall or explain or ask questions about what you have read, then you are reading passively.

Reading actively means constructing your own meaning from the text, the ideas expressed and how they are organised. It means trying to discern the author's argument and to evaluate how effectively the thesis of this argument is supported by reasons. If the material doesn't contain an argument, active reading means finding the overall controlling focus of the material and the information used to support this idea. Such reading involves criticising the material to uncover how the argument (or focus) has been affected by the author's background, purpose, world view or theoretical framework. You also need to pay attention to visual images and materials such as graphs, tables and diagrams instead of skimming over them. And active reading involves determining how what you are reading relates to other material in the field and to your own learning and purpose for reading. An active reader is aware of the author's writing style and method of presentation.

> ... she continued with the process of taking a fragment here and a sentence there, and built them into her mind, which was now the most extraordinary structure of disconnected bits of poetry, prose, fact and fantasy. (*Doris Lessing*)

This chapter is about reading actively. It focuses on you the reader, and on how you can become involved with what you read so that you come to know and understand it fully. The chapter is designed to help you formulate your purposes for reading, and suggests a range of techniques appropriate for different purposes and materials.

You are likely to use the chapter most often in conjunction with material you are reading thoroughly, such as a course text, or when discussing material with others. It is a long chapter, so first look through the headings and then either start at the beginning and work through it slowly, or dip into sections which are most immediately useful to you.

Use the previewing section to help you decide, for example, whether to read a book which is one of a dozen suggested references. If you want to improve your notemaking or write a book review, read rapidly through the chapter to that section. The techniques described in 'Approaches to reading' apply to reading a whole book, a part of a book, a journal article, a research paper, a government report or online course materials.

Preparing to read

Your purposes

Your purpose for reading influences any preparation you do before you read, your reading rate, and whether you underline or make notes. Before you read, clearly articulate why you are reading. Ask yourself questions such as: 'How thoroughly do I want or need to understand this material?' 'Do I need to read for an in-depth understanding?' 'How much do I want to remember?' 'Do I need to critique the material?' 'Do I need to relate the reading material to the material in the lectures or discussions on the topic?'

Imagine that you are reading to prepare for a discussion on an unfamiliar topic. A few days before the discussion you look through a couple of references and try to identify some of the main issues of the topic, using guides such as the introduction, index, chapter titles or layout to help you. Or imagine that you have to write a detailed critique of an article. First, you read for an overview and then you read slowly, underlining or making notes on the theoretical framework and the argument, and re-read if necessary. To critique the article you might read other texts on the topic that present different or conflicting perspectives.

Sometimes you read the same material for several purposes. For example, you may be required to read the same text for background information for a course as well as to understand it in-depth to answer an assignment question. You approach the material differently to meet each of these requirements.

If you are required to read large chunks of text online, you may find it preferable to print out the material and read it in hard copy using the techniques later in this chapter that apply to other printed material.

> Computer-mediated communication can be used for the transmission of lengthy lecture-type materials, but because reading screen after screen of material with no opportunity to respond is difficult and boring, this form of communication is better accomplished by textbooks or printed materials. (*Linda Harasim*)

Examining your material

When browsing in a bookshop or library, why does one book appeal to you more than another? When leafing through an academic journal why do you pause over some articles and not others? When surfing the Net why do you pay more attention to one Web site rather than another? Perhaps a book's appearance or title attracts you or the author is someone whose writing you usually enjoy. Perhaps an article seems relevant to one of your interests or useful for a particular purpose. Perhaps the visuals on a Web site complement the written text rather than detracting from it. The layout, writing style or author's approach to the subject may lead you to buy a book, borrow a journal or bookmark a Web site. Each book, article or Web site is different, and your response to each will depend on who you are as a reader.

Previewing

Systematically previewing material helps you to read actively and is one of the first steps you take to become thoroughly familiar with material. Such preparation gives you some understanding of why the material was written, its theoretical framework, the author's argument or focus, and how that information is organised and presented. Previewing can indicate which parts of the text could be most useful for your purpose and how thoroughly you want or need to read different sections.

Previewing a book, article or chapter

To get the feel of a book you might glance through it, read the back cover blurb, look at the pictures or diagrams, think about the meaning of the title and perhaps check through the table of contents and read the introduction.

There are various systematic steps you can take when previewing a book, but the order of these depends on your preference. You might start by reading the first chapter to become immediately involved with the content and the author's style, or you may prefer to check through the information that surrounds the text, such as the publication details and the index. As you preview, write down any ideas, questions or statements which seem relevant to your purpose and which might help you understand and critique the book. Try to determine the author's position on the topic. This previewing helps you read actively because you have a framework into which the information fits; and as you read you consciously look for answers to your questions, and for information that supports or disagrees with your original ideas on the book.

Apply the questions in Table 9:1 for a fuller sense of what a book is about. For example, a quick thumb through the index can tell you the major areas covered by the book; and a glance at the publication details gives information about the book in its field, such as how recent it is, whether it has sold enough copies to be reprinted, and whether it has been published in more than one country.

Previewing a book which is an edited collection written by a range of authors is different from reading a book written by one author. Many course textbooks are such collections and you need to preview them by adapting the questions outlined in Table 9.1. Identify any articles that are familiar, those that look interesting and those that you think will be particularly difficult or easy.

Most of the steps described for previewing a book also apply to previewing parts of books or articles, so firstly read Table 8.1 and adapt the questions to the article or chapter. As you preview read the introduction and conclusion and any section headings.

Previewing online

In online courses, make full use of any navigation guides and overall maps as the basis for your exploration of the material available through hypertext links. When previewing written text online, first scroll through to determine the length of the material and to find any headings and subheadings. Work out if all of the headings are at the same level or if they are at different levels. Apply the appropriate questions from Table 9.1 to the material and read the introduction and conclusion. Make sure you note the source of the material, when it was written and the credentials of the author.

Table 9.1 The anatomy of a book

Title/subtitle

What is the author trying to convey in the title (and any subtitle)?

Cover/dustjacket

What information does the cover of the book give about the contents, the author, and the book within its field?
How reliable is any information on the cover of the book?

Author/editor/translator

Is there any information inside the book about the author's (or editor's or translator's) background, other publications, or experience relevant to the subject?

Do you know anything else about the author or any other of his/her writings?

Publication details

When was the book written?

What is the publication date of your copy of the book?

Has the book been revised?

Which edition is the book? Has the book been reprinted?

If the book is a translation, what is the date of this?

Who is the publisher?

In which countries has the book been published?

Table of contents

Is the table of contents sufficiently detailed to be helpful?

Which sections appear to be interesting, familiar or difficult to you?

How do the contents relate to your purpose and to other material you are studying?

Preface/foreword/introduction

If the book includes a preface, foreword or introduction, have they been written by the author or editor, or by someone else?

What information do these sections give you about why the book was written, its place in its field, how to read it?

Has the book been written to argue a case or is it an exposition describing or outlining a subject?

Is the author's position on the subject explained? Does the position fit within a theoretical paradigm?

Text of the book

What do the introduction and conclusion tell you about the book? Are there guides to your reading of the book, such as summaries of chapters, sub-headings?

Does the author spell out the argument of the book in the introduction or conclusion? If the whole argument is not made explicit, can you identify the thesis?

How does the structure of the book, for example in chapters or sections, develop the argument?

Layout

How are headings and sub-headings used?

How is emphasis indicated within the text? For example, are italics used?

Graphics and visuals

Does the book contain much graphic or visual material?

Is any graphic material—such as diagrams, photographs, graphs, tables, charts, maps—easy to follow?

How does any visual material—images or representations—seem to relate to the written text?

Glossary

If the book has a glossary, are many words unfamiliar to you?

Bibliography and references

How comprehensive are any footnotes, endnotes or a bibliography?
Does the author use recently published items in references and the bibliography?
Is the list of works at the end of the text a bibliography (that is, all sources consulted) or a list of references (that is, those sources cited in the text)?
Is the bibliography divided into subject areas?
Is it a comprehensive or selected bibliography?
Do the references include sources other than written materials?

Index

What does an examination of the index add to your understanding of the contents of the book? Which subject areas are given prominence?
Does the index list mostly ideas and concepts, or more factual entries such as names of places and people?
Has the index sufficient detail to enable you to locate your areas of interest easily?

Complexity of material

... one of the stupidest things [to] do is insist that children comprehend everything they read, and read only what they comprehend. People who read well do not learn to read this way. They learn by plunging into books that are 'too hard' for them, enjoying what they can understand, wondering and guessing about what they do not, and not worrying when they cannot find an answer. (*John Holt*)

How complex material seems to you depends on your knowledge of the subject, your interest in it, and whether or not the material accords with familiar theoretical perspectives or world views that you hold. Even if you are familiar with a topic, material can be complex because it expresses new ideas in unfamiliar language, because of its style and format, or because it is poorly written, organised or presented. ('Evaluating your selection' in Chapter 7 looks at determining the complexity of material when deciding whether to use it in research.) If material seems too simple for your purpose, you may need to check that you really do understand it thoroughly—even basic material sometimes has one or two points to offer, and can provide useful revision.

Here we suggest how to read material which seems difficult, and the first step in doing this is to try to articulate why this is so.

- If the material is difficult because the subject doesn't interest you, read a little of it and use the techniques described later in this chapter to make your reading more effective. On closer acquaintance the material may become more interesting and you can try to relate the subject to one which interests you.
- If the material conflicts with your 'common sense' understandings or with your beliefs and biases, discuss these conflicts with a sympathetic person who doesn't share your attitudes. It can help you see your

beliefs and biases in a new light if you play devil's advocate to them. Understanding different or conflicting perspectives is essential to thinking critically.

- If the theoretical perspectives or key concepts on which the material is based are unfamiliar to you, you may need to read other material which deals with the same perspectives or concepts, and it may take you time to understand the material fully.
- If the material is in an area unfamiliar to you or if you have a mental block about the subject, preview the material first, then read the easiest sections before you attempt more advanced ones. If you can't get past the basics, ask for help.
- If the material appears complex, first preview it, then read it slowly and look for the argument or controlling focus—sometimes material which at first seems complex becomes clear after a careful reading. Making notes or drawing a diagram or pattern of the material as you read can help your understanding. You may later find it both easier to understand and very stimulating.

The discipline area

She took the book to her refuge, the tree, and read it through; and wondered why it was that she could read the most obscure and complicated poetry with ease, while she could not read the simplest sort of book on what she called 'facts' without the greatest effort of concentration. (*Doris Lessing*)

How you read is also influenced by the discipline area of the material. The methodologies and conventions for communicating in writing vary from discipline to discipline; and within disciplines writers have different styles and ways of presenting information. This influences the way you read. For example, in maths understanding what you read can depend on mastering information one step at a time. In geography, you frequently refer to maps and other visual material as you read. In literature, reading a literary work to savour the language differs from reading literary criticism to select the central points. How much you are expected to read varies from one discipline to another, and this in turn also influences how you read. For example, in disciplines in the social sciences and humanities you are usually required to spend more time reading than in the physical sciences.

As a newcomer to a discipline area you may find the specialised language of that discipline difficult to understand, and even familiar, everyday words may have new and distinct meanings. For example, the word 'program' has different meanings in psychology, computing and education, and the meaning of 'character' is different in literature, mathematics and biology. Some words embody concepts that have changed over time; for example, the words 'culture', 'power', 'subject', or 'class' can have specific meanings in different disciplines, and these meanings change with time. You need a subject dictionary to understand the meanings of some words and to be clear how the words are used in the context of your reading. You might also need to become visually literate (to read images and other representations) or numerate (for example, to learn how to read tables and different kinds of graphs).

In the materials you read there are varying amounts of quantitative information. This information may be obviously mathematical in forms such as graphs, tables, formulae or symbols, or it may be embedded in prose so that the mathematical meaning is within words such as 'rate', 'decreasing inflation', 'exponential growth' and 'inversely proportional'. The degree to which you deal with this quantitative information depends to a large extent on your purpose in reading, the nature of the material itself, and your attitude towards those mathematical representations.

People usually read non-fictional materials to gain information. In doing so it is essential to consider the inferences and conclusions based on evidence of both qualitative and quantitative kinds. Although it is common for people to skim over graphs, tables, numbers and symbols, it is only by paying due attention to them that you can decide whether to accept the inferences and conclusions of the author that are based upon the data. This does not necessarily mean that every single number of a table, for example, needs to be considered in detail. However, an ability to make inferences, consider comparisons, see the 'big picture' and to pick up inconsistencies is a valuable skill. In some cases it is helpful to make transformations between the kinds of representations; for example, from a table to graph, from formulae to words, or from words to a graph. In general it is advisable to change your reading speed and consider these quantitative aspects more slowly than the rest of the text.

When you have to learn a new 'language' the following tips are useful.

- Talk about difficulties with a teacher or with other students in a discussion group, listen carefully to relevant lectures, ask for a glossary of terms, or consult a specialised dictionary on the subject.
- Read some basic books on the subject.
- Make a real attempt to understand the new language, then if you still have difficulties or think too much is expected of you, let your teachers know. The language may be second nature to them, and they can easily forget that it may be incomprehensible jargon to you.
- Compile your own list of terms.

  'Twas brillig, and the slithy toves
  Did gyre and gimble in the wabe:
  All mimsy were the borogroves,
  And the momeraths outgrabe. (*Lewis Carroll*)

Developing your vocabulary

If you read widely you can improve your vocabulary, that is, your understanding of the words you read and hear and the words you use in writing and speaking. You can actively work at improving your vocabulary by consulting a general dictionary, technical glossary or subject dictionary and by developing a system for recording and using your new words. Try a notebook or card system or keep a document on the computer in which you write the unfamiliar term, the context in which it appeared, its dictionary definition and your own sentence using it. If you have a learning log set aside part of it for this purpose. Practise using these words in your writing and speaking. Try them out on other students and your friends. Ask for feedback from a teacher on your use of the words. Learn a new term a day or several a week.

When you begin studying in a new discipline or embarking on a new course or subject, pay particular attention to the vocabulary. If you find there are many terms or concepts that you don't understand, start with those that are central to the area or those that keep recurring. When you understand these terms start on the others.

Before you read, use your preview to look for frequently used or unfamiliar words and concepts and look these up before you read. Use the index or leaf through the text to find these terms. This will help you read more quickly and you will not be slowed down by continually consulting a dictionary. However, if you are reading and you do come across terms that you don't understand, don't skip over them. Take the time to stop and look them up.

> The student's success is not simply a function of the number of words he or she has read and remembered. Rather, it is the degree to which the student—through that reading—has gone inside of the literature, has become used to the shape of relevant academic conversations, and has grappled with the unfamiliar language until it becomes his or her own language. (*Ronald Barnett*)

As you read

How you read material depends largely on why and what you are reading. You probably read a detective story straight through to find out 'What happens next?' With many academic books you affirm or reject what you read on the basis of your world view, theoretical perspective, experience and interests. Maybe you read with pencil in hand, jotting notes or underlining anything which strikes you as useful, significant, puzzling or appealing. Perhaps you ask yourself questions about what you are reading. Are you conscious of varying your reading rate according to your material? Do you talk about what you are reading with your friends and urge them to read it too?

How you read is also influenced by whether or not you share your reading, perhaps discussing what you have read afterwards. Reading with others, either silently or aloud, gives you the opportunity to share immediate reactions to material. Some material, such as poetry, plays or novels, lends itself readily to being spoken and listened to with another person or a group; and listening to material read aloud can also give you new insight into the use of language, and the pace and style of the text. You may also like to share with your teachers and other students, either face to face or online, the problems and pleasures you have with material. Because peoples' perceptions of what they read differs, opinions vary, and so hearing different viewpoints can help you understand material more fully. (To set up a group to read each others' writing, see 'Share your writing' in Chapter 12.)

> It is possible to question readings of stories which may seem 'natural' and normal by paying attention to the ways a story conforms to or differs from familiar patterns. (*Bronwyn Mellor, Annette Patterson & Marnie O'Neill*)

Approaches to reading

> Some books are to be tasted, others to be swallowed, and some few to be chewed and digested; that is, some books are to be read only in parts; others to be read but not curiously; and some few to be read wholly, and with diligence and attention. (*Francis Bacon*)

Different reading techniques are sometimes given names, such as 'skimming' or 'scanning', and actual reading rates of words per minute are suggested for each. Such terms can be confusing, and while generalised reading rates may apply, in practice how you read varies. It depends on your purpose, the material and your concentration when you read.

This section describes six different reading approaches which arise from your reading purpose and the material, but it doesn't assign reading rates to each approach. It looks first at the breadth and depth of the understanding you are seeking from your material and then at reading rates.

Imagine you are planning a visit to a city that you have never visited before. Why are you going there? Six possible purposes are:

- to stroll around the central shopping area for pleasure
- to experience the city atmosphere
- to visit a famous art gallery or a zoo
- to familiarise yourself with the key features of the city
- to explore thoroughly as much of the city as possible, or
- to evaluate whether or not you could live in the city.

Your purpose in visiting the city influences how you go about preparing for your visit, what you do when you arrive, and how long you stay.

Imagine that you are planning to read a book you have not read before. Are you going to read this book:

- for entertainment?
- to gain an overall impression of it?

- to locate a specific idea or section?
- to familiarise yourself with the argument or controlling focus?
- to understand and get to know the whole book in depth? or
- to critique or review the book?

These six purposes and how they influence your approach to reading are explained below.

1 Entertainment reading

What do you read for relaxation? A favourite magazine? A detective story? A collection of poems? An abstract philosophical work?

Entertainment reading (that is, reading without any specific intention of criticising or remembering what you read) can be more than reading for relaxation on free evenings or holidays. When studying, it can be a pleasurable way of getting yourself into the right frame of mind for in-depth study on a topic, and can provide you with general background on the subject.

When you read for entertainment, you probably read fairly quickly or browse through the material. You might pause to ponder over a particular passage, image, or item of information, but you probably do not make a conscious effort to remember what you read. You might use entertainment reading as part of formal study when you intend:

- to read the quotes in a chapter of this book as stimulus for reading the chapter in detail
- to enjoy an historical novel before beginning an intensive study of the era in which the novel is set, or
- to read a biography of a scientist whose discoveries you are studying.

2 Overview reading

Reading for an overview of material entails reading quite rapidly, reading the introductory and concluding paragraphs, noting the argument or controlling focus, noting how any graphic or visual items fit into the material, and forming an overall impression of what you read. You are not concerned with specific details or a complete understanding of the material. Read for an overview when, for example, you want:

- to find out how this book might be useful to you
- to decide whether to read a book in more depth, or
- to add to your store of information on a familiar subject area or topic.

3 Reading for specific information

I have always been able to forget what I have read, retaining, however, a sort of geographical memory that would send me quickly to the right page in the right book to find something I had half forgotten but wished to remember. (*Arthur Ransome*)

To locate (or re-locate) a specific item or section in material, read through most of the material quite rapidly, using such features as the table of contents, the index, chapter headings and sub-headings to guide you to the item or section you want. Then read the section thoroughly, possibly making notes or underlining. (If you are reading online you might choose to print out the relevant section.) Use this technique if, for example, your purpose is:

- to look for a specific section in this book
- to locate biographical details on a literary figure, or
- to find evidence for or against a case you will debate.

4 Reading for the argument or controlling focus

To familiarise yourself with the argument or controlling focus in material (see 'Genres', Chapter 6), first take an overview of it. Examine the structure of the material and find the thesis and supporting premises.

Read for the argument or controlling focus when, for example, you want:

- to familiarise yourself with the main approaches to study presented in this book
- to read an article as background for a research paper
- to describe an item which is part of an annotated bibliography
- to prepare for a discussion on the material, or
- to understand the central conclusions in an experimental report.

5 Reading for an in-depth understanding

When reading to understand an entire book or article as thoroughly as possible, first preview the material. Determine the structure of the material, then read to identify the thesis and supporting reasons, or if there is no argument, the focus and supporting points). Then take the material section by section, reading the supporting evidence and identifying more fully the relationship between the thesis and support. Seek out material that shows objections to the argument. Ferret out its theoretical perspective and any underlying assumptions.

Reading in this depth doesn't mean laboriously reading every page (or screen) word by word. It does involve making sure that you read actively, understanding each section so that, with the material set aside, you can clearly construct your own understanding of what you have read and can see how each section fits into the whole argument or exposition. Seeing clearly how material is organised or structured can help you to understand its content. (Refer to Table 13.2 'Transitional words and phrases' to alert yourself to the words and phrases that are signposts to the structure.) Make notes or underline important information to help reinforce your understanding.

Read for an in-depth understanding if, for example, your purpose is:

- to identify the assumptions underlying this book
- summarise or paraphrase material
- to follow a complex argument
- to understand each stage of an experiment in order to repeat it yourself, or
- to understand material thoroughly so you can build on it in further learning or so that you can critique it as outlined below.

6 Reading to question and critique material

To question and critique what you read, you need to read for an in-depth understanding of the material as outlined in 5 above and apply the suggestions below.

Before reading you should already have evaluated the material to find out if it is useful for your purpose, how complex it is for you and to check if its subject matter is relevant and interesting (see 'Evaluating your selection', Chapter 7). You begin to critically evaluate material during your preview and as you read, but you also need to think about it critically when you have finished reading and can see the text as a whole.

To critique material as you read it, take the text section by section. A section may be a group of chapters, a chapter, a paragraph or even a sentence, depending on the length of the text, how much graphic or visual material is involved, your purpose and how complex or familiar the material is. Before you begin a large section, preview it. As you read, ask yourself the questions in Table 9.2. These questions should help you identify the author's theoretical perspective, purpose and assumptions; understand the argument or focus and its structure; and evaluate the style and format of the material. At the end of the section, recapitulate what you have read. Check if you understand the contents of the section as thoroughly as you need to, and try to understand the relationship of the section to the whole. When you finish reading each section, put the material aside and evaluate its usefulness for your purpose. Decide which information you want to underline or include in your notes.

If you have difficulty answering the questions in Table 9.2, discuss the material with other people. First, try to reach agreement on the argument—the thesis and supporting material—or if there is no argument, the controlling focus. Then discuss any differing opinions on the argument or focus for the material as a whole and for individual sections of the material. (Note that the questions asked in Table 9.2 are similar to those you should ask when you evaluate your essays as in 'Working with your rough draft', Chapter 13.)

Specific instances of when you might need to do this include:

- to write a critical review of this book
- to include a critical summary of the material in an assignment
- to prepare for an in-depth debate on the material, or
- to critique the theoretical perspective taken by an author.

Table 9.2   Asking questions as you read

As you read a section of a book or article, look for information to help you answer the following questions.

The author's purpose

- Why has the author written the material? Are these purposes explicitly stated? Are there other implicit purposes?
- For whom is the material intended?

The author's approach

- What theoretical perspective has the author taken? How does this perspective relate to other material in the field?
- Has a contemporary issue or a particular paradigm or philosophy influenced the author's purpose?
- What are the author's underlying assumptions? Are these explicitly stated?
- Is there any evidence of covert or overt bias, such as interpretation of material or choice of sources or information? (See Appendix A for examples of discrimination in language and attitudes.)

Content

- What is the argument, or if no argument the controlling focus in the material?
- What evidence, examples or explanations are used to support the thesis or controlling focus?
- How does the author develop the thesis from one reason to another?
- Do the supporting evidence, examples and explanations seem well researched and accurate?
- Is the factual information correct as far as you know?
- Which aspects of the topic has the author chosen to concentrate on and which to omit?
- Is the material presented in breadth and/or depth? Is the material dealt with fully and accurately or is the subject treated superficially?
- Is any irrelevant material included?
- Does any graphic or quantitative material illustrate or restate the written content?
- How are any visual images linked with the written text?
- Which of your questions about the subject does the author answer? Which are not answered?
- How do the contents relate to what you know about the topic?
- Do any items puzzle or intrigue you?

Structure

- What framework is used to organise the material? Is the framework clearly explained and logical?
- How is the argument (or if no argument, the focus) reflected in the structure?
- How are the main points ordered, linked and balanced?
- How is the supporting material organised and developed within the framework?
- How does the author introduce the argument?
- Does the author recapitulate what has been said at appropriate points?
- How does the conclusion relate to the introduction and to the rest of the material?

Style and format

- In what style has the material been written? For example, is it formal or informal, simple or complex, descriptive or critical, didactic or persuasive, narrative, analytical?
- How does the style and format influence your reaction to the material?

Reading rates

> Speed, which becomes a virtue when it is found in a horse, by itself has no advantages. (*Idries Shah*)

When feeling overwhelmed by long reading lists or by the time it takes to get through a book or the plethora of Web sites, you might wish you could increase your reading rate or speed. Although learning to read more rapidly can save you study time, fast reading rates are useful only if you can understand and recall what you read as fully as you need to. They do not in themselves ensure better comprehension. Reading effectively involves varying your reading rate according to your purpose and to the difficulty of material for you (see Table 9.3).

You can improve your reading rate while still constructing an understanding of what you read.

- Check how fast you can read while still understanding what you read. Time the number of words you read per minute for:
  - a light novel you are reading for background
  - a journal article you are reading to familiarise yourself with the central ideas, and
  - a chapter in a course text that you have to understand in depth.

  Read at least ten paragraphs of each one. In each case, when you finish reading, set aside the material and try to recall it in as much detail as you need. If you have trouble remembering the material, your reading rate probably needs to be slower and you may need to try the techniques in the following points.
- Preview all material before you read it, perhaps jotting down the major headings. Although this may appear to take extra time in the beginning, if you have a framework in which to put what you read, as you read it you can vary your rate according to the importance of the information and ideas. This framework will also help you remember the material later.
- Push yourself to read as fast as you can for 10–15 minutes each day for a week, then check your rate and comprehension. Remember your reading rate will regress if you seldom read and if you don't practise reading faster.
- Make a habit of reading material which is as complex as your study material. Becoming accustomed to reading material which is more demanding than light fiction or the sports pages makes it easier to read most of your study material.
- If you find that it slows you down to consult a dictionary or technical glossary as you read, make a list of unfamiliar terms as you read and then look them up as you need them. (See a method for doing this in 'Improving your vocabulary'.)
- Pay attention to any quantitative material such as tables and statistics, and ask for help if you have difficulty in interpreting these.

- Use any visual material or any layout clues to help you quickly understand written text.

The aim of improving your reading rates is to save you time, but you only save this time if you understand and remember what you read as thoroughly as you need. Without understanding, you have to go over the material repeatedly until you do understand it, and your initial time-saving is lost.

Table 9.3 Varying your reading rate

The following example suggests how you might read a chapter in this book.
Chapter 10 'Lectures'

Your purpose	The material	Your rate
To warm up	Boxed quotes	Fast
To read for an overview of the chapter	Whole chapter, especially the introduction and conclusion	Quite fast
To locate specific information to help you make more useful lecture notes	Section on 'Making notes'	Fast until you locate the section you want, and then slowly within the section itself
To familiarise yourself with the controlling focus	Whole chapter	Slowly, making use of the introduction and the headings
To gain an in-depth familiarity with the chapter	Whole chapter	Slowly and thoroughly, underlining or making notes
To critique the assumptions and controlling focus of the chapter for a discussion	Whole chapter	Slowly and thoroughly, section by section

Notemaking and/or underlining

> Books that you may carry to the fire, and hold readily in your hand, are the most useful after all. (*Samuel Johnson*)

You might underline your own books because you want to make your responses to what you read part of the book itself. You might make notes because you don't want to mark your books, because referring to the book later is difficult, or because a précis of the information is more useful for your purpose (see 'Buy, copy or borrow material?', Chapter 7).

On rare occasions you come across a piece of writing which encapsulates ideas that are especially significant for you, so that you want to photocopy, download or buy the material. However, usually it is better to close the book or file and try to express what you read in your own words, as this helps you remember it. Avoid photocopying or downloading to disk material which you will never read. When under pressure and short of time, you may tend to photocopy everything rather than read any one item carefully (see 'Selecting, recording and filing information', Chapter 7).

Why make notes or underline?
You might do this:

- to help you see the structure in what you read
- because what you read strikes you as useful, puzzling or interesting
- to remember what you read
- to be able to refer to it later, for instance, for an assignment or for an exam in a few months time, and
- to help you concentrate on and understand what you read.

What to note or underline
This includes:

- the author's purposes, theoretical framework and assumptions (explicit and implicit)
- key elements, such as the argument, the controlling focus, major characters or crucial information
- single phrases or sentences which encapsulate key elements or the author's purposes and assumptions
- details or facts which appeal to you, such as a useful statistic or a vivid image, and
- items to follow up, such as a question, an idea that offers further possibilities, a puzzling comment, an unfamiliar word, an explanation you don't understand, or an opinion you question.

How much to underline or note
The amount of underlining you do or the quantity of notes you make depends on what you read, why you read and whether you have easy access to the material again.

If you have limited time and access to material, it is easy to opt for the apparent safety of making notes of everything you read 'just in case' you need the information later. However, if your are researching an essay topic and you analyse your question before reading, you need fewer notes and underline less. Having a clear idea of your reading purpose prevents you finishing up with masses of notes and no idea of how to organise or use them (see 'Organising and integrating ideas and information', Chapter 7).

Check that you understand what you have underlined or written down (see 'Questioning and evaluating', Chapter 7). Underlining a lot or making detailed notes can be necessary, but it may indicate your inability to discriminate what is important from what is not, and can give you a false sense of achievement because you have a large quantity of work to show, regardless of its quality.

If you often record lengthy quotes or paraphrases to use in assignments because the material 'says it much better than I can', try instead to select a limited number of quotes and paraphrases to support your own argument. Although in western higher education your teachers usually expect you to display familiarity with argument and ideas in the key literature in a field, relying mostly on authorities shows a lack of confidence in your opinions and a belief that there is a Right answer for a question (see 'Questioning and evaluating', Chapter 7, and 'Independent study', Chapter 4).

You probably don't need to underline or make many notes if you are reading mostly for entertainment, if you are familiar with the subject or if you have an excellent visual or conceptual memory. But if you need the material later, take down at least a bare outline of its contents and notes on where to find it again. Two weeks and six books later you will find it surprisingly difficult to recall what you have read unless you have some record of it.

'The horror of that moment,' the King went on, 'I shall never, never forget!' 'You will, though,' the Queen said, 'if you don't make a memorandum of it.' (*Lewis Carroll*)

How to make notes or underline

Develop your own method of note making or underlining which differentiates between the thesis or focus and supporting material (see 'Genres', Chapter 6). Work out a way of indicating the author's position and assumptions or attitudes, the details which appeal to you, and items to follow up. If you have a strongly visual memory, you might decide to develop a mind map or patterned notes (see Table 10.1 for ways to do this). If you use patterned notes creatively, when planning an essay for example, the open-ended nature of the pattern can enable your brain to make new connections far more easily. Note that you can create a pattern as part of your assignment preparation to help you to link the concepts in your assignment.

When beginning to make notes:

- write down full details of author, title and publication.
- on each page of notes, write the title or author and list the page numbers of the book or article in the margin of your notes. This habit is essential for quoting exactly, referencing assignments, and checking the content of an idea you want to paraphrase.
- use quotation marks to clearly indicate the beginning and end of material you have copied exactly.

- clearly identify the beginning and end of material you have para-phrased (see 'Paraphrasing and plagiarism', Chapter 15), and
- note any numerical information accurately.

(To integrate your own ideas with those from your reading try the sys-tem suggested in 'Organising and integrating ideas and information' in Chapter 7. See Table 10.1 'Notemaking' for more ideas on how to make notes.)

After you read

> Some of the girls sell their textbooks when they're through with them, but I intend to keep mine. Then after I've graduated I shall have my whole education in a row in the bookcase, and when I need to use a detail, I can turn to it without the slightest hesitation. So much easier and more accurate than trying to keep it in your head. (*Jean Webster*)

When you have finished reading, do you close your book or article with a sigh of satisfaction or relief and not think about it again unless you have to use it? To remember and use what you have read, review the material as a whole, and use it as soon, as often and as widely as possible (see 'Transferring and using what you learn', Chapter 5).

- Look at the material in relation to your reading purpose. If you are researching an assignment, ask yourself the following questions. Does the material lead you to revise how you have analysed your question? Is the book central or peripheral to your understanding of a topic? Does the material provide the necessary level of information for your research? What parts of the material particularly apply to the thesis or focus of your essay?
- Find out whether your initial impressions and any questions raised during your preview have been confirmed or answered. To help revise what you learnt from the text, look again at those parts of the material you examined during your preview. Check through the index, for instance, to help recall what you read and to give you a fuller understanding of the scope of a book.
- Look at the material as a whole and ask yourself the same questions about the purpose, approach, content, structure, style and format as you asked about each section while reading.
- Review your notes or underlining to ensure that you remember what you have read and to see how the various sections fit together. Draw up patterned notes of the whole chapter or article or write a summary of it.
- List questions which the material has raised and which you want to follow up. Edit your notes, or summarise them further if necessary, and file them (see 'Selecting, recording and filing information', Chapter 7).

- Think about the material and how your construction of its meaning is shaped by your world view, your knowledge, your experience, your interests. Did any of the ideas affect your beliefs or actions?
- Reflect on how the material's style and format compares with your own writing. Perhaps the material is in a genre that can provide an example on which you can model your own writing, especially in relation to how you might structure what you write or how to use the languages of a discipline. The material might also provide an example of what not to do.

Whether or not you think about what you have read when you finish reading depends largely on the impact it had on you and whether you are required to use it. You might remember an argument which changes your thinking or recall particular ideas or information. You may read further works by the same author or on the same subject, and in time re-read the original work. If an article or Web page pleased or irritated you, stimulated or satisfied your curiosity, you are likely to reflect on it and discuss it with other people. Articulating your ideas and responses to material helps clarify them, and you may also be required to articulate your ideas about a book or article in a written review (see Table 9.4).

Table 9.4 Writing a review

'... What is the use of a book,' thought Alice, 'without pictures or conversations?' (*Lewis Carroll*)

The overall purpose of a review is to interest and inform potential readers and to give your considered opinion of a book or article. As well as summarising or describing the contents of the material, the review should evaluate the overall strengths and weaknesses of the material from your perspective. The review should give enough of the content of the material for the reader to be able to understand your critique of it without having to read the original. Depending on your specific purpose for the review and any word limit, you should include some or all of the following information.

The context of the material:
- full details of title, author and publication
- when the material was originally written and/or revised
- the author's qualifications and experience.

Summary of the material:
- a brief outline of the book's contents
- a summary of the book's argument and structure
- the author's purpose in writing the book.

A critique of the material would include an evaluation of the following:
- the theoretical perspective taken in relation to other perspectives on the topic
- the material in relation to other material in the field, including whether the book is introducing any new concepts or data and/or reviewing, contradicting or supporting previous material

- the depth and thoroughness of the treatment of the subject matter in relation to the length of the material
- any data presented
- the conclusions—are they based on the reasons or evidence, and any suggestions or recommendation—are they theoretical or practical; are they applicable or possible in a real situation?
- how the book relates to your knowledge, your experience, your interests, your beliefs
- the author's style
- comments by other reviewers have said about the book (check indexes such as *The Australian Book Review Index*)

Presentation of material:

- the standard of the index, a bibliography, graphic or visual material
- the overall quality of the presentation, such as layout, quality of paper and binding.

The review should follow the conventions for writing an essay with an introduction, body and conclusion. The body of the review should contain a summary of the book and the critique of it. Your review should be an argument with a thesis which expresses your judgement of the material. Support any statements you make, including your opinions, with evidence, explanations and examples. A few well-chosen quotations can convey the flavour of the author's style as well as illustrating a point. (Give the page reference for a quote immediately afterwards.)

Your own honest and well thought-out opinion of the material is of more value to your learning and to your readers than your version of someone else's opinion. A review can be technically excellent but dull to read unless you convey to your reader the impact the material has on you.

Reviewing the chapter

1 Look through this chapter, taking each heading in turn and recalling what you can about it. Which section can you recall in most detail? Why?
2 Choose one section which is useful to re-read. As you re-read it, think about how you are reading and why.
3 Could you explain the structure and contents of the whole chapter to someone else?
4 Summarise this chapter using patterned notes. (See 'Making notes', Chapter 10.)

Further reading

Drewry, John E., 1974, *Writing book reviews*, Greenwood Press, Westport, Connecticut.

Kress, Gunther, 1985, *Linguistic processes in sociocultural practice*, Deakin University Press, Deakin University, Victoria.

Mellor, B., Patterson, A. & O'Neill, M., 1991, *Reading fictions*, Chalkface Press, Scarborough, WA.

Morris, A. & Stewart-Dove, N., 1984, *Learning to learn from text: Effective reading in the content areas*, Addison-Wesley, Sydney.

Packham, G., McEvedy, M.R. & Smith, P., 1985, *Studying in Australia: Reading efficiently and note-making accurately*, Nelson, Melbourne.

CHAPTER 10

LISTENING TO LECTURES

Depending on who you are—your experience, your world view and how you are feeling—you react to and select from what you hear. Each person responds differently to the pitch and intensity of sounds. One person's music is someone else's noise. If you live in the country the noise of traffic can be deafening when you visit the city; for an enthusiastic motorbike rider the roar of a 750 cc engine is melodious to the ears; and the 'snap, crackle and pop' of a favourite breakfast cereal can be irritatingly loud to someone with a hangover.

Do you consider yourself a good listener?

Do you listen closely to your friends when they talk about their troubles?

Have you ever felt your eyes glaze over as you listened to a teacher's monologue?

Have you ever found your mind far away from the lecture theatre towards the end of a lecture?

There is a difference between hearing sounds passively, and actively listening. Concentrating on what you hear is one of the basic requirements for listening to lectures. But even when you are keenly interested in a subject, it can be difficult to concentrate for a long time while sitting passively without the opportunity to respond.

This chapter is about understanding lectures well enough for them to be genuinely useful for your purposes in learning, rather than attending classes largely because you think you should. The chapter looks at how you can actively prepare for a lecture and how you can concentrate on what is being said and on making notes. It suggests that after a lecture you need to review and use the material which has been presented to you.

Lectures are essentially a one-way communication process. The lecturer lectures and you listen, whether the lecture is delivered to ten students in a high school classroom or to several hundred people in a large lecture hall, whether the lecture lasts for five minutes or two hours. A lecturer may follow the customary format of university and college lectures and talk for almost the entire time with little or no student participation, or he or she may set aside part of the lecture for students to respond to and discuss what is said.

Why lectures?

Lectures have for a long time been the most common form of tertiary teaching, so it is worth thinking about their purposes. These can include:

- imparting information to large numbers of people
- providing a common ground for formal discussion in a subject
- serving as a starting point for private study
- drawing together the main ideas in a new research area
- providing a preliminary map of difficult reading material
- reviewing literature which is difficult to find, and
- adapting a topic for a particular audience in a way that a standard course text can't.

However, educators debate the effectiveness of lectures in achieving many teaching aims. For example, it is often stated that lectures don't encourage students to think for themselves and that students should discuss ideas thoroughly rather than simply listening to them in lectures. It is also argued that lectures are widely used not because they are effective, but because they are the cheapest way of teaching large numbers of students. In online courses, the text of any lectures which have been transferred to this medium without change will be no better than the original and may in fact be more difficult to read critically. You probably have your own opinions on how valuable lectures are in achieving your purposes for learning.

> I cannot see that lectures can do so much good as reading the books from which the lectures are taken. (*Samuel Johnson*)

Some lecturers think seriously about how much can be learnt and retained from lectures and about what they want students to learn from a particular lecture. These lecturers adapt their lecturing methods to their purposes, and are willing to depart from the traditional lecture format.

- Depending on the learning objectives of a course, the lecturer may present either an argumentative or expository lecture. Be aware of these different frameworks (see 'Genres', Chapter 6).
- If the lecturer intends to take a class in stages through difficult subject matter which involves a sequence of reasoning or events, he could use a series of five-minute lectures, each of which is followed by a few minutes for students to discuss or work on a related question.
- If the lecturer wants to exchange questions and comments with students in a small class, she doesn't plan a set lecture or time for student participation beforehand. Instead she relies on knowing the subject well and on being able both to present it logically and to restructure it in response to discussion.
- If a lecturer's purpose is to encourage maximum participation from a large class, she might lecture for half the time and divide the remaining time equally between a preliminary class discussion, individual student work, small group discussion and a brief summary by the whole class.

> 'Should a lecturer cover the ground laid down in his [*sic*] syllabus, even when some students don't understand, or go at a slower pace and get behind?' ... If lecturers considered their courses in terms of the learning being achieved by students rather than as a succession of performances by lecturers, this question would seldom be asked. (*Donald A. Bligh*)

A lecturer's effectiveness partly depends on their personality, particularly if—as is often the case—they are not trained in the skills of communicating to an audience. And because lecturing styles and abilities differ, you inevitably learn more from some lecturers than others. Skilled lecturers vary their method of presentation, pace of delivery, voice, and position in relation to the audience. They may be story tellers, actors or humorists or someone whose pleasure in the subject is catching. Some lecturers read their lectures, while others use brief notes or speak extemporaneously. A lecturer who is sensitive to an audience and responsive to their shifts in mood and attention is always more enjoyable. You may or may not share a lecturer's enthusiasm for a topic, but a talented lecturer is a pleasure to listen to and can hold your attention almost regardless of the subject.

However, all lectures require at least some effort on your part. If you consistently prepare for lectures, actively concentrate on what is said, and think back over it afterwards, you will get more out of lectures, even poor ones.

Preparing for a lecture

Usually you will hear a face-to-face lecture only once, so preparing beforehand will help you understand it more fully.

- Think about how useful a lecture could be in achieving your purposes in learning. For instance, if you are attending a lecture as well as discussing a topic or reading a book on it, why? You might do so to find information which is difficult and time-consuming to locate elsewhere, or to listen to a gifted lecturer present a familiar topic in a new way. Your main incentive could be to absorb information for exams and assignments; or you might attend out of habit or because attendance is compulsory.

- Prepare for a lecture by thinking about where the topic fits within the broader framework of a course—review previous lectures and the course outline. Do some of the suggested reading on the topic and look for other relevant material. You may find material (such as a summary of main points of the topic, a map, a time line or a list of biographical dates) you can take to the lecture to help you follow it. List any questions or ideas that come to mind as you prepare. You can use these as reference points when listening to the lecture, so that you are less likely to be overwhelmed by a mass of unfamiliar information and should be able to listen and make notes more intelligently.

- Consider your alternatives for recording the lecture. You probably make notes on a lecture, so think about how you can best do this. Will you take linear or patterned notes? You may want to arrange to compare your notes with someone else's after the lecture (see 'Making notes'). You might decide to share attending lectures in turn with another students, and agree that you will each take clear and thoughtful notes when it is your turn.

  Check if the lecture will be taped. If not, you may want to tape it yourself if, for example, the topic is unfamiliar or if you want to listen without making notes. However, don't tape lectures indiscriminately—think first about your reasons for wanting a tape rather than notes (and preferably ask for the lecturer's permission before using a tape recorder).

- Immediately before a lecture, think about how you feel. If you are feeling physically or emotionally low, do what you can to make yourself feel better. (See 'Emotions', Chapter 1, for suggestions on how to put your worries aside.) If you need to miss the lecture, have someone else tape it or make notes for you.

To help you follow a lecture, arrive before it starts to collect any handouts and so that you don't miss the introduction. In an introduction the lecturer often outlines the lecture; relates the topic to reference material, to a theoretical framework or to the rest of the course; states a problem the lecture will address; or tells a joke or a story to lead into the topic.

As you listen

'I think I should understand that better,' Alice said very politely, 'if I had it written down: but I can't quite follow it as you say it.'
'That's nothing to what I could say if I chose,' the Duchess replied, in a pleased tone. (*Lewis Carroll*)

Thoughts can move faster than speech, so your attention can easily wander during lectures unless you actively concentrate on what is being said (see 'Overcoming concentration difficulties'). To sustain your concentration so that you understand more fully what you hear, try to question what is being said, anticipate what will be said and frequently review what has been said. Make notes, and try to deal with situations which make concentration difficult.

Questioning and evaluating

Ask yourself questions about the purpose, approach, content, structure, style and format of the lecture. Most of the questions suggested in Table 9.3, 'Asking questions as you read', also apply to lectures. You may have other questions specifically related to lectures such as 'What is the lecturer conveying by his or her stance, distance from the audience and voice tones?' The questions you ask as you listen can form the basis for any notes you make.

Making notes

'Write that down,' the King said to the jury; and the jury wrote down all three dates on their slates, and then added them up, and reduced the answer to shillings and pence. (*Lewis Carroll*)

It is impossible to reproduce most of the content of a lecture exactly and very rarely do you want as much detail as this. Instead your notes should be your consciously selected version of the material offered, so that you make notes rather than take them. The previous chapter on reading suggests why you might make notes and what your notes could include (see 'Notemaking and/or underlining', Chapter 10), and the same points apply to lectures. But how you make notes when listening to a once-only live lecture differs from making notes from printed material you can re-read. (Table 10.1 offers some suggestions on note making that you can apply to both your reading and lectures.)

Table 10.1 Notemaking

You make notes from your lectures, from your reading and from discussions. The term 'note making' is used here to indicate that you need to take an active role in creating your notes and that your notes are more than a passive record of a reading or lecture. As a learner you should be making your own individual notes, processing and selecting information so that you make notes which are useful for your own purposes. These notes should show at a glance the relative importance of information—that is, you should use methods of note making that clearly separate the main points from the minor points.

Linear notes
Most people find the easiest way to make notes from reading and lectures is to start at the top left hand corner of a page and write from left to right until they reach the bottom right hand corner. If you prefer a linear note making method, try some or all of the following suggestions:
- use headings and subheadings which break up your text
- note key words
- use numbering
- use different coloured pens to differentiate the relative importance of information.

Another idea to try is to divide your page into two columns by folding your page lengthwise, then to use the left hand column for headings and main points and the right hand column for minor points or details. This method ensures that before you write anything you have to decide the relative importance of the information.

As you become adept at the method add a third column, a narrow left or right hand column, in which you record your responses to the information. These responses might include: references to check, points of particular interest, questions to ask about the material you don't understand, aspects you know about, or exclamations.

Patterned notes
These notes are also called 'explosion charts'. (See the graphic below for an example). The method involves starting in the centre of the page and branching to the edge. The theme or argument of the information is in the centre of the page and the main and sub-points radiate from it. The minor points or details radiate from the sub-points. You can also show 'cross-connections' between, for example, main points. The pattern can be drawn to represent the structure of the material as presented, or the structure that most closely suits your intended use of the material. Patterns of notes are a visual aid to learning the material that complements the usual oral/textual format in which we store information.

The advantages of this system over the linear form of note making are outlined by Buzan:

1 The centre or main idea is more clearly defined.
2 The relative importance of each idea is clearly indicated.
3 The links between the key concepts are immediately recognisable because of the proximity and connection.
4 As a result of the above, recall and review is both more effective and rapid.
5 The nature of the structure allows for the easy addition of new information without messy scratching out or squeezing in.
6 Each pattern looks and is different from the other patterns. This aids recall.

From: Lorraine Marshall, 1997, *A learning companion*, Murdoch University, Western Australia

Online courses at times present information in the form of electronic lectures (electures) which may have the same purposes as face-to-face lectures. Straight text lectures may need to be downloaded for easier reading and underlining.

Find a balance for each lecture between making useful notes and listening carefully—making notes constantly or making none at all are both of dubious value. In lectures which are meant to stimulate your imagination, spend most of your time sitting back and listening. In lectures which are densely packed with information and ideas you will take more notes, but select from and condense what is said so that you can listen closely enough to understand. For instance, if you are given a lot of data or examples, you can often summarise what they mean rather than frantically trying to copy them all. Sometimes a sketch version of a graph can be useful to trigger your memory. Lecturers may use phrases such as 'the following three factors are ...' or 'It's important to note that ...' to help you identify the structure of the lecture and indicate which points to note (see Table 13.2 'Transitional words and phrases').

If you prepare for a lecture and go over your notes very soon afterwards, you can usually strike a happy balance between making satisfactory notes and listening attentively to what is said. Try the following methods to experiment with how detailed your notes need to be and how much time you need to spend listening.

• Make as many notes as you think you will need. Go over these immediately after the lecture, asking yourself if you understand all you have written, and try to reproduce the way in which the lecture developed. If you can't, you have possibly spent too much time writing during the lecture—or the lecture itself was very confusing.
• If you have access to a tape of a lecture or if you can make your own tape, don't make notes but sit and listen intently. Immediately after the lecture and before you listen to the tape, see if you can write down a satisfactory summary of what you have just heard, perhaps in a patterned format. Then listen to the tape and compare your notes with what you hear.

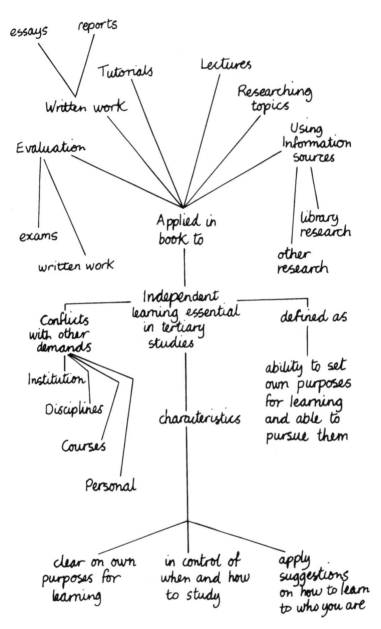

A student's patterned summary of the points they found relevant in *A Guide to Learning Independently*.

- If you are listening to a taped lecture, listen to the whole tape once without making notes. Write notes on the lecture before you listen for the second time. A taped lecture gives you the advantage of being able to stop and replay it at any point—something you can't do with a lecturer.

The above are suggestions, and you should develop your own method for distinguishing the structure of what is said—the thesis or main points, sub-points and supporting details. Lecture notes in which you can see the structure are easier to remember. Leave space for your own comments, questions or references to follow up, and items to think about further. Include on each page the lecture title and date, and the lecturer's name.

Overcoming concentration difficulties

Now I lay me back to sleep,
The speaker's dull, the subject's deep.
If he should stop before I wake,
Give me a nudge for goodness' sake. (*Anon.*)

Try to overcome difficulties which prevent you concentrating on and understanding a lecture (see 'Concentrating', Chapter 2). Your concentration is usually better at the beginning of a lecture—if you are able to put aside the thoughts or distractions which were occupying you before the lecture began. You also concentrate better when you know that the lecture is nearly over—unless you are impatient to leave. During a lecture your maximum concentration span is probably about twenty to twenty-five minutes. In a long lecture, revive your concentration by changing your sitting position, by quickly reviewing your notes, or by asking the lecturer a question.

- Try to minimise distractions in your physical surroundings—a hard chair, a wobbly desk, a cold room or loud hammering nearby are not conducive to full concentration.
- If you find it difficult to listen to a lecture tape because you can't see the lecturer's expressions or gestures, listen intently and replay parts of the tape if necessary. If you still have trouble, ask the lecturer for a written copy or an outline of the lecture.
- If a lecture seems to offer little that is new to you, ask yourself 'Am I really listening to what is being said?' If you are, try to anticipate what will follow, relate what is being said to what you already know about the topic, and review any notes you have made as you listen. Make a game of trying to find new information.
- If a lecture contains too much unfamiliar material, make a list of questions on points you don't understand, and ask the lecturer to clarify a couple of these points.

- If the content of the lecture seems irrelevant or uninteresting to you, jot down at least an outline in case the topic becomes relevant or interesting at a later date. You might prefer to leave the lecture quietly and do some other work rather than feeling that you are wasting time.
- A lecturer may make it difficult for you to follow a lecture because he or she doesn't organise material clearly, doesn't provide a written or oral lecture outline, or doesn't adequately prepare overhead transparencies and other aids. When you can't follow a lecture easily, leave plenty of space for your notes so that you have a chance to go back and add and edit as you write. For online lectures with long passages of text, you might need to print out a copy for easier reading.
- If a lecturer's style is difficult or dull for you, think about why this is so. You can probably do little to change the idiosyncrasies of lecturers' styles, but let a lecturer know if you can't hear or follow what is said. Don't dismiss lecturers you find difficult to follow as useless after only a couple of lectures. They may know their subject well, and as you become more familiar with their individual styles, it is often easier to concentrate on and understand what they are saying.

After a lecture

Before I came here I was confused about this subject. Having listened to your lecture I am still confused. But on a higher level. (*Enrico Fermi*)

As you hear most lectures only once, *reviewing your notes* as soon as possible—preferably immediately after a lecture or the same day—helps you remember what you have heard.

- Do you understand everything you have written?
- Can you identify the argument of the lecture—the thesis and reasons? If the lecture has no argument can you distinguish the controlling focus, main and sub-points, and how the lecture developed from one point to another? It may help to underline or highlight the main points as you review your notes.
- Is there a clearly identifiable theoretical framework for the lecture?
- Do you need to edit your notes so that they reflect the lecture more accurately and read more easily? Do you need to expand your notes so that you can still understand them in a month's time?
- Do you have a relevant article or other material to file with your notes? Could you usefully include references to a couple of multimedia items?
- Would it be useful to express all or part of your notes in another form, for example as a flow chart, or diagram or in a pattern? (See Table 10.1 'Note making'.)

If you have *persistent problems* in identifying the structure of lectures and understanding your notes:

- listen to lecture tapes or read a hard copy of the lecture if you need to
- make sure that you are preparing thoroughly for lectures
- compare your notes with someone else's, and discuss the differences to help clarify ways to improve your notemaking
- read some more on the topic so that the lecture isn't your only source of information, and
- ask a lecturer for help with the problem (see 'Contacting people', Chapter 3).

Your problems with lectures may be due to the lecturer. If you have difficulty understanding an important lecture, go and see the lecturer soon afterwards to talk about the topic. Sometimes a person who's awkward in front of an audience is helpful when discussing information on a one-to-one basis. (Think about how you feel when delivering a seminar paper and when discussing the same topic with one other person.) Lecturing is a talent which few people possess naturally, so constructive comments can help lecturers improve their skill. Such comments can be made tactfully by asking questions on points you don't understand and possibly suggesting alternative lecture formats (see 'Why lectures?'). Part of being an active listener is to suggest tactfully to lecturers how their lectures could be more effective.

Since most lectures are a one-way communication, *using and discussing the lecture material* is essential if you are to understand it fully.

- Do you have items you want to follow up, for example an idea which interested you, a reference you noted, a point you didn't fully understand, a quote you want to check out?
- Did the lecturer suggest any follow-up to the lecture such as a reference to read, a problem to solve, an exercise to do, or a couple of questions to think about?
- File your notes for easy future reference (see 'Selecting, recording and filing information', Chapter 7).

Some lectures contain ideas or information that are especially significant for you. These lectures are easy to remember and use. Otherwise, you are most likely to use what you have heard and written down if you need the material for an assignment or an exam, for a seminar or online discussion group, or when talking to friends or a teacher. In a discussion over coffee after a lecture, for example, you can compare notes, clarify points you didn't understand, exchange ideas which excited you, and decide on questions or suggestions with which to approach the lecturer if necessary.

■ ■ ■ ■ ■

If you find some lectures boring and pointless, is it because you are sitting back and expecting to be entertained? If you are, think about your purpose for attending a lecture and prepare to take an active part as a hard-working listener. Inevitably some lectures seem a waste of time, and very few people deliver an ideal lecture. To make the most of the range of knowledge and lecturing styles you are offered, take the time to learn how to get the most out of lectures and, if necessary, pluck up the courage to try to change them.

Further reading

Bligh, Donald A., 1972, *What's the use of lectures?* Penguin Education, Penguin Books, Middlesex, England.

Brown, George, 1978, *Lecturing and explaining*, Methuen, London.

Buzan, Tony, 1989, *Use your head*, BBC Books, London (revised edition).

CHAPTER 11

PARTICIPATING IN DISCUSSION GROUPS

Do you think of yourself as a 'talker' or a 'listener'?

Which people or situations encourage you to talk?

Who do you talk to in your daily life, about the weather, about personal matters or about current issues?

Do you find that many of your conversations are about other people, yourself, sex, ideas, events, technology, religion, politics?

To whom do you particularly enjoy listening?

Do you think that you learn more from talking with people, from reading, from writing, or from watching TV or video?

Do you chat to others by writing letters or e-mails?

Your discussions with other people may be intense debates, rambling conversations, casual chats, exchanges of brilliant repartee or rituals of polite remarks about the weather. These discussions may be very brief, go on for several hours, or continue intermittently for weeks or even months. Perhaps you use discussion to sort out your ideas, share experiences, play with words, or learn something new.

As a tertiary student, you probably learn a great deal from informal ad hoc discussions over endless cappuccinos in the cafeteria or from e-mail chat groups. In universities, debates and arguments and discussions are central to the culture (see 'Thinking critically', Chapter 3). All members of the different disciplines, whether teachers or students, are participants in ongoing debates on a whole range of subjects, topics, questions and problems which have been written about and discussed from a wide range of world views. Within a tertiary education that focuses on critical thinking, students are encouraged to identify their world views and to be aware of their underlying values and assumptions.

Why discussion groups?

Sharing your learning in discussion groups can be a collaborative exploration of ideas which offsets the competitive pressures on you as a student. Discussion groups also provide an alternative to the solitary activities of private study and listening to presentations such as lectures.

Any discussion groups can offer an opportunity:

• to integrate what you learn from your reading, writing and lectures
• to clarify your ideas and feelings on a subject
• to stimulate you to study and think
• to sort out misunderstandings and problems in your work
• to practise communicating ideas to others
• to solve problems collaboratively, and
• to develop critical thinking skills and attitudes in a group context.

More specifically, student-organised study groups which meet regularly can be an invaluable support, and a source of feedback on your work before you submit it. Within a course, groups which form to work collaboratively on a particular project can stimulate you to think in new ways. Formal tutorials and seminars can provide closer contact with a staff member and informal teacher feedback on your progress.

Online discussion groups may be formal or informal and can provide a much-needed source of support and contact, particularly for distance and isolated students. Informal discussions in an online course may focus on academic matters and/or provide social interaction. The academic discussions might take the form of regular formal tutorials or seminars, the collaborative production of an assignment, or shared informal problem solving.

Online groups offer advantages to all students. Since the contributions are text-based, an active discussion list can construct a shared knowledge base, and a record of the group discussions builds up which can be stored and edited and easily revisited.

> ... learning networks are groups of people who use CMC [computer mediated communications] networks to learn together, at a time, place and pace that best suits them and is appropriate to the task ... The use of computer networks ... introduces new options to transform teaching and learning relationships and outcomes ... [N]etworking technologies can improve upon traditional ways of teaching and learning. (*Linda Harasim*)

This chapter discusses different types of groups and it outlines techniques for setting up groups which can be used in informal discussions with other students as well as in tutorials and seminars. The chapter also deals with some aspects of how discussion groups work, and suggests how you can learn from and enjoy groups by attending to what you do before, during and after a group meeting. Ideas are given on preparing for discussions, participating actively, and reviewing and using what is discussed.

Types of discussion groups

Variety is the spice of discussion groups, whatever their origin, purpose and focus. Within a group, people of different ages, experiences, backgrounds and world views have much to offer each other when exchanging ideas, and a varied format and content for group meetings is stimulating.

> I dogmatise and am contradicted, and in this conflict of opinions and sentiments I find delight. (*Samuel Johnson*)

Most structured discussion groups in undergraduate higher education can be characterised according to who establishes them, what they focus on, and how much collaborative learning is involved:

- Groups may be set up by teachers for all or part of a course, or by students who establish study groups which meet regularly.
- The content of the discussions might focus on a particular part of the content of a course, an assignment or other course work, study skills, and/or provide student support.
- The amount of collaboration depends on factors such as the purpose of the group and a teacher's role in a group.

Traditionally, formal small group discussion in higher education is mostly conducted in tutorials and seminars. Such face-to-face groups meet specifically for discussion as part of a course, and usually consist of a teacher as leader and a particular group of students. These formal group discussions vary widely in structure and content. For example, they may be:

- a mini-lecture where the teacher imparts information
- a group in which the teacher remains relatively unobtrusive and the rest of the group manages itself
- a seminar series where each member takes a turn as chairperson
- a group which uses interactive exercises such as role-playing to learn about human values and attitudes, or
- a session which emphasises the less subjective, rational aspects of learning.

Both tutorials and study groups may focus on:

- formal debates on issues, solving a specific problem, or working on a particular piece of research
- discussions structured around a paper given by a group member or based on set reading, or
- sharing experiences and feelings as well as discussing intellectual issues.

Collaborative learning groups

... these shared spaces can become the locus of rich and satisfying experiences in collaborative learning, an interactive group knowledge-building process in which the learner actively constructs knowledge by formulating ideas into words that are shared with and built upon through the reactions and responses of others. (*Linda Harasim*)

Collaborative learning groups can be informal out of class or be part of your formal learning; and they can be with one other person or several people. Collaborative learning in class can be a five-minute buzz group where you share information with a group of students, or a formal group which has a life cycle of perhaps a few days or a few months. Weekly tutorials can be collaborative learning groups which are led by a tutor.

As learning in teams has recently been acknowledged as a generic skill that is important for all students to acquire before they graduate (see 'Developing skills and attitudes', Chapter 3), many courses set up collaborative learning groups as part of the formal course work. These formal groups are usually student-led and organised; they may be face-to-face or online; and they may be short term, or a major part of a student's course workload. The groups may vary in size, but usually consist of 3 to 5 students. They might involve a group written project, and may involve group assessment of the discussion process and of any work produced.

To work successfully in a collaborative group it is important to understand how groups work and the stages through which they pass.

Stages of group development

To develop a well-functioning group and to maximise your own learning, it will be helpful if you utilise the following stages or life cycle of effective groups. The stages outlined below[1] involve both an analytical and a reflective component. For a group to be effective these four stages should occur at the micro level, that is during each work meeting of the group, and over the life of the group.

- First, it is important to *find common ground* with the other members of the group. This involves some socialising to get to know the others and find out what you have in common with them. It is also important to understand each person's expectations of the group, identify conflicts and work at resolving them. Socialising—as long as it does not dominate the group's time—is not a waste of time but is important for the success of the group.
- Second, early on you need to *clarify the different roles and goals* for each person in the group. This involves setting up ground rules for the group (see 'Ground rules').
- Third, you need to *achieve the outcomes* on which the group has agreed.
- Fourth, it is necessary to *reflect* on what the group has achieved both in terms of the group's product and the group process. The process of evaluating the group preferably involves both individual and group evaluation.

These stages should also apply to online groups. A few social comments about yourself before you get down to the business at hand can work wonders to situate you to the person or people 'listening' to you elsewhere on the network.

As well as pursuing your academic goals, it will help if you work actively to develop the skills for participating in the group process. Such work involves actively reflecting on what is happening to you as you work with the group, and taking initiatives both within the group and with your teacher to alleviate any difficulties (see 'Taking your part during discussions').

Setting up discussion groups

Your teachers will probably have addressed the issues discussed in this section when establishing formal tutorials for face-to-face or online courses. If you are in a collaborative group which you either establish with other students or to which you are formally assigned within a course, you should also address these issues. You also need to consider them if you are setting up a study group with other students from within a course or across related courses. (If you want to set up a group to concentrate specifically on writing see 'Writing groups', Chapter 12.)

First things

The size of a group

A group should be small enough to enable everyone to say something within the time available. Traditionally seven to twelve people is recognised as an effective number for tutorial groups, but this varies with the purpose of the discussion (and possibly because of funding cuts to tertiary education). Most people feel hesitant about speaking up in front of a large group, but the group should be large enough to provide a variety of ideas. If a group is too small, combine it with another group if possible. If the group is too large, break it into smaller groups for a part of each session or permanently. However, for informal study groups three or four people can be ideal. This is also an ideal size for an online work group which needs to make decisions quickly.

Where and when you meet

How will you arrange when and where you meet? Agree on the length and frequency of meetings according to the size and purpose of the group. With an electronic group, your meetings can be time-independent (asynchronous) and place-independent. You will need to decide if you need to include any realtime meetings online (or through teleconferencing, audioconferencing or 'phone hook-ups) or face-to face.

Give some thought to where you might meet so that you can spend some uninterrupted and relaxing time together. Discussions are influenced by the physical setting in which you meet, so in formal settings seek out a comfortable room if possible. Otherwise, consider how you can adapt an unfriendly meeting place to the group's needs. A cold box-like room occupied by standard institutional chairs and tables and a blackboard is more conducive to monastic silence than heated debate. What can you do with an inappropriate room? It is often possible to rearrange seating or desks so that everyone is more comfortable, and most importantly, can see everyone else. A leader need not be isolated in front of the group; a large open space in the middle of a group can be closed up; and if the room is carpeted people may be more relaxed sitting on the floor.

Sometimes another place can be found for a group, or you can meet outdoors or in a private home. Meeting outside a formal setting—to have coffee or go to a movie, for example—can have a positive impact on the discussions of a formal group.

The first few meetings

Getting to know each other

Instead of plunging straight into talking about a course topic or assignments and assessment, people in a group can devote some time to becoming acquainted, perhaps over a cup of coffee or a glass of wine. Names and faces become more familiar if each person, including the teacher, introduces themselves briefly and talks about their interests and hopes for the course. Try icebreakers such as naming games or round robins (see 'Further reading' for a reference with ideas on this). If the group divides into pairs for a brief period to discuss a specific question about a topic or the course, people have another opportunity to get to know each other. The group as a whole can also begin to get a sense of the resources, strengths and expertise of group members. Remember that sharing some socialising is not a waste of time but actively contributes to the group process. It should not occur only in the first meetings but needs to be built into each meeting (see 'Stages of group development').

The group's role and focus

In the early stages of a group, it is very useful to establish some shared initial expectations about what being in the group might involve. Some people in the group may see the group's main role as enabling students to exchange ideas, while other people might see the meetings as an occasion for the teacher to tell them more about a subject. Some people may hope that group meetings will be a forum for discussing lecture topics or their special interests.

If the group is part of a formal course, one of the first topics for discussion should be the group's role in the course as a whole and how it should operate. Group members also need to decide (or be told) if participation in the group will be assessed formally or informally, and if so, how.

If the group is to work collaboratively on a project or assignment, how will the group arrive at an initial understanding of how much work will be done together? How much and what will each person be responsible for working on? It is valuable to develop a couple of tasks that you can immediately work on together.

An online group does not have to be limited in its role and focus because of the medium. Consider setting up a virtual cafe (bring your own coffee), a debating team or a learning circle.

Your ongoing meetings

Attending meetings

The same group of people need to attend the meetings regularly (or via e-mail, contribute regularly). People find it easier to make their own contributions if discussions are ongoing over a period of time and everyone knows what was discussed previously. Regular attendance also helps group members feel comfortable with each other and feel confident about suggesting ideas, asking questions, admitting ignorance, and responding honestly to what is said by someone else. Developing this sense of 'give and take' lessens the pressure to say something on most topics and to impress others. In online groups participants need to agree on how frequently new contributions should be submitted, on the time frame for comments, and on how frequently group members are expected to log onto the group's discussions.

Ground rules

> It is crucial to establish ground rules in a group because you've always got issues of power, and if you don't have ground rules it's basically a free for all. *(Julia Hobson)*

Establishing a code of behaviour or ground rules, for the group and abiding by these can help the group work harmoniously and can help ensure that the group achieves its stated aims. For example, if the aim of a discussion group is to foster critical thinking skills and attitudes in members of a group, the ground rules will need to reflect this. Similarly, in a writing group the ground rules will reflect the output aims of the group (see 'Writing groups', Chapter 12).

It is preferable if these ground rules are arrived at collaboratively when the group first meets. If everyone contributes and agrees to the rules, then all members are likely to abide by them. If a group does not seem to be working well the ground rules may need to be renegotiated or members of the group may not be abiding by them. Some possible ground rules might be: everyone will prepare for meetings; when someone speaks everyone listens; everyone will be on time; discriminatory comments will not be allowed. The ground rules to foster critical thinking and attitudes may be substantially the same as those for effective groups, but might also include: avoid being dogmatic; don't silence others; explain assumptions; respect cultural differences and other people's opinions.

For online groups, in addition to ground rules such as those above, you also need to abide by guidelines on online protocols.

■ ■ ■ ■ ■

Once a group is established, you need to consider how to make most effective use of the time you spend together. The rest of this chapter elaborates on key aspects of the group process.

Preparing for a discussion

If everyone in a group prepares, the discussion at least has the basis for success. If you prepare, you will have a clearer idea of what you want to discuss and you will remember the discussion more clearly. You can also challenge others who do not prepare and who rely on 'talking off the top of their head'. Everyone will occasionally have times when they can't prepare as fully as they would like. However, if most people don't prepare it would be useful to discuss why not, and to ensure that being prepared is a ground rule with which everyone agrees.

Be sure you know as precisely as possible the topic planned for discussion, what preparation is required, and why. If you find the preparation required is too much or too difficult, if you have trouble obtaining necessary materials, or if you have other demands at the time which make it difficult for you to prepare fully, ask the group leader as soon as possible for suggestions or information.

- Do any required preparation such as reading or exercises.
- Formulate in writing at least one brief item to contribute to the discussion—a thought, a definition, a question, a piece of information, or a comment on your reading or lectures on the topic (see 'Asking your own questions', Chapter 4).
- Revise your relevant lecture notes.
- Check reference books and audiovisual material on and around the topic and follow up with more specific reading if necessary.
- Read any notes you made during or after the last group meeting.

Immediately before the group meets, be aware of how you feel and try to put distractions behind you (see 'Your emotions', Chapter 1). You might read thoroughly a section from a relevant book to focus your mind on the discussion topic.

Preparing for a discussion paper

Prepare thoroughly if you are to give a paper. Your efforts will be assessed according to the content, how you structure your material, and your presentation.

- Research, plan and prepare the content of your paper. In a short paper, limit yourself to one or two main points. You need a clear introduction, and a summing-up which could be a statement or question for the group to debate. This is especially important if you do not make copies of your paper, as your listeners will have the material presented to them only once. (See Chapter 7 for information on researching, and Chapter 13 for ideas on how to plan and structure the content of a discussion paper.)
- Prepare visual materials or handouts, perhaps as a patterned summary, to help your audience follow you. If you plan to use data, maps or other information which may be difficult to absorb quickly, prepare photocopies or a whiteboard display so the group can read the information.
- Decide whether to speak from notes or read a paper. You may feel more confident if your paper is written out fully. Rehearse aloud, so that you know how long your presentation takes. Most listeners become restless after 15–20 minutes, so time your presentation with this in mind.

- Practise varying your presentation to hold the group's attention. You are more likely to engage your listeners if you invite questions or ask the group questions at appropriate points in your talk.

Taking your part during discussions

'The time has come,' the Walrus said,
'To talk of many things:
Of shoes—and ships—and sealing wax—
Of cabbages—and kings—
Of why the sea is boiling hot—
And whether pigs have wings.' (*Lewis Carroll*)

Most groups spend time talking about academic or practical matters such as the next topic for discussion, the set reading, or who will deliver a seminar paper, but they usually neglect to consider explicitly group processes and interpersonal interactions within a group—the 'hidden agenda'. Even group interactions of which every member is aware, such as frequent silences or an over-talkative person, aren't usually discussed by the whole group. The following are a few examples of this agenda.

- The particular combination of people in a group plays a large part in shaping the discussions. For example, groups made up of school leavers who are full-time students approach a subject differently from groups made up of part-time students from a variety of backgrounds. People who are in a minority in a group, such as women in a predominantly male group or Aboriginals in a mostly white group, often feel less free to speak.
- If people always sit in the same place or two or three people always sit together, this can set up habits of who talks to whom and where discussions centre.
- A person who decides the direction of a discussion may not be a teacher or a person who talks a lot, but someone who asks pertinent questions or who brings an aimless discussion back on track.
- How people contribute to a group is influenced by whether each person's participation is assessed, and if so whether it is assessed by a teacher or by the whole group.
- When people contribute to a group discussion, they may be trying not to appear naive/over-clever/aggressive while at the same time seeming to be witty/intelligent/confident/sexually attractive.

[in] working together across differences ... the 'outsider' should sincerely attempt to carry out her attempted criticism of the insider's perceptions in such a way that it does not amount to, or even seem to amount to, an attempt to denigrate or dismiss the validity of the insider's point of view. (*Uma Narayan*)

If you have little experience of taking responsibility for formal discussions and are anxious not to appear foolish in front of the other students and a teacher, you are unlikely to initiate discussions on how a group is working. If a teacher is unskilled in dealing with group dynamics, he or she is unlikely to initiate discussion with students about what is happening in a group. But the personal interactions within a group can't be separated from its intellectual discussions, and a group needs to spend time talking about both if it is to realise its full potential (see 'Collaborative learning'). If you feel that a 'hidden agenda' item is being ignored at the cost of group effectiveness and your own learning, try to work up the courage—perhaps with someone else in the group—to bring the problem constructively into the open, using some of the suggestions which follow. A basis for discussing both academic work and the interactions within the group can usually be established in the first two or three meetings.

Contributing to a discussion

Each member of a group, even if remaining silent, influences how that group operate. The success of a discussion group depends largely on whether everyone plays a part in establishing ground rules, takes responsibility for how the group operates and feels free to contribute fully.

Talking and listening skills

'... I find discussion as a whole ... difficult, because I've never had to discuss anything before and haven't put my feelings into words ... It takes me an awful long time to think about what I want to say and, sometimes, by the time I've thought about it, it's gone.' (*A student*)

Participating fully in a group discussion requires practice in the skills of talking clearly and concisely, asking useful questions and listening carefully. These skills take time to acquire, particularly with a group of people who initially are strangers, and for each combination of people you need to find your own balance between talking and listening. In particular, studies have shown that men often dominate discussions in which both sexes are involved. Some people don't see asking questions as an essential part of conversations, so they may need to practise the skills of asking questions and genuinely listening.

Participating in a group is not the same as talking a great deal. Some of your alternatives are:

- listening closely for most of the time, occasionally contributing a well thought-out question or piece of information
- attempting to paraphrase what someone else said, to make sure you understood them
- asking questions which begin 'Do you mean that ... ?' 'What do you think about ... ?' or simply 'Why?'

- commenting in response to someone who has spoken, as long as you really are responding and not just waiting until they have finished so you can have your say, and
- affirming an idea that someone else has put forward.

If you have prepared for the discussion you will have your own thoughts and questions to contribute. If a discussion group is to help you sort out your ideas and become aware of your beliefs and biases, articulate these and bring them out from inside your head so other people can respond to them. Don't hold back because you feel you have to utter perfectly complete thoughts or always be serious.

You may come from a cultural background or an educational system in which you do not expect to speak up unless addressed directly by the teacher or in which your main contribution is to respond to factual questions asked of the class. In universities and colleges, you are expected to contribute ideas as well as information and to comment thoughtfully on what the other members of the group say. Practise this, and talk to the group leader or to other students about how you can more effectively contribute to the discussion.

If you lack confidence in a discussion group, remember that it takes time to gain experience in the skills of formal discussion and to settle into a new group of people. Even if you like the group members at first meeting, you may still be cautious about venturing opinions until you know them a little better. If you continue to feel uncertain of yourself in a group or if you are not confident about a topic, you can gain confidence by preparing for the discussion, getting to know some other members of the group outside the formal discussion time, and talking to the group leader or a helpful staff member about how you feel. Others who at first seem to know more than you often don't; and even if they do, you still have your contribution to make (see 'Your cultural and social self', Chapter 1).

> Very few people know how to listen. Their haste pulls them out of the conversation, or they try internally to improve the situation, or they're preparing what their next speech will be when you shut up and it's their turn to take the stage. (*Peter Hoeg*)

If you talk too much and are aware of this, you will probably also be aware that other people stop listening or find it difficult to follow what you say. For several meetings try to ask other people questions whenever you feel tempted to talk—you will probably be surprised at how much they have to contribute.

How much time do you usually spend in talking and how much in asking questions and listening to what others say?

How much response do you usually give to other people's ideas?

Your answers to these questions will probably vary for each group to which you belong. Can you work out why you put more effort into some groups than into others?

Online discussion groups have some distinctive features when it comes to talking and listening. Since they are independent of time and place you can decide when and where you want to contribute to the discussion. This gives you the opportunity to reflect on an unfolding discussion before you contribute first, and to edit your initial response before you send it. This can be particularly useful if you prefer time to think before you write, if you have physical difficulties with writing, or if English is not your first language. Another advantage is that you don't have to compete to contribute, and can be heard uninterrupted. If you are shy, you don't have to wait for a group leader to pick up visual signals which indicate you want to say something.

Online group discussion is likely to be egalitarian because it is physically anonymous and so, for example, you are not judged by your appearance before you speak. However, because of the absence of visual cues online discussions are likely to be less rich and nuanced than face-to-face interactions. You will also have to learn the skills of talking in chunks rather than being part of a conversation with its interruptions and interweaving of half-completed sentences. In addition, sometimes you may feel that you are talking into space, a feeling that heightens the usual writers' sense of being exposed when they commit thoughts to paper or screen.

As well as learning some of the above skills of contributing online, you also need to become familiar with the mechanical skills such as keying in text.

> The interface design must provide ease of navigation, a sense of human interaction, and helpfulness and responsiveness to the needs of learners studying in an information rich, self directed medium. Learners need to feel confident that they know where they are at any one point in the course and that they can easily make contact with others as the need arises. (*Allison Brown*)

Taking responsibility

Each person in a group influences the nature of the discussion, and the absence of even one person can change the atmosphere of a group. Everyone needs to prepare for and participate in discussions rather than seeing the group solely as the leader's responsibility. If only one or two people contribute, even a skilful leader can do little to make the group function satisfactorily.

The amount of time each person in a group talks depends on factors such as their enthusiasm for a topic, amount of preparation, and well-being at the time. A common difficulty in a group is having one or two people who are persistent talkers or non-talkers.

Some people prefer to contribute to a discussion only occasionally, but the person who rarely says anything needs encouragement. Most people indicate by facial expressions or body movements when they're ready to speak, and if other people are sensitive to these signs they can give a shy person an opportunity to speak. Someone who is quiet may gain confidence if the group divides into smaller units for part of the discussion. You could suggest that each person prepares a specific contribution for each session or takes a turn to comment briefly on a topic which comes up, as this gives reticent members of the group practice in speaking while limiting more garrulous individuals.

However, the whole group needs to discourage a person who talks too much, and usually this can be done politely but firmly by remarks such as 'That's interesting—I'm curious to hear what other people have to say now'. If what the talker says is irrelevant, the whole group will be grateful to someone who restates the original topic. But if the offender fails to take the hint, someone in the group needs to deal with the problem after the meeting.

Leading and monitoring a group

The official group leader may not always be a teacher—he or she may be a student who is giving a paper or is responsible for chairing the discussion. Most groups also have unofficial leaders, even if 'leaderless'.

Some groups rotate the leader or moderator so that everyone has the opportunity to develop leadership skills.

If you are the group leader even for one session, consider the following ideas.

- When preparing for the discussion make sure you devise a list of discussion questions (and possible answers to them) in case no one asks any questions (see 'Asking your own questions', Chapter 4), and perhaps share these questions with the teacher.
- Think about different ways of organising the session, you might break the group into smaller buzz groups or allow members time to reflect and/or write before they speak.
- Perhaps assign different roles which group members can play, such as observers, monitors, reporters or questioners. Observers of the group process can check if the ground rules are being followed. Monitoring is particularly important for online groups if many members are new to this form of discussion and if the appropriate protocols are still evolving.
- For online groups, remember that unless group members have to use a password to access discussions, others can 'overhear' your stored discussions by using search engines for a subject search which taps into what you have been discussing.

- If you are giving a discussion paper, let the group know if you are happy to deal with questions or comments during your presentation, or if you would rather these were kept until you finish. If you are responsible for the discussion afterwards, try to encourage other members of the group to take part. As well as helping them and improving the discussion, directing this effort to others usually reduces your anxiety about being the centre of attention.

'Begin at the beginning,' the King said, very gravely, 'and go on till you come to the end: then stop.' (*Lewis Carroll*)

The teacher's authority in a group

The authority of those who teach is very often a hindrance to those who wish to learn. (*Cicero*)

Where a teacher is responsible for a group in a formal course, their authority usually overrides that of a student, even when the teacher tries to prevent this.

A teacher may have authority in a group because she or he is:

- a group leader appointed by the educational institution
- an assessor of the group members' work
- a specialist in a particular field of knowledge
- a skilled group leader
- a person older than most students in the group, or
- a dominant personality.

Leadership styles

He was leader by default—by de fault of de rest of de group. (*Anon.*)

Some teachers consciously try to step back from a position of authority in a group, to encourage students to articulate their own ideas and learn from each other. Such teachers face the challenge of trying to be *a resource person* in a subject rather than an expert or an appointed leader. They try to use their personal skills with people or groups to foster the development of individuals and the whole group, instead of attempting to direct this process. If you are accustomed to having your learning firmly directed, you may find this approach disconcerting.

There are teachers who consciously prefer to be *the definite leader* in a group. This choice is consistent with a model which defines formal education as students receiving information from experts. Teachers who base their teaching on this model are likely to expect to be the focus of the group's comments and questions and use group meetings to give mini-lectures. (For help with making notes in such groups see 'Making notes', Chapter 10.) This approach can work when both teacher and students feel under pressure to cover a prescribed amount of material, but it discourages discussion between students and ignores much of the potential of small-group work.

Some teachers remain as *automatic leaders* because they haven't given much thought to the bases of authority in a group—and even teachers who want to encourage student participation occasionally fall into accepting this authority. An inexperienced teacher may be glad of the security that the role of leader offers, and some older teachers expect younger students to defer to them. Some teachers, because of their personality and experience, are accustomed to leading most groups in which they find themselves.

> The role of the teacher in an online environment is radically different to more traditional teacher–learner relationships. Once teachers have completed the syllabus and instructional design of the online course their role is then to observe, monitor, facilitate and provide information as appropriate, not to deliver a course in a fixed and rigid one-way format.
> (*Allison Brown*)

Coping with a teacher's authority

If you are a student in a group where the teacher takes the authority you may find it helpful to cope with this authority if you can work out why the teacher is the group leader. For example:

- Some teachers don't recognise that their familiarity with the concepts and language of a subject gives them a position of authority in discussing it with students. It is often difficult for these teachers to understand how complex a subject can be for beginners (To develop your vocabulary, see 'Developing your vocabulary', Chapter 9).
- Other teachers have their own plan for a tutorial or seminar because they are anxious to cover a syllabus or eager to convey what they see as the important or exciting issues in a topic. Such teachers may ignore or belittle contributions which don't fit their plan, or ask questions for which they have a Right answer in mind. They may attempt to start a discussion at too advanced a level or at a pace too fast for most of the group, so that discussion is only possible if there are one or two students who are self-confident and familiar with the subject. Other students are left either to drift off or to try to guess the teacher's plan, rather than having a chance to think about and articulate their own ideas.
- Teachers who don't know how to encourage participation may leave a group floundering because they fail to realise the need for a clearly defined starting point for discussion. Or they may hover over a group—rushing in to break up any silences instead of allowing people to collect their thoughts, asking questions to which the answer is obvious, or answering questions so conclusively that further discussion is pointless.

All the tutors say, you know, do ask a question if you don't understand me, but if you really have no idea of what on earth they're going on about you can't very well say 'Well, would you start again at the beginning'. You can't ask a question because you just don't know what to ask it about. (*A student*)

How can a group cope with a teacher's authority? Start with the assumption that it is the responsibility of the whole group, not only the teacher, to make a group work and ask yourself if you have contributed as fully as possible. A teacher who takes a dominant role may appear to determine a group's character, but she or he can only dominate if the rest of the group allow this to happen—if, for example, you seldom address comments or questions directly to each other. As a group, work out clearly what you expect and want from the discussions, and develop ground rules to help the group work harmoniously. Keep in mind that if you aren't prepared to take action, you can't expect the situation to change.

- What aims would you each like the group to have?
- What do members have to offer each other in discussions, and what skills and knowledge does the teacher have which are valuable to the group?
- If you find the teacher difficult, can you work out why and together decide on ways to handle the problem?
- What activities could the group undertake which would help each person participate fully?
- If you think that assessment of contributions to the group is preventing full discussion, can you suggest alternatives?
- If you don't understand an aspect of the discussion, are you each willing to ask about it?
- If the discussion seems aimless, are you each willing to say so, explain why, and suggest a definite direction the discussion might take?
- Are you each prepared to renew the discussion after a silence?

You may want to talk about these and other questions during or outside group meetings. If at all possible, talk directly with the teacher concerned about any problems rather than suffering in silence or grumbling and doing nothing. Teachers who are concerned about their students and their teaching know that they can often learn from students and welcome thoughtful suggestions. Such a direct discussion may require considerable courage if a teacher is authoritarian, and more than a little tact if a teacher is well-meaning but unskilled (see 'Approaching teachers', Chapter 3). It is usually easier to talk with a teacher if you have met on a one-to-one basis early in the course, so that you see each other more as individuals with particular interests in a course rather than as a 'Teacher' and a 'Student'.

After a group

After a group meeting, review the discussion to think about how it relates to you, your learning and the course. To help you remember what was discussed, as soon as possible make a brief summary and follow up anything you haven't understood. If you gave a paper, think back over your presentation and the ensuing discussion. If required, see the group leader to evaluate your paper. Make sure that you know what the next topic for discussion will be and precisely what you are expected to prepare.

Another way to learn more from a formal discussion is to get together afterwards with one or two other students to talk informally about the topic. You can sort out points you didn't understand, make some of those comments which were lost in the larger group, and consolidate and build on what you did understand. The moral support that such discussions can give is invaluable, particularly for less confident students.

> ... all my confidence diminished as I was to hear someone talk of *The Plague* all the time referring to the Germans in France during the War. What in heaven's name was she talking about? I had also read *The Plague* and found it a most interesting story of a town infested by bubonic plague, but it never entered my head that these things were all symbols. From that moment I was frightened to open my mouth. At coffee break, however, I was to learn a couple of others felt the same reaction to this piece of news. (*Brian's Wife Jenny's Mum*)

You may have persistent problems in a group and feel dissatisfied or unhappy. If you have contributed as fully as you can, you may want to discuss your feelings privately with the group leader. You could sound out the other group members to see if they share your feelings and if so, arrange to devote some of the formal discussion time to dealing with the problem. The group needs to revisit the ground rules and perhaps amend them. You may be able to change to another group if these attempts to deal with the problem don't succeed. Such a change often only involves asking the teachers concerned and is preferable to wasting your time.

■ ■ ■ ■ ■

Do you usually enjoy discussion groups? Most students feel confident and interested in some groups, and uncertain or bored in others. Perhaps the most important thing about groups is that even good groups have their off days. The success of a group as a whole depends on every member assuming responsibility for it; the success of a group for you as an individual member depends on your willingness to participate in critical debate and to speak and listen.

Students should be enabled to develop the capacity to keep an eye on themselves, and to engage in critical dialogue with themselves in all they think and do. ... the student interrogates her/his thoughts or actions. (*Ronald Barnett*)

Further reading

Bozek, P. E., 1991, *50 one-minute tips for better communication*, Crisp Publications, California

Dashwood, A., 1992, *Speaking: English for academic purposes*, University of Southern Queensland, Toowoomba.

McEvedy, M.R., Packham, G. & Smith, P., 1986, *Studying in Australia: Speaking in academic settings: Oral skills for seminars, discussion and interacting with supervisors*, Nelson, Melbourne.

Macbeth, Jim & MacCallum, Judy, 1996, *Collaborative learning: Working together in small groups*, A Gripping Films Production, Murdoch University.

Peel, M., 1992, *Successful presentation in a week*, Hodder & Stoughton, London

Schmuck, R.A & Schmuck, P.A., 1992, *Group processes in the classroom*, 6th edn, Wm. C. Brown, Dubuque, Iowa.

Stevens, M., 1987, *Improving your presentation skills: A complete action kit*, Kogan Page, London.

Young, Robert & Lovat, Terry, 1988, *Communicating all around* in Terry Lovat (ed.), *People, culture and change*, Social Science Press, Wentworth Falls.

Notes

Schmuck, R.A. & Schmuck, P.A., 1992, *Group processes in the classroom*, 6th edn, Wm. C. Brown, Dubuque, Iowa.

CHAPTER 12

DEVELOPING YOUR WRITING

From time to time I feel a need, sharp as thirst in summer, to note and to describe. And then I take up my pen again and attempt the perilous and elusive task of seizing and pinning down, under its flexible double-pointed nib, the many-hued, fugitive, thrilling adjective ... The attack does not last long; it is but the itching of an old scar. (*Colette*)

If writing is one way you often express yourself and communicate, you probably enjoy writing and feel at ease with the process. Your formal academic writing will be enriched by your experience with the craft. In tertiary institutions, written expression is emphasised, and learning is assessed primarily through writing essays, reports and examinations. You may have opportunities to take an oral exam, to deliver a paper orally, to present an assignment in film, on tape, as a collection of photographs or drawings, or by writing a play, a short story or poem. Don't overlook these. However, the reality is that to pass courses in tertiary institutions you must be able to write prose. In particular, you are expected to become familiar with the languages and methodologies of your discipline and you may find that you acquire some more quickly than others (see 'Disciplines and courses', Chapter 6). Similarly, although you might find that while essay writing comes easily it may take you time to learn to write reports in the style expected.

> This chapter is the first of three dealing with writing. It discusses academic writing and suggests ways to develop your writing. Whether you currently find writing a pleasure or a chore, the suggestions offered in this chapter can help you explore, develop and have confidence in your writing. The chapter suggests three ways to develop your writing: that you make writing a regular activity in your life; that you write for different purposes and in different genres; and that you share your writing with others in a non-threatening and constructive way. The next two chapters deal with two of the dominant genres used in tertiary study: essays and reports.

Does writing usually come easily to you?

Do you enjoy putting ideas, thoughts, feelings on paper or tapping away on a keyboard?

Has the use of a word processor for writing changed how you write?

Do you enjoy playing with different writing styles?

If you enjoy writing and write frequently, then you already have an enormous advantage when it comes to writing for academic purposes. You probably have worked out an effective range of approaches to your writing—sometimes waiting until the ideas settle in your mind before beginning, perhaps writing to a detailed plan, or maybe just sitting down and beginning to write. Be aware that the many genres of informal writing differ significantly from those of academic writing, but that if you like to write you have the major advantages of a positive attitude, a fluency with written language, and practice with the craft of writing.

Do you lack confidence in your writing because your ability to write was undermined by severe criticism?

Do you have difficulty with writing because you think that what you write falls short of the standards expected by a teacher?

Do you think your vocabulary is limited?

Does your writing seem to deteriorate when you are writing about unfamiliar material or concepts that you find complex?

When you are grappling with new concepts and trying to present them in an unfamiliar genre, your writing may not be as clear as when you write about material you understand in depth. You may find it easier to write in one discipline area than in another.

The 'academic style' which is appropriate for tertiary level writing is largely dependent on the disciplinary convention, and does not necessarily include long technical terms and convoluted sentences. Sometimes you do need to make use of particular terminology to convey a precise meaning, but such terminology can easily degenerate into jargon if used carelessly or to impress. When in doubt, opt for simplicity. The main aim of academic writing is to communicate what you want to say to someone, and the basic need to be lucid and direct applies as much to scholarly writing as to any other.

There is no one perfect academic style of writing. Each student will assimilate and present ideas in an individual way. The forms and conventions must be followed but they are there to be used for your own writing purposes (see 'The discipline area', Chapter 9). You are not expected to be an expert or a renowned author in your field; and it is preferable when writing essays or reports to express your own honest, carefully considered response, rather than paraphrasing or plagiarising other people's words and opinions or indulging your prejudices (see Appendix, 'Discrimination').

You have your own way of using words when you speak and, while you may not be a Shakespeare, you probably have your own style of writing. Use it in your academic writing. If your style includes irony, metaphor, an occasional flash of wit, use them unless they meet with strong disapproval from the people who assess your work.

The process of writing

Communicating is surely an important objective of writing but not the only one, nor the first ... the first use of writing is to think with—to articulate ideas—and by shaping these thoughts on paper, to communicate them. (*V.A. Howard*)

Unless you are writing to articulate your thoughts purely to yourself, writing is communicating. This involves thinking about the genre in which you write and about your audience, the person or people who will read your writing. You are trying not only to express your thoughts fluently and accurately, but to do so in a certain style and in a way that your reader will understand. To do this you must be clear about what you want to say and why, and you will draw on any language, experiences and beliefs that you and your readers share.

Find a subject you care about and which you in your heart feel others should care about. It is this genuine caring, and not your games with language, which will be the most compelling and seductive element in your style. (*Kurt Vonnegut*)

Writing is a process that involves both a creative dimension and a critical dimension, and it is important to work on both of these in developing your writing. The creative phase is the process of generating words on the page or screen, of turning the thoughts, ideas, inspirations or dreams in your head into written words; and the critical phase is when you reflect on, constructively criticise and edit these outpourings. Your instruments for either phase can be pen and paper, typewriter and paper, or computer screen—which of these instruments you use and how you use them will depend on your personal preferences and your finances.

The **creative or generative phase** of writing involves thinking, reflecting and imagining as much as putting words on paper or tapping out sentences on a computer screen. This writing phase may at times involve writing to a plan or using a required genre. But essentially the writing process can also be a way of actively constructing knowledge. The process can stimulate new thoughts and directions to which you respond in writing as you write. As you write you can uncover areas of seemingly forgotten knowledge, or clarify unanswered questions about the content of your work. So the process of writing can in itself be a learning process. Sometimes the creative phase of writing flows easily, while at other times the words just will not come. At these difficult times it can be a good idea to put your work aside and come back to it later, or to write about whatever else it is that you have on your mind. Sometimes, especially when there are deadlines to meet, you need to struggle on in the hope that the flow will come.

> Thinking to oneself can be silent, or talking aloud to oneself, or writing. While all three are equally thinking, the most ... accessible form is that which leaves a record on tape, disk or paper. (*V.A. Howard*)

The **critical or editing phase** of the writing process is different from the creative. In fact the two phases are incompatible and it is difficult, if not impossible, to both create or generate and edit simultaneously. It is claimed that the creative facility resides in one hemisphere of our brain and the critical in the other, and that our brains are not capable of creating and criticising simultaneously. If this is so, it makes sense to separate these two processes in your writing.

Do you procrastinate about writing because you don't know where to start writing on a topic? Do you feel that every sentence you write must be perfect? You perhaps sit for a long time over one sentence or paragraph. When you are generating thoughts try not to edit. Think about having two hats: a creative one and an editing one, which you change as required. When you wear your creative hat, you might generate most of an assignment, or you may write for only a short time and cover only a section or even a paragraph of a total piece of work. Just don't stop the thinking and creating process by editing or criticising as you go. Write, let it flow (see 'Freewriting'), and when you cannot generate any more thoughts, when you are written dry, only then go back and reflect and edit.

Word processing ... with its 'soft' stage in the activity of writing, encourages the writer rapidly to string together the basic thrust of what is to be said. Thorough acquaintance with the word processor invites a kind of compositional free association. At a later point, the user assumes he or she can return to the text and expand, delete, and reorganize. To some degree such a compositional strategy may be used with a pencil and paper or a typewriter. But there is almost inevitably a careful habit of mind which comes into play with these instruments because of the time and energy involved in composing and reformulating with them. Typewriter and pencil impose, even at the opening stage of composition, the value of economy. Working on a word processor displaces the sense of care in the activity of writing. The manipulative power of the technology encourages the writer to become full-of-care only at a later phase. Word processing, in sum, makes second nature for the writer a sense of the flexibility of the text. The technology enhances the writer's sense of the possibility and importance of reformulation; this means many organizational and developmental elements of composition become focal interests only after the primary associational stage of writing. (*Phil Mullins*)

Once you have finished with the creative process of writing, do you put your work aside and not look at it again? Do you hand in the 'final' draft of your assignments to your teacher with only superficial changes from first to last draft? If so you are not fully developing your writing, as an essential part of the writer's craft is reflecting on what you have written and learning to edit your work. This chapter and the two which follow provide help with editing. It may be useful to recognise that experienced writers often sit for hours over a page of work, or produce several extensively revised drafts often introducing different ideas, changing the content, and editing ruthlessly before producing the final draft. Even so, rarely is an expert writer entirely happy with the final version.

Developing your writing, including your formal academic writing, is a continuing process. You need to learn to vary elements of your style according to the discipline and the genre in which you are writing, and according to the topic, your audience and your purpose for writing. One way to do this is to experiment with different ways of writing.

Write often and reflectively

Learning to write again is ... not a tightening up process. It is not a matter of learning lots of techniques. It is learning to relax one's muscles and one's brain. (*Brian's Wife Jenny's Mum*)

One of the most effective ways to improve your writing is to write, write, write—and then write some more. Make writing an integral part of your life, and write regularly and for extended periods. Play with words and write in as many genres as you can. Write informally about yourself and your life and write about your academic work—your lectures, readings, discussions and ideas. From time to time re-read your informal work, because as with your formal writing it is important to cast a critical eye over your creative endeavours. Assess your strengths so you can build on them, and work on your weaknesses. To improve your writing reflect on how you write, and evaluate it in relation to what others say about the process.

Experiment with different writing methods

Free writing

Free writing is the best way to learn—in practice, not just in theory—to separate the producing process from the revising process. Freewriting exercises are push-ups in withholding judgement as you produce so that afterwards you can judge better. (*Peter Elbow*)

When you free write, you write without attending to a plan and without editing as you write. The process of writing is the stimulus that helps you discover the focus and approach for what you want to say and how you want to say it. Free writing can help you generate meaning and coherence from ideas and words which are lying dormant or jumbled in your head. This method is particularly valuable if you freeze up when you have to write, or if you have a mental block when writing an assignment (see 'Free writing', Chapter 12 and 13).

Sit quietly for 10–15 minutes while you write down or type the thoughts that flow through your mind. Don't stop to select, organise or edit what you are writing, and don't worry about details such as spelling and punctuation. If your mind suddenly flashes elsewhere, explore that sidetrack. Don't stop writing. If you can't think of anything to say, write 'I don't have anything to say' over and over until a thought hits you. It can help to imagine that you are writing to someone else explaining your thoughts, as long as you don't stop to reflect on or edit what you are writing.

Practice in this way can develop your writing—try free writing about your dreams or problems, about people or events. Incorporate this method into the initial stages of an essay or seminar paper. To help break the habit of always editing as you write, try free writing directly on computer, or by speaking your thoughts onto a tape recorder and then transcribing them. Once you have the words on the page or screen you can look at them critically and begin the editing process.

Structured writing

It was his habit to prepare an extremely detailed synopsis, complete with chapter titles, so that he knew exactly what was to happen in each chapter. He then began writing whatever chapter took his fancy or seemed easiest, leaving the most difficult to last ... Reading the smooth flowing narrative, building up to a climax, it is difficult to believe the book was written in this extraordinary way, but so it was. (*Arthur Ransome*)

Sometimes you need to write according to a plan because you are required to write in a specific genre or format. Using a plan is the writing method frequently taught and expected in formal education, and you are likely to use it when writing a report, an essay, an article for a paper or a business letter. However, even if you are working closely to an overall plan, as you express your ideas and information in words try not to edit as you write. Once your ideas are sorted out on paper, you can always go back and find the precise phrase you want.

Write in different genres

... creativity has much more to do with mastering a genre and then adjusting it to meet one's own purposes than with writing stories ninety percent of the time one puts pen to paper. It is surely creativity of this more general and practical kind that schools need to foster in young writers. (*Jim Martin*)

While developing your writing is largely a matter of writing and receiving feedback on it, writing in different genres is a way to explore different ways of structuring your writing. Just as reading published diaries will give you ideas for the format and content of any journal writing, analysing well-written models of other people's work can give you insights into a genre. Well-written students' essays or reports can inform your own academic work, so when required to write a report or an essay in a topic, ask your teacher for copies of previous students' work on another topic and ask for comments on why they meet the teacher's expectations or the course objectives. Take these points into consideration when you are editing and rewriting your own assignments.

Letters, articles, poems and other forms

I am not urging you to write a novel ... although I would not be sorry if you wrote one, provided you genuinely cared about something. A petition to the mayor about a pothole in front of your house or a love letter to the girl next door will do. (*Kurt Vonnegut*)

Do you write letters to family and friends, turn out business letters and reports as part of your job, keep a journal, keep in touch with colleagues by e-mail, write an occasional poem or short story, or send 'letters to the editor'? Many people who write in these forms don't see themselves as able to write because they are not producing a book or because writing is not a major part of their job. But regular practice in a variety of writing genres can help you develop your writing.

If you haven't thought of letters, articles or poems as part of your writing, try experimenting with:

- writing letters or e-mail messages instead of 'phoning your friends (and keep copies of your correspondence)
- capturing an experience or playing with words in poems, lyrics, short stories or dialogue
- writing a letter to the editor of your local paper if you feel strongly about an issue, or
- writing an article for the newsletter of a community group in which you are active.

If you are accustomed to writing letters, poems, plays or articles you could occasionally use these familiar forms in your assignments (but first check that this is permitted as your teacher may wish you to concentrate on learning how to write in a certain genre). For example:

- an essay comparing Freud with Jung could take the form of an exchange of letters setting out the basis of the disagreement between the two men
- an assignment on evolution could be written as a dialogue between Bishop Samuel Wilberforce and Thomas Huxley, or
- a preface or introduction to an essay may be written as a poem or a personal letter.

Electronic e-mail communication and contributions to chat groups are usually informal free flowing writing, perhaps more akin to speaking than most other writing forms. This informal writing can be an important part of your overall writing output and can provide a space to write for an audience.

Personal journals or diaries

I never travel without my diary. One should always have something sensational to read in the train. (*Oscar Wilde*)

If you have ever kept a diary, what did you record in it? As a teenager, did you record those major events in a small notebook that you kept hidden, or did your entries read something like, 'Got up early this morning. School was OK except I got into trouble on the way home. Watched TV.'? When travelling, have you ever kept a diary as a record of places and events? During periods of emotional trauma, have you written pages and pages that you destroyed afterwards? For some people, the thought of keeping a diary or journal conjures up images of monotonously recording facts and details, or pouring out secret feelings on paper. A journal can be these, but it can also be much more.

What is a journal?

A journal is your reflective space—it is a place where you reflect in writing on whatever interests or concerns you. In a personal journal you write for yourself. As such, it is a place where you can be honest with yourself, where your thoughts and ideas won't be judged by others, and where you are free to write in whatever style you like. You may use a journal to make an occasional entry, or write intensively for a couple of months and then let it lapse. You might write in a journal daily to describe the events, experience, feelings, people and ideas from each day.

Keeping The Daily Log

Think back to how you felt when you awakened in the morning. Describe the mood, the sensations—physical, mental.

Do you have the feeling that you were dreaming during the night? What was the general atmosphere of those dreams? How much of them can you remember and write down?

What was your mood as the day started? How did the morning unfold?

What thoughts kept coming into your mind without your deliberately thinking them? Worries, hopes, fantasies? What emotions? Angers, loves?

What events took place with people, works, groups?

Did unusual situations occur, situations of intensity, crisis, joy?

How does the day proceed? Note the rhythms of the day as you move from the morning to the afternoon, into the evening. Does the quality of your feelings, your mood, your emotions change?

Recapitulate your experiences of the day—all the occurrences that you can perceive both within your mind and on the outside of your life.

Write these without judgement: nothing to be proud of, nothing to be ashamed of; no praise, no blame.

Now feel the day as a whole. Write a few adjectives and a metaphor for how the day feels to you. (*Ira Progoff*)

A journal might be about yourself:

- your dreams, daydreams and fantasies, descriptions of the circumstances in your life that connect with these, and discussion of them
- your emotions
- how your body feels
- your reflections, thoughts and reminiscences on your past, and
- your ideas, theories or inspirations.

It might be about your world:

- descriptions of a particular situation or event
- observations about people, and
- comments on public happenings or issues.

It could include items such as:

- poems, short stories, song lyrics which you write or collect
- important letters to you or copies of letters from you
- clippings from newspapers or magazines and your comments on them, and
- notes on books, lectures, movies or television programs.

If you write about your private life and thoughts in your journal, do you worry that other people might read it? You don't have to write about personal matters, but if you do, be careful not to leave your journal where it might be found. You can use symbols instead of names and places, or write as if describing a fantasy or a dream that makes sense only to you.

A format

First, date each entry in your journal.

You can keep your journal entries chronologically or organise them into sections. A loose leaf format enables you to organise or reshuffle your writing into sections, to easily remove pages you want to share, and to elaborate on entries started long ago. You can also carry a couple of pages in your pocket or bag, in the glove box of your car, or attached to your clipboard, and write when the impulse moves you. If you make your entries on computer, you can also set up files to reflect these sections. Some entries you might print out in hard copy to intersperse with handwritten material, or you might leave your journal as a computer folder. If you make your entries electronically, laptop computers can provide flexibility.

> Never have I seen as clearly as tonight that my diary-writing is a vice ... I glided into my bedroom, closed the curtains, threw a log into the fire, lit a cigarette, pulled the diary out of its last hiding place under by dressing table, threw it on the ivory silk quilt, and prepared for bed. I had the feeling that this is the way an opium smoker prepares for his opium pipe. For this is the moment when I relive my life in terms of a dream, a myth, an endless story. (*Anais Nin*)

If you are already an avid journal writer, you will understand how Anais Nin felt about writing in her diary. If you haven't already done so, read the diaries of some well-known diarists such as Anais Nin or Charles Darwin to enrich your own journal writing. If keeping a journal is not a part of your life and you think you would find it valuable, set aside a regular time so that you can enjoy writing it.

Learning journals or logs

A learning journal or log is a space where you keep track of your learning. It is a place where you reflect in writing on the ideas from your reading, discussions and other study tasks. It is where you document what you learn from a particular course or from your learning overall. Keeping a personal learning journal as part of your studies can help you become aware of the experiences, enthusiasms, beliefs and biases you bring to your learning, and to understand who you are as a learner. Since a journal also provides an opportunity to experiment with and explore different writing styles without being judged, it can have a positive impact on your formal writing. Writing is a way of constructing your knowledge, so the process of writing regularly in a log can be a learning process in itself.

The format for keeping a learning log or journal is similar to that for a personal journal. You can keep your log in looseleaf format or on a computer. Develop a system for dividing your log into sections that reflect the different areas about which you will write. For example, you might create sections for each of the courses you are taking. Alternatively, you could use your log for work within only one course, and set up sections that separate your notes on your reading and assignments from your reflections on the unit content overall. If you are using the log to write about yourself as a learner, you could use it to respond to questions you are asked throughout this book such as those asked in Chapter 1. If you haven't kept a log before, you can also use it to reflect on and explore your writing processes or the experience of keeping a log itself.

In some courses you may be required to keep a working journal, perhaps in the form of a reading log, and if so the content, format and style should be specified. For example, field journals in natural history or ecology courses can have strict rules on what to include and how to structure both the original field notes and the journal entries that follow. If keeping a log is a formal requirement of a course, use a looseleaf format so you can easily remove entries that you don't want anyone else to read.

Share your writing

The essential human act at the heart of writing is the act of giving ... This central act of giving is curiously neglected in most writing instruction. Otherwise people would have shared their writing—just given it to another human being for the sake of mutual pleasure—as often as they gave it to a teacher for evaluation and advice. For most people, however, the experience of just sharing what they have written is rare. (*Peter Elbow*)

Do you ever write solely for yourself, or for one or two close friends?

If you write letters, short stories or poems, do you share these with friends?

Do you belong to an electronic discussion group in which you share your writing?

Writing alone is a traditional method of producing assignments, sitting for hours at your desk or computer with the aid of innumerable cups of black coffee the night before the assignment is due and never discussing your thoughts and ideas with anyone. Since usually only your teacher reads your formal assignments, you receive only one person's perception and evaluation of what and how you write.

Many students do not share with anyone else their written work or their ideas about how they will approach a written assignment. Before you start any sustained writing, it can help you clarify what you want to put on paper if you explain your ideas with someone else. This is useful when you are beginning to formulate ideas on a topic or when thinking how you intend to present your work. It is not necessary to talk to someone who is familiar with your area, although the feedback will be more valuable if you can find another student from your course or discipline. If you cannot find such a student it can help to explain your ideas verbally or in writing to a friend or member of your family who will listen carefully—or even to express them aloud to the family pet. But the ideal is to find someone taking similar courses with whom you can share a mutual exchange of ideas and comments on written work. A working relationship such as this is invaluable, and from it you can both learn and improve your written work.

Computer-mediated communications have added a dimension to the sharing of written work. If you have Internet access, not only is it possible to share your ideas on an assignment electronically with other students before you begin writing and as you write, but it is also possible to share rough drafts and a final version of an assignment.

Contrary to what many students believe, discussing your work with other students and receiving their assistance with writing is not cheating. Cheating is when you take other people's ideas and use them as your own without acknowledgement, or if they write parts of your work for you (See 'Paraphrasing and plagiarism', Chapter 13).

Comments from others on your writing can be extremely useful. Have one or two friends read your writing and respond to it, or tell your teachers that you want to improve your writing and ask for detailed feedback on your work. Perhaps you would like to share what you write with a wider audience but feel unsure of the criticism you might receive. If you work on your writing with a friend or a group of people who feel as you do, sharing your work and actually writing in their company is likely to give you confidence in developing your writing style.

Writing groups

Writing groups can be established with other students either face-to-face or electronically. They can be used to discuss informal writing or writing for assessment. Sometimes writing groups are set up by your teacher, and they can be important in collaborative group projects. If there are no formal mechanisms for establishing a writing group, you might decide to set one up yourself.

Why join a writing group?

1 If other people read (or listen to) what you have written and each comments on it immediately or shortly after you submit it, you receive a variety of feedback which you can question and discuss. If this feedback is positive and is accompanied by useful suggestions, you won't be devastated by criticism and you will have some ideas on how to change your writing.

2 Each member of the group will have their own way of expressing themselves. So reading or listening to other people's work gives you access to a variety of styles, of approaches to topics and of pieces of writing in a genre.

3 After some time, giving feedback on other people's work and receiving comments on your writing can help you evolve your own standards for evaluating your own and others' writing.

4 Actually writing in the same place as other people who share a common writing purpose can provide a new stimulus for what to write about and how to write. And although in some cases you may be physically separated, it is possible for a group to meet in cyberspace in realtime to compose electronically.

The written word is uniquely suited to the construction, group revision and sharing of knowledge. Practically all education is built around textbooks and written assignments, and computer-mediated communication (CMC) networks introduce an interactive text to enable information sharing and group knowledge building. Most CMC networks are asynchronous, a feature that with the text-based nature of communication, allows each participant to work at his or her individual learning pace and take as long as needed to read, reflect, write, and revise before sharing questions, insights, or information with others. (*Linda Harasim*)

Setting up a writing group

The steps outlined below can be applied to face-to-face or electronic groups.

1 Find people with whom you share a purpose in writing, such as writing essays for a course, making journal entries, or putting together a student magazine.

2 The group should be small enough for each person to contribute, yet have sufficient people to provide variety and depth in feedback.

3 Attend regularly (or via e-mail, contribute regularly), as people who get to know each other feel more comfortable about sharing their writing. After the first few meetings or contributions don't admit new members. In an online group clarify whether some, all or none of your writing will be read by a teacher.

4 Agree on the length and frequency of meetings according to the size and purpose of the group. With an electronic group, agree on how frequently new pieces of writing should be submitted; on the time frame for comments; and on how often members of the group will log onto the discussion group to receive messages.

5 Between meetings, do any necessary rewriting or preparation for the next meeting.

6 If a group member contributes a piece of writing to be discussed, provide copies for everyone to facilitate discussion.

7 For the first meeting, consider writing about yourselves as a way of getting to know each other.

8 The group might decide to write on one of the following:
   - free write on a set topic (as described earlier in this chapter)
   - practise a particular style (such as narrative or expository) or form (such as a dialogue or a scientific report), or
   - focus on a specific subject, such as the theory of evolution or a piece of music.
   For a face-to-face group, participants might chose to write for part of the time they are together.

9 There should be no compulsion for people to share their writing as some people need more time to feel confident about this, but allow all members the opportunity to present their work. In some sessions the group might discuss everyone's work, while in others it may concentrate on the writing of one or two people.

10 Work out how much you expect to read and critique each others' work. For example, you might read some of each other's work for each meeting, or after some initial exchange of everyone's work, you might focus on only one person's work at each meeting. Perhaps each person might present each meeting with a key issue or a dilemma or a brilliant idea they want to try out. Another option is to decide what to do only for the first meeting and then decide at each subsequent meeting on what to focus next time.

11 Allow sufficient time for each piece of work to be read with care. In a face-to-face group, perhaps read the piece both silently and aloud. In an electronic group, allow enough time for online comments to be returned and read.

12 Agree on a standard for responses which should include the following.
- Feedback should be constructive, emphasising strengths rather than weaknesses. Initially negative criticism which points out weaknesses should be avoided because it can undermine a beginning writer's confidence which the group is aiming to build. Destructive criticism is always taboo. When negative criticism is given, suggest how to make changes. Give feedback by responding to the piece spontaneously, or according to agreed-upon criteria such as those set out in the next two chapters.
- Agree on a code of conduct which does not permit discriminatory language and comments (see Appendix, 'Discrimination'). For online writing groups agree on communication protocols.
13 Choose a member of the group to monitor the process. This is particularly important for online groups where problems can arise as protocols are still evolving.

Whether you write on your own or with other people depends on your purpose and subject. You could make journal entries with a group of other students in a course, write a report with one other person, or write poetry by yourself. Trying alternatives to find out which ones you enjoy is one way of discovering and exploring your writing voice.

■ ■ ■ ■ ■

A writer does not just sit down and instantly write a great book. She spends time practising the craft of writing and puts in many hours on the individual book. Writing has become part of her daily life as well as a talent which delights readers. You may not be a world-famous author, but writing frequently and experimenting with different genres can help you develop your writing and give you pleasure as a writer. And just as a great writer refines her skills and thrives on the response of both her fellow writers and her readers, so you can polish and enjoy your writing if you share it with others.

Further reading

Darwin, Charles, 1972, *The voyage of the Beagle*, Bantam Books, New York.

Elbow, Peter, 1981, *Writing with power*, Oxford University Press, Melbourne.

Holly, Mary Louise, 1984, *Keeping a personal-professional journal*, Deakin University Press, Victoria.

Progoff, Ira, 1975, *At a journal workshop: The basic text and guide for using the intensive journal*, Dialogue House Library, New York.

Rainer, Tristine, 1980, *The new diary: How to use a journal for self guidance and expanded creativity*, Angus and Robertson, Sydney.

Stuhlmann, Gunther (ed.), 1974. *The journals of Anais Nin*, Vols. I–IV, Quartet Books, London.

CHAPTER 13

WRITING ESSAYS

... I always try to write on the principle of the iceberg. There is seven-eighths of it under water for every part that shows. (*Ernest Hemingway*)

Writing an essay is more than putting words on paper—defining your purpose, analysing your question, and carrying out research are integral to what and how you write. Each activity requires careful thought as you integrate your purpose with what is expected of you, and as you bring together your ideas and the information you find. Each activity can also have its own pleasures—discovering new information, turning ideas on a question over in your mind, talking about them with other people or trying them out in different combinations and sequences. When you have more or less analysed a question and researched it, you can begin to focus on the task of writing the essay as a whole.

This chapter looks at the processes involved in producing written work. Although primarily concerned with writing persuasive or expository essays, the ideas in the chapter can also be used in producing other written assignments including those that you write collaboratively. The processes outlined are intended as a framework from which you can develop your essay writing. This framework can help you understand written comments on your work, or can be used as a basis for discussing your essays with a teacher or other students. When writing an essay you might use the entire chapter, or you might prefer to use parts of it to help with specific problems such as planning an essay or writing coherent paragraphs.

However, the framework offered is useful only if you write frequently and if you receive feedback from others. Each essay is not an isolated end in itself—what you learn from writing one can help you with the next, even if the content and format of each differ and each is in a different discipline. Improving your writing takes time and practice, and your writing may seem worse before you notice any improvement—it takes time to change old habits and develop and refine new methods. Saying exactly what you want and in the style you want is easier if you have confidence in your writing abilities (see Chapter 12, 'Developing your Writing').

Before you begin writing

An essay develops from how you have analysed the question which was set for you or which you developed to guide your research (see 'Your revised definition', Chapter 7). As a result of your thinking and research, perhaps you have written sentences or paragraphs which capture thoughts you want to use. You will also have notes from your research.

Your definition of the question

Your written definition should reflect the argument and structure of your essay. Clearly and fully developing a definition of the question is crucial if you are writing an assignment collaboratively (see 'Group writing projects', Chapter 6) and particularly if you are doing this online. Your definition of the question should do the following.

- Make clear your purposes for the essay. Ask yourself, 'Why am I writing an essay in the first place?' 'For what purpose was this piece of work set?' 'What is my purpose for writing this particular essay, and for choosing this question?'
- Clarify your thesis or controlling focus (see 'Genres', Chapter 6). For an argumentative essay, ask yourself, 'What thesis will I advance for the topic?' and 'What reasons will I use to support my thesis?' If your

essay is expository, ask yourself 'What evidence, explanations and examples will I use to support my controlling focus?'

- Propose a possible structure which indicates how you will present the main points of the essay and how they are connected. Ask 'Exactly what is my question?' 'How many parts are there to the question?' 'What are my main points for the question?' 'How might I order the main points so that they support my thesis or controlling focus?' and 'How do the directive words in the question (see Table 6.1) influence the structure of my essay?'
- Indicate how you will approach your essay. Ask yourself 'How will I handle the subjectivity of my work?' 'How many of my own opinions will I include?'
- For an argumentative essay, outline:
  - the extent to which your argument reflects your personal opinions, and
  - the world view or theoretical framework in which your argument is situated.
- Ask yourself, 'If I write the essay in this way, will I be answering the exact question?'

Your readers

I wish thee as much pleasure in the reading, as I had in the writing. (*Francis Quarles*)

Before you start writing the whole essay, think about your readers. Is your teacher the only one who will read your essay? Are you writing a paper to be read by a group of students, perhaps in an online course? Is there a possibility your paper will be published in a collection of student work or elsewhere? Which positions on the question would you expect your readers to take? If you are uncertain of the level at which to pitch your writing, a good rule of thumb to use is to write for another student who is taking the course but does not have an in-depth understanding of your topic. To communicate effectively:

- have clear in your mind the argument or controlling focus that you are presenting
- keep in mind your purpose for presenting it
- be aware that you are communicating with someone
- take care to say exactly what you want to, and
- say it simply and succinctly.

Writing your rough draft

We would be given an assignment. I would take one look at it and think, 'That's the end of that. I won't be there next week so I won't have to worry about it.' After two harrowing days, when I kept thinking, 'Will I, won't I?' I'd sit down to look at it. (*Brian's Wife Jenny's Mum*)

For each essay you write, start with a rough draft. You may produce several drafts if your definition of the question changes as you write or if you have the time. Your final draft will then be a matter of editing your last rough draft.

When you write the rough draft of an essay, your main concern should be the structure of your essay and the clear expression of your ideas. Concentrate on saying what you want, in the order you want, and as accurately as you can. When you are in the creative or generative phase of expressing your ideas, don't worry about a detailed structure or niceties of style or about having the precise word. And don't become bogged down with concerns about perfect spelling or being absolutely correct and detailed in conventions such as footnoting. Be as precise as you need to be to express your ideas clearly and fully, and leave the perfecting formalities to your final draft.

Most skilled writers produce several drafts of a work before arriving at a final version. Many students, however, sit down with pen and paper and expect to start writing the first sentence and to write straight through to the end, producing a more or less complete essay in one draft. This is not the way to produce a satisfactory essay—any method of writing relies on thoughtful research and time to mull over a question before writing, and any method should lead you to a rough draft which has three clear sections, an introduction, a body and a conclusion. How these sections should be organised and written is outlined in 'The parts of the essay'. Once you have produced your draft, use the checklist of questions in 'Working with your rough draft'.

Writing methods

Working from your definition, you can produce your rough draft by free writing, working from a detailed plan, or a combination of these two methods. Any of these methods can be effective.

Writing to a plan

An essay plan might be written down or might be something you hold in your head. You plan might be linear (as in Table 13.1) or be an explosion chart or pattern (see Table 10.1 'Notemaking'). When writing an essay more or less to a written plan, this plan structures and limits what you write and prevents you going off on tangents. A plan includes a statement of:

- your thesis or controlling focus
- an introduction and conclusion, and
- the structure—how the main points are ordered, balanced and linked.

Don't be surprised if you don't follow your plan exactly. As you write, the process of expressing your ideas can stimulate new thoughts and directions and lead you to see familiar ideas in new ways (see 'The process of writing', Chapter 12). Actually expressing your ideas with clarity involves searching for and choosing words, phrases and sentences, so part of the structuring can only be done as you write. Integrating new ideas into your plan and making choices as you write can further clarify what you want to say and can lead you to revise your plan. Hopefully such revisions will only be minor at this stage of your work.

Free writing

In free writing you use the act of writing to clarify your thoughts, without editing them as you write. Free writing can help start you on your writing and can help you come up with a statement of your thesis or focus. You will often be surprised how much knowledge of the topic you have (see 'Free writing', Chapter 12 and 13).

If you have a mental block when writing essays, particularly when starting to write, it may be because you don't feel confident about your writing or about your knowledge of a topic or how to organise your information, or because you are anxious about your study or have other pressures in your life (see 'Emotions', Chapter 1). Perhaps you are having difficulty defining or deciding on a thesis or controlling focus. If you do block, but you have to or want to write, sit down at your computer, or at your desk with lots of paper and a pen. Don't worry about notes or plans or references. Start writing or typing anything on your question that comes to mind and write continuously for about ten minutes. If you can't think of what to write, write about why you can't think of what to write, or about the thoughts which are coming between you and the question. When the time is up, look over what you have written. Some of it may be useful later, or it may stimulate new thoughts. This free writing activity is often enough to shift a mental block and to stop you procrastinating, but if it doesn't you may need to leave your work for a few hours or days, or longer if possible. And remember that even for skilled writers, sometimes writing refuses to flow smoothly.

> The writer wandered to the water cooler, washed his hands, looked up the weather report, made some unnecessary phone calls, looked at his tongue in the mirror for symptoms of fatal disease and, when he had at last exhausted methods of killing time, went to his typewriter. (*Russell Baker*)

You can use free writing to produce an entire essay in draft form. Review your ideas and notes on the topic, clarify any overall directions you can see for the essay but don't plan what to write. Begin writing as outlined above. Keep in mind your question and your definition of it. Write a first draft of all or part of the essay without any editing as you write. Then re-read what you have written and quickly sum up the essence of your writing in one statement. Write a second version, again without editing, and repeat the looking over and summing up process. If your argument or focus is still unclear, write a third draft. When you have a draft that is clear enough, use it as the basis for your final one, and so proceed to the editing stage. Be prepared, however, to throw away much of what you have written. Since you will have to produce several drafts, using this process can be time-consuming unless you start with some clarity about what you want to say. Without this initial clarity, allow somewhat more time than you normally would for writing from a plan.

Other writing methods

Two extreme ways of producing the rough draft of an essay are completely free writing from your written definition but without a plan, or writing exactly to a detailed plan. Between these two lie many alternatives, of which the following are a few.

- Use a plan and, with your notes and references in front of you, edit your thoughts and words as you write and use free writing whenever you are stuck. You could:
  - write the body of the essay first, and then the introduction and conclusion, or
  - begin with the introduction and write in the order you planned, right through to the conclusion, or
  - begin writing the section where your ideas are clearest, and proceed section by section until you have written the one which is least clear to you.
- Make a plan and then with your notes and references put aside, free write your rough draft. If you don't understand a section well enough to write about it or if you need a quote or item of information, turn to your notes and references to refresh your memory—and then close them before you start writing again. When you finish writing your draft, check your work against your notes for completeness and for references you could cite.

It took me two hours to write this. I bit my finger-nails, cut my toenails, had a snack, crunched an apple and generally procrastinated. But I did it! (*Brian's Wife Jenny's Mum*)

■ ■ ■ ■ ■

The parts of your essay

An essay is constructed like a freight train. The argument is the engine, supplying power and direction and pulling the rest behind it. The cars are the paragraphs, each carrying a topic sentence and a load of specific sentences; the couplings are transitions holding the cars together, and the caboose is the conclusion, letting the reader know that the essay has come to an end. It is important to realise that the train exists to carry the freight: the essay is the vehicle for getting the meaningful specifics of your topic to the reader in an orderly condition, so they can unload and use them.

No matter which method you use to produce an essay, your rough draft should finish up with the following parts. (Adapted from Frank Morgan, 1968, *Here and now: an approach to writing through perception*, Harcourt, Brace & World, p. 153.)

Table 13.1 A sample essay plan

You are writing on the topic 'Critically evaluate the theory that the moon is made of green cheese.' After reflection and research you decide to argue that the moon is made of green cheese. You think that the most important and interesting aspects of the topic are: the beliefs for and against the question; twentieth century scientists' attitudes to the relevant theories and evidence; and astronauts' discoveries myths about the green cheesiness or otherwise of the moon. You define the topic accordingly. The following model is a basic one you could use to structure your essay.

Topic: Critically evaluate the theory that the moon is made of green cheese.

Introduction	
Thesis:	That the moon is made of green cheese.
Supporting reasons	(a) Historical beliefs for and against
	(b) Twentieth century scientific research
	(c) Astronauts' discoveries

Main Point (a)	**Main Point (b)**	**Main Point (c)**
Historical beliefs for and against theory	Scientific research	Astronauts' discoveries
1 In Greek times	1 Geology of the Mice Age	1 Mice on the moon
2 In 19th century industrial Europe	2 Properties of green cheese	2 Feline interest in the moon
3 In mid-20th century	3 Causes of craters on the moon	3 The Lunar Costa Verde
4 The Green Cheese Revivalist Movement		
Brief summary of these beliefs	Critical evaluation of key points in the research	

Conclusion
That the moon is made of green cheese
(a) Historical beliefs for and against theory
(b) Twentieth century scientific research
(c) Astronauts' discoveries
Personal conclusions and two implications for future research

The introduction

The introduction outlines *what you are going to say*. It should make clear your definition of the question and make your reader want to read on. You should:

- outline your thesis or controlling focus
- indicate your main points, and
- state how your essay is structured.

To orient your reader to the question you might:

- outline your theoretical position on the topic
- outline your reasons for focusing on specific aspects of a general topic
- explain the significance of the question
- provide a context for the essay
- define any key concepts or terms, and/or
- indicate the scope and limits of your essay.

To engage the reader and add interest or variety you might:

- briefly review literature, or
- give selected data to establish an issue as worth writing about, or
- use a quote which conveys the key ideas you will discuss.

The body of your essay

Here you say *what you want to say*. You should order your main points effectively and provide links which make this order clear to your reader; present each main point as fully and accurately as necessary; write coherent paragraphs; and keep a balance between your main points.

1 Ordering your main points

After the introduction, your argument or focus should be developed clearly and logically throughout the essay and restated in the conclusion. The following suggestions may help you decide on the order in which to develop material you have selected.

- Refer back to your purposes and definition.
- Keep your thesis or controlling focus firmly in mind and, as you write, show the links from your main points by referring back to this.
- By now you should have decided on your main points. Ask yourself why you chose these and how they are connected to each other. In the moon topic, shown in Table 13.1, you might have chosen your points because they reflect significantly different aspects of the topic. Does an understanding of one point depend on explaining another point first? You might have decided to put the point about historical beliefs first as a background for current scientific research and astronauts' discoveries.

- If, however, you still have several supporting points from which you will choose as you write, write each point out as a separate section of your essay. See what links emerge from what you have written and re-write your final points as necessary to clarify the links between them and to develop an ordered whole.
- As you write, if you are not using a computer use a separate page for each paragraph. When you come to order your whole essay, you can add or delete paragraphs and arrange them in the order which seems most logical.

2 Linking information

As well as coherently developing each main point in turn, your argument or controlling focus depends on you indicating the links between these points and the reason for their order. In addition, within each main point you should make clear how your choice of examples, explanations and evidence works to support the point. If you assume that this connecting information is not essential, your reader is left to second-guess what you intend.

To convey these linking relationships, use transitional words or phrases (see Table 13.2) and use pointers such as 'Having discussed idea X, I now want to examine ...' or 'However, Y contradicts idea X which I have just discussed ...' or 'Firstly, I discuss X, then secondly, I discuss Y ...'. Use subheadings (if allowed) and include a plan or a detailed table of contents. Remember that to make clear the order of the main points in your essay and to indicate the links between them, they need to be clear in your mind.

> 'Then you should say what you mean,' the March Hare went on.
> 'I do,' Alice hastily replied; 'at least—at least I mean what I say—that's the same thing, you know.' (*Lewis Carroll*)

Table 13.2 Transitional words and phrases

These are words and phrases which show relationships between two ideas or facts. They indicate:

Addition

in addition, again, also, and, besides, finally, first, further, last, moreover, second, too, next

Cause and effect

accordingly, as a result, consequently, hence, otherwise, therefore, thus

Comparison

similarly, likewise

Contrast

in contrast, although, and yet, but, however, nevertheless, on the other hand, on the contrary

Examples or special features

for example, for instance, in other words, in illustration, in this case, in particular, specifically

Summary

in brief, in conclusion, in short, on the whole, to conclude, to summarise, to sum up

Connections in time

after a short time, afterwards, as long as, as soon as, at last, at length, at that time, at the same time, before, earlier, of late, immediately, in the meantime, lately, later, meanwhile, presently, shortly, since, soon, temporarily, thereafter, until, when, while.

---

3 Presenting each main point fully and accurately

Saying what you want to also entails presenting each of your main points fully and accurately. To support a main point you might explain a point further, cite statistics or facts, refer to reputable research or use quotations.

Don't expect your reader to be a mind reader. Remember that you have been researching and thinking about the topic recently, so a sentence you write which conveys a whole collection of ideas to you may not do so to your reader. Don't skim over points which need explanation. Don't assume that your reader automatically knows who or what Alcibiades is, or precisely what you mean when you use terms such as 'instinct', 'natural', 'good' or 'Western society'. When you make general statements, support them with explanations or examples. Consider if it is appropriate to include quantitative material—in disciplines such as psychology, for example, tables might be included as an appendix.

Even if your teacher is the only person to read your finished work, check if you are expected to write without assuming his or her knowledge of the topic so that you demonstrate your own knowledge fully. If you are in doubt about the level of writing at which to aim, imagine that you are writing for a reasonably intelligent student just about to begin the course and with an interest in your topic. This helps to avoid pitfalls such as writing on the implications of Hegel's ideas without actually describing the ideas because you assume that your teacher knows what they are.

Paragraphing

Each main point should consist of one or more paragraphs. Each paragraph should contain one key idea or cover one aspect relevant to a main point. This idea or aspect is frequently set out in a key sentence, which may come anywhere in a paragraph or may be implied by the total content of the paragraph rather than stated explicitly. Each of the other sentences in the paragraph should explain or illustrate the point which the paragraph is making, but each should also have a purpose of its own.

Stop for a moment and think about what you have just read. Now look at the next paragraph. What is its key point? Is there an explicit key sentence? How does each of the sentences in the paragraph relate to the key point of the paragraph?

A paragraph should be coherent, so that your reader is led smoothly from one sentence to another and understands the connection between them. For example, if the paragraph uses a central metaphor, each sentence may echo and expand that metaphor. Words and phrases such as 'similarly', 'because', 'besides', 'in contrast', 'meanwhile', 'therefore' or 'for instance' help to indicate the links between sentences (see Table 13.2). If a paragraph is not coherent, your reader will be faced with bewildering jumps of thought, events out of sequence or facts illogically arranged.

> Just as the sentence contains one idea in all its fullness, so the paragraph should embrace a distinct episode; and as sentences should follow one another in harmonious sequence, so paragraphs must fit into one another like the automatic couplings of railway carriages. (Winston Churchill)

A paragraph may vary in length from one or two sentences to many (and such variety makes more interesting reading). As a *very* approximate rule of thumb for assignments, each paragraph averages about 100 words. Thus in a 2000-word assignment, you would have approximately twenty paragraphs, which you might divide up with two each for an introduction and conclusion, and an average of four or five paragraphs on each of three or four main points. Thinking of your assignment in this way can help you understand how many main points you can make fully and clearly.

4 Balancing main points

Decide if all your main points should have equal weighting within the essay. In the moon topic (Table 13.1), you might decide to look more closely at twentieth-century scientific research, or you might devote more space to the astronauts' discoveries because they are more recent.

Even with the most careful planning, as you actually write you may find that you need to devote more of the total essay to a point to explain it fully, to give less emphasis to a point, or to delete a point which no longer seems essential to your thesis.

Some essays have a strict word length requirement. What do you do if you discover part-way through your essay that it will be too long if you present all the points you have planned to cover? You may need to reduce the number of points or to eliminate repetitive sections. Conversely, does your essay look as though it will fall short of the length required? If so, check that your plan hasn't been too skimpy on the number of points you cover, and check that you have supported each of your main points thoroughly.

When in doubt about whether or not to include or omit material, refer back to your purposes for the essay and your argument or focus, and ask yourself if the material fits with these. Learning to discard material is an essential but often difficult part of writing—you may have to force yourself to do it.

> Have the guts to cut ... If a sentence, no matter how excellent, does not illuminate your subject in some new and useful way, scratch it out. (*Kurt Vonnegut*)

The conclusion
This draws together *what you have said* in the body of your essay. It should:

- sum up your argument
- restate your thesis or controlling focus
- draw together your main points, and
- refer back to your introduction.

You might also:

- suggest a question that needs to be explored further, or
- raise one or two further research implications

You should not introduce a new major point or a statement which needs detailed explanation. As well as drawing together what you have said, the conclusion serves to round off your essay—don't make it so abrupt that your reader is surprised that the essay is finished.

> There are two things I am confident I can do very well; one is an introduction to any literary work, stating what it is to contain, and how it should be executed in the most perfect manner; the other is a conclusion, shewing from various causes why the execution has not been equal to what the author promised to himself and to the public. (*Samuel Johnson*)

Working with your rough draft
Working with your rough draft is essentially a checking and rewriting stage, since by now you should have a clear idea of the purposes, content, structure and basic writing style of your essay. Part of your work with the rough draft will probably be remedying oversights. For example, you may need to find full details for bibliography entries, or check on the precise wording of a quote or exact data for part of a graph. What else do you check for at this stage?

Purposes
- Does the essay reflect your purposes in:
    - undertaking an essay in the first place
    - doing this particular essay
    - choosing this particular topic or question, and
    - selecting your argument or focus within the question?
- Does the essay reflect the purposes for which the essay was set?
- Have you checked that you have met all requirements for the essay?

Argument or exposition
- Does the essay have a thesis or controlling focus?
- Have you clearly stated this in your introduction?
- Do the main points support your thesis or focus?
- Are you clear about the theoretical framework in which your argument or exposition is situated?

Content
- Is your topic or question clearly defined?
- Does the essay answer the question or address the topic?
- Is all your material relevant to your definition of the question?
- What are the main points of your essay?
- Are the main points presented as clearly and fully as necessary?
- Have any central terms been clearly defined?
- Are quotations and examples which you have used integral to your essay?
- Do you have too much or too little material for the length of your essay?
- Is there any unnecessary repetition of minor points?
- Have you avoided any discriminatory attitudes or language?

Structure
- **Introduction**
  Does your introduction:
  - accurately outline your definition of the question
  - state your thesis or focus
  - clearly indicate to your reader the stages by which you develop your argument or exposition, and
  - intrigue your reader?
- **Body**
  - What is the structure of your essay?
  - Does your structure logically and effectively develop your thesis or focus?
  - Is there a balance between your main points?
  - Are the main points clearly linked ?
  - Does each paragraph within the body of the essay contain only one key idea, and is this idea clearly relevant to the material it is supporting?
  - Have you clearly connected your paragraphs using transitional words, phrases or sentences?
- **Conclusion**
  Does your conclusion:
  - reinforce the thesis or focus of the essay
  - relate to your introduction
  - finish the essay smoothly, and
  - suggest any further areas or questions to be followed up, without introducing any major new ideas?

Approach
- Is your position on the question explicit?
- Have you acknowledged how your beliefs, values and assumptions affect your interpretation of the material?
- Have you been uncritically biased in your selection of material?
- If allowed, have you incorporated your own ideas which develop the thesis, and have you supported these ideas?

Style
- Have you expressed your ideas clearly and simply?
- Is your writing style your own?
- Have you incorporated any formal requirements regarding style and conventions into your writing?

> Reheating a piece of writing after it has cooled, tempering it, and sharpening it is enjoyable—if you know how. Otherwise it may turn out worse, brittle and misshapen. (*Ken Macrorie*)

If you have thoughtfully researched, planned and written your essay, you are less likely to have to make major revisions to your rough draft. However, sometimes when you re-read your draft you are struck with a new idea about the structure or content, or you suddenly see a major flaw in what you have written. If you have sufficient time, you may want to rework an initial rough draft substantially. Be prepared for this, but realise that at some stage you have to stop working on your essay and let it stand as it is, warts and all. If you are writing your essay at the last minute, you are unlikely to have the time for detailed rewriting. In this case, the amount of work depends on how clearly you really knew what you wanted to say before you started writing.

When you have finished writing and working on your rough draft, you have done most of the work on your essay. Wherever possible, write a rough draft, work on it and put it aside for at least a few days before you write the final one. You might discuss it with others, or have someone else read it and comment. If you are writing an assignment collaboratively, swap your pieces with other members of the group. You may want to change a phrase, add a word, rewrite a sentence or a paragraph. In any case, give yourself time to stand back from what you have written, time to reflect on your whole essay before you finally sit down and edit it.

Editing your final draft

In the final draft, you edit what you have written to polish your writing style and to complete details of formalities such as punctuation or footnotes. It can help you proofread your work if you produce your final draft in a new form, for example, in a different font or in double spacing if your drafts have been single spaced.

- Often a good essay is difficult to read because of inadequate proofreading. (Chapter 15 is designed to help you check details such as presentation, writing conventions and spelling.) Using a spelling or grammar checker on your computer is no substitute for thorough proofreading.
- The craft of improving your writing style involves imagination as well as hard work (see Chapter 12). When polishing your writing in an essay, check carefully for points such as unnecessary repetition, inaccurate use of words of whose meaning you are uncertain, and ambiguous use of 'it', 'this', 'they', 'them'. Reading your essay aloud (particularly to someone else) is an effective way of checking for these items. If possible, ask someone else to comment on your writing style in the essay.

Evaluating your essay

Ask yourself:

What were my purposes for the essay?

How well have I achieved these?

How would I change what I researched, planned and wrote if I repeated the essay? Why?

Has working on my essay led me to any ideas or questions I might follow up?

You should be the first person to evaluate the strengths and weaknesses of what you write. You will provide your readers with a basis for constructive criticism if you include your written evaluation (as well as your plan or detailed table of contents) with your essay.

> It's not healthy for the tightrope walker to be misunderstood by the person who's holding the rope. (*Peter Hoeg*)

The next stage is up to your readers. If your essays are usually read only by your teacher and the teacher provides helpful feedback, you will be encouraged to write more even if you have difficulties to overcome. If your teacher provides only curt or cursory comments on your writing, find one or more other people who will spend time and care commenting on your work. If such help is not possible, you can discover a new perspective in your writing by reading your work aloud to a tape recorder and listening to it. Even if you have comments from other people, learning to evaluate your own work is part of the craft of writing.

If your way of writing essays or reports is criticised explicitly because it does not conform to the accepted conventions of your discipline at tertiary level, you may need to learn how to use the appropriate genre and to adapt to what is expected. Find out from your teacher why your written work does not meet the requirements, and read the relevant sections in this book.

The more useful the feedback you receive on an essay, the more you can evolve your own style and craft as a writer. Think carefully about any comments you are given and discuss them with your reader to learn more about your strengths and weaknesses as a writer. Remember that for your writing, yours is the final evaluation. (See Chapter 16 for more on evaluating your own work.)

■ ■ ■ ■ ■

Hopefully, writing an essay is not a postscript to research, or a duty that you scribble through at the last minute. If you think of essay writing as a craft to be practised and as part of all the writing you do, you will understand that it can reward you for the time, care and imagination you put into it in ways which are more satisfying than achieving a good grade.

Further reading

Anderson, J. & Poole, M., 1994, *Thesis and assignment writing*, 2nd edn, John Wiley, Brisbane.

Arnaudet, Martin L. & Barrett, Mary Allen, 1984, *Approaches to academic reading and writing*, Prentice Hall Regents, Englewood Cliffs.

Axelrod, R.B. & Cooper, C.R., 1994, *The St. Martin's guide to writing*, 4th edn, St. Martin's Press, New York.

Baker, S., 1990, *The practical stylist*, 7th edn, Harper Collins, New York.

Bate, Douglas & Sharpe, Peter, 1990, *Student writer's handbook: How to write better essays*, Harcourt Brace Jovanovich, Sydney.

Clanchy, John & Ballard, Brigid, 1991, *Essay writing for students*, 2nd edn, Longman Cheshire, Melbourne.

Hult, Chrisine A., 1996, *Researching and writing in the humanities and arts*, Allyn & Bacon, Sydney.

Lovell, David W. & Moore, Rhonda D, 1992, *Essay writing and style guide for Politics and the Social Sciences*, Australian Political Studies Association, Australian Defence Academy, Canberra.

Manalo, E., Wong-Toi, G. & Mansen, M.–L., 1998, *The business of writing: Written communication skills for business students*, Addison Wesley Longman, Melbourne.

Murphy, Eamon, 1985, *You can write: A do-it-yourself manual*, Longman Cheshire, Melbourne.

Osland, D., Boud, D., McKenna, W., Sulusinsky, I., 1991, *Writing in Australia: A composition course for tertiary students*, Harcourt Brace Jovanovich, Sydney.

Peters, Pam, 1985, *Strategies for student writers: A guide to writing essays, tutorial papers, exam papers and reports*, John Wiley and Sons, Brisbane.

Taylor, Gordon, 1989, *The student's writing guide for the arts and social sciences*, Cambridge University Press, Melbourne.

CHAPTER 14

WRITING SCIENTIFIC REPORTS

Some of the worst (articles in scientific journals) are produced by the kind of author who consciously pretends to a 'scientific scholarly' style. He [*sic*] takes what should be lively, inspiring and beautiful, and in an attempt to make it seem dignified, chokes it to death with stately abstract nouns; next, in the name of scientific impartiality, he [*sic*] fits it with a complete set of passive constructions to drain away any remaining life's blood or excitement; then he [*sic*] embalms the remains in molasses of polysyllable, wraps the corpse in an impenetrable veil of vogue words, and buries the stiff old mummy with such pomp and circumstance in the most distinguished journal that will take it. Considered either as a piece of scholarly work or as a vehicle of communication, the product is appalling. The question is, does it matter? (*F. Peter Woodford*)

Yes, it does matter—whether your report is published in a scientific journal or is a course requirement. Communicating your findings and observations in a report is an integral part of science, and communicating clearly is interwoven with thinking clearly. Unless your reports are clearly thought out and written, your practical work—no matter how good—is of limited value.

What do you bring to an experiment or field trip which affects the quality of your written report? Your knowledge of a subject—of underlying theory and specific detail—is obviously important and can be improved with preliminary reading. Your care in observation, your practical skills, and your expertise in experimental design and using research techniques also affect the standard of your scientific work and writing.

Purposes of reports

Another facet which is basic to good research, experimental design and report writing is an awareness of your purposes. Some of your purposes are very specific—to test a particular hypothesis, to observe a certain phenomenon. However, you also need to think about why you are doing the research in the first place. And as one of your purposes is to communicate your findings, think about who will read the report. You might:

- write a report on a routine laboratory experiment for your teacher, where both carrying out the practical work and writing about it are exercises in using a meticulous scientific method, or
- write a public report for a government department or the popular press or a report for your work in an interdisciplinary course. Readers of such reports need emphasis on key ideas without too much scientific detail or too many bland descriptions.

Each individual research project and its report has a different purpose. Keeping your purposes and your readers in mind when researching gives you a basic framework for clear report writing.

This chapter looks at basic principles of writing highly structured reports. It is mostly concerned with reports based on gathering primary data from laboratory experiments and field work, and less concerned with reporting on secondary data gathered from reports of other people's research (see 'Identifying primary and secondary sources', Chapter 8).

How you use the chapter depends on the detail in your laboratory manuals, on the number of practical sessions you have each week, and on the extent to which you design your own research. For example:

- if your laboratory manual describes in great detail the experiments you are to carry out, focus on planning the experiment and use each section of the chapter as you write your report

- if you have to write up three laboratory sessions each week, you could use this chapter to help you write any difficult sections, and
- if your research is substantially your own, the sections on writing styles and conventions may be particularly valuable.

Writing as you plan

If I had eight hours to chop down a tree, I'd spend six sharpening the axe. (*Abraham Lincoln*)

If you are expected to design all or part of an experiment, write as you do so. Your written design can then be built on as you carry out the experiment, providing a detailed and organised basis for your final report. Clearly state the purposes of the report, the problem you want to solve and your hypothesis or predictions. Write down the nature, frequency and duration of the necessary measurements and observations. For example:

- how you will choose samples
- the range and degree of precision required in measurements
- any controls needed to test for one or more variables
- how you will ensure reliability by avoiding systematic errors and assessing the size of any random errors
- methods for checking the accuracy of measurements and observations
- how you will record each measurement, the scales you will use, and
- if you will be presenting numerical data, samples of the likely format for tables and figures.

It is possible to measure something other than what you expect to measure. For example, people frequently talk in everyday language about measuring intelligence. Yet it is not clear what is being measured: it may be ability in a specific subject, adaptability, expression, or something quite different. Alternatively you might be trying to measure a physical property like the fire retardant ability of a chemical. How can you be sure that your measurement is a valid measure of the retardant effect, and that it will give similar results to other measurements of fire retardant, or will be a good predictor of measurements of the fire retardant for other materials? (*Lorraine Marshall*)

Beginning a report

Is 'writing up' something you see as a task to be done after the 'real work' of an experiment or field work is over? In practice, the process of writing can help you to clarify your thoughts and stimulate new ideas, so write at all stages of your laboratory and field work rather than leaving this activity to the end.

Your laboratory or field notebook

> ... a lab notebook. Everything gets written down, formally, so that you know at all times where you are, where you have been, where you are going and where you want to get. In scientific work and electronics technology this is necessary because otherwise the problems get so complex you get lost in them and confused and forget what you know and what you don't know and have to give up ... Sometimes just the act of writing down the problems straightens out your head as to what they really are. (*Robert M. Pirsig*)

Begin writing for a report during your practical work as you record methods and results, and immediately afterwards while the work is still fresh in your mind. Writing in this way helps you think critically about what you are doing, and can lead you to repeat an experiment while it is still set up, or to fill in gaps in your field observations. Your notes should be a complete and chronological record of what you did and when, including calculations and diagrams of apparatus.

Write the name of each of the sections of your report on separate pages of your notebook and record your ideas, observations and results under the appropriate heading. Don't worry at this stage about your writing style or the order of material within a section—concentrate on putting ideas and information down as clearly and concisely as possible.

Measurements, observations and calculations

As you carry out and record research, your results are usually in the form of numbers. For example, if you are interested in how long it takes a one-celled animal to divide, you would measure the time from one division to the next with a number of these animals and then derive the average time. The results would be a set of numbers called data. In the early stages of analysing data, ordering them in tables or figures can help you see patterns emerging in your results. After collecting, recording and analysing initial data, check your data to determine if you need to make further measurements. In your notebook include a brief discussion of your main results or observations, and record any unexpected developments in your experiment. Also make sure that you:

- label each measurement—including the units used—so that you can identify it later
- decide when measurements can be estimated and when precise, and how precise they need to be
- take enough measurements and observations to be as accurate as necessary in the time available, but don't spend time on additional measurements which don't significantly improve accuracy, and
- if making calculations, decide how you will double check for mistakes.

Planning your writing

- Before you start writing your whole report, plan *what* you are going to say and how you are going to say it—this is where sheets of paper and separate pages in a computer document for the various sections are useful. Discussing your work with others—teachers, students, friends—gives you practice in explaining your ideas and results and helps clarify what you want to say and how.
- Consider *how* you might write your report. You could tackle it in stages, editing each section as it is completed and possibly starting by writing up Materials and Methods and the Results, drafting your Discussion and the Conclusions, and leaving your Introduction until last. Another method is to write the rough draft of the whole report from start to finish, concentrating on conveying your ideas and information accurately, and then editing what you have written.
- *When* you write your report probably depends on when it is due and your overall workload, but the earlier you begin writing, the more time you will have to set your completed report aside and think about it (see 'Writing to a plan', Chapter 13).

As you write your report

A scientific or technical report usually follows a highly structured format, and is expected to follow certain conventions in data presentation and writing style.

Report genres

Think about your report as a whole, rather than as an assortment of sections. However, each section should by itself convey intelligible information to your reader.

When considering the sections which make up a report, it is important to realise that there is *more than one report genre*. For example:

- biomedical reports often consist of an Introduction, Materials and Methods, Results and Discussion
- reports in descriptive field sciences are likely to include an Introduction, Materials and Methods, Geographical Context, Analysis of Data, Results, and
- more theoretical papers may consist of an Introduction, Theoretical Analysis, Applications, and Conclusions.

While reports in the Social Sciences have similar sections, they are different again.

In a first-year student scientific report, you are probably given a title, expected to write a one- or two-sentence Introduction, and to describe the Materials and Methods as in the laboratory manual. Most of your own effort on the report is spent on your Results and Discussion sections. Occasionally reports require a cover page, a table of contents, illustrations or preface, and they may include recommendations, appendices and acknowledgements. It is not unusual for two sections to be combined when this makes sense such as the Results and Discussion, or the Conclusions and Recommendations.

It is the *purpose of each section* of a report which is important. Even if you are told which sections to use in your report, don't follow the instructions blindly. Take the time to reflect on the function of each section in the whole report.

The following descriptions of report sections include some points which apply more to articles for publication than to conventional student reports. These points are mentioned because they relate to the purpose of a section, and as such need to be thought about early in your report writing career.

1 The title, or 'What is the specific problem or the specific question being asked?'

Your title should attract a potential reader and should be short and specific, for example 'Resources and Environmental Management: Fundamental Concepts and Definitions,' or 'Numerical Data Bases for Australian Science and Technology.' Use a subtitle if a fuller description is necessary, and for the sake of brevity omit words such as 'a', 'the', and 'on' where possible.

The title should state the problem posed or the question asked and can indicate how this problem or question was approached; but a title is not a summary of your report. On the page headed 'Title' in your notebook, list key words and write the title before you write your full report. Check it for accuracy afterwards and ask yourself, 'Do the results and discussions actually answer the particular question or problem set out in the title?'

2 The abstract or synopsis, or 'What are my main findings?'

Your abstract or synopsis is a précis of the content of your report, and is meant to be read in conjunction with the title. It is usually no more than a paragraph, and will include information on the field, the hypothesis, the research design and the main results. An abstract should enable your reader to decide whether to read the whole report, so it should be intelligible by itself and should not be full of technical jargon. To help you clarify your ideas and plan your material, it may be useful to write the abstract before the rest of your report. After the whole report is written, revise the abstract to ensure that it presents the essential content of your report in a balanced manner.

An abstract differs from a *summary*, the latter being a review included at the end of a report to help your readers understand your conclusions or recommendations. Such a summary includes more detail than an abstract and may contain tables and figures. The term 'abstract' is commonly used in academia, while the term 'synopsis' is used in government reports.

3 The introduction, or 'What did I investigate, and why?'

In Part One of formal scientific method, which is the statement of the problem, the main skill is in stating absolutely no more than you are positive you know. It is much better to enter a statement 'Solve Problem: Why doesn't cycle work?' which sounds dumb but is correct, than it is to enter a statement 'Solve Problem: What is wrong with the electrical system?' when you don't absolutely *know* the trouble is in the electrical system. What you should state is 'Solve Problem: What is wrong with cycle?' and then state as the first entry of Part Two: 'Hypothesis Number One: The trouble is in the electrical system.' (*Robert M. Pirsig*)

The introduction should state the specific problem or question under consideration, perhaps as an enlargement of the title.

- State clearly the purpose and scope of your work. If you are testing an hypothesis, introduce the relevant theoretical background.
- Discuss selected research studies which, when taken together, show that your particular experiment or observation is logical and worthwhile within its field. For example, you may have focused on gaps or dilemmas in a field, or have tested a new application of previous work.
- Don't cite a large number of studies in the introduction. Either refer to any papers which review the research literature relevant to the research question and methodology or, if you want to critically review a large body of research literature, add a separate section after the introduction or a review which is separate from your report.
- Explain any unusual or complicated theoretical aspects of the subject which aren't covered by the literature, particularly if your readers include people without a strong background in the field.
- Address any research findings which run counter to your proposed approach to the topic.
- State the assumptions and limitations of your work, and define any technical terms as you introduce them.
- Paraphrase your conclusions if necessary, but without attempting to provide a review of these or of your results.

4 The materials and methods, or 'How did I go about what I did?'

This section describes what you did, usually in the order in which you did it, *so that a reader with experience in the same field could repeat the experiment or observations*. Strike a balance between being concise and giving sufficient detail. To this end, a diagram of apparatus used can be preferable to a long written description of the same apparatus.

- Broadly outline your overall experimental design unless this is obvious from your introduction.
- Under 'Materials', describe any field work locations and list the equipment used including software, and items such as questionnaires.
- Refer to any preliminary experiments and any changes of techniques you have made.
- State the conditions and procedures of the experiment and observations. Indicate how any safety or ethical concerns have been handled.
- Describe the main features of your samples and any sampling and control devices used.
- Describe measurement techniques used.
- Include your reasons for choosing a particular method if there were alternatives.

5 The results, or 'What did I observe or find?'

The purpose of this section is to present in a logical order a statement of your findings and observations in a particular experiment. These should be supplemented with tables or graphs derived from an analysis of data recorded (see 'Data presentation'). In a student practical report, present your results accurately but don't simply provide large amounts of raw data—you are expected to show that you have thought about the raw data and summarised them into an appropriate format. Your results should be presented with your hypothesis in mind, and provide the building material for the discussion where you interpret the results.

The Results section should be coherent on its own. You may be able to report the results fully in a few words or numbers or in a clear table or figure, accompanied by comments on the most significant patterns in the data. If your results led to further experiments which produced further results (and so on), you might want to combine your Results and Discussion sections.

- Display data in a reliable and systematic manner.
- Any raw data, or data to more decimal places than appropriate for the summaries in your results, should be placed in an appendix.
- State the number of results obtained, and your reasons for omitting any of these from this section.
- Give the results which support your conclusions (or lack thereof), but be careful that your selection doesn't distort the results in order to reach a particular conclusion.

6 The discussion, or 'How have I interpreted the results and what are my answers to the specific question asked?'

I am appalled by the frequent publication of papers that describe most minutely what experiments were done, and how, but with no hint of why, or what they mean. Cast thy data upon the waters, the authors seem to think, and they will come back interpreted. (*F. Peter Woodford*)

In some student practical reports you are only required to discuss whether your hypothesis is tenable or whether you have answered the question asked. Nevertheless, the Discussion is the heart of your report and the section where you have the greatest opportunity for critical analysis. Your aims here are to interpret your results; to show their significance in relation to your introduction; to explain how the results add to what is already known; to say whether or not your hypothesis is sustainable; and to discuss your work in relation to the theory underlying similar studies.

- Discuss the precision of your results. Refer to or take them as read, rather than summarising them.
- Explain any irregularities, shortcomings or unexpected results. Note that these discrepancies, rather than being a problem, can often alert you to significant findings.
- Avoid any obviously subjective judgements, such as talking about 'excellent results' or 'highly useful data'.
- Indicate the limits of your research.
- Compare your results with the findings of studies that you mentioned in your introduction. If you have time, to do this satisfactorily check the original studies to find out exactly what other researchers did, how they did it, and the conclusions they drew, then report these findings accurately.
- Consider any positions which apparently contradict your own.
- Give theoretical explanations for the data discussed.
- If appropriate, briefly suggest one or two possible directions for future research in the area.

The points in your discussion should be logically argued and developed, but the section should not be too discursive. Use subheadings to help your reader follow the stages of your argument unless your discussion is brief. The reader should be able to judge the validity of your conclusions from the information in the discussion.

7 The conclusions, or 'What conclusions can justifiably be drawn?'

The TV scientist who mutters sadly, 'The experiment is a failure; we have failed to achieve what we had hoped for,' is suffering mainly from a bad scriptwriter. The experiment is never a failure solely because it fails to achieve predicted results. An experiment is a failure only when it also fails adequately to test the hypothesis in question, when the data it produces don't prove anything one way or another. (*Robert M. Pirsig*)

State succinctly the conclusions which can justifiably be drawn from your work, and indicate their significance for your original research question. If your results are inconclusive (for example, after a short student practical session), say so, give reasons for this, and suggest improvements or further work to be done. Don't present another summary of your results.

8 The references, or 'Which studies did I cite?'
Your list of references should be in alphabetical order, and should consist only of reports or studies cited in your report, not literature consulted. When citing from references which report on other people's experiments, each reference should be checked if possible to ensure that any errors in citing the original experiment are not repeated (see 'Conventions' and 'Questions and mistakes').

■ ■ ■ ■ ■

Teachers' purposes for asking you to write reports include teaching you about a scientific method and a subject area, as well as providing an exercise in writing. In this case you will be faced with the often conflicting aims of showing your teacher how much you know about a subject, while including only necessary detail as expected in a professional report. When confronted with this dilemma, don't rehash textbook material on basic theory, and don't bury your Discussion and Conclusions under a mass of detail. Do talk about the problem with your teacher for suggestions on how the different aims can be reconciled or which one should have priority. When deciding what to include and what to omit, remember that in professional reports the readers usually know less about the subject than the author, while the reverse is presumably true of the readers and writers of student reports. However, don't assume that because your teacher knows a subject you should not explain it fully and clearly. Your teacher needs to know that you understand the basic principles of a subject.

Data presentation
Your data must be ordered, presented in a clear format, and interpreted, or your readers won't be able to make sense of them. How you order and present your data depends on a host of factors, but the guiding principle is always clarity. To achieve clarity, data are usually presented in tables and graphs, accompanied by an explanatory text.

Why use tables or figures?
Use tables or figures if they enable your reader to understand the data more clearly. Use them if, for example, they present data more concisely than words could; or use figures such as graphs and charts at the beginning and end of your results analysis to show the overall relationships between variables. Don't use tables or figures simply for the sake of having them in the report.

How will you present data?
This depends on the information you have to convey. For example, don't use graphs if you have data for an insufficient number of points.

Do use bar or line graphs, pie charts or flow charts if you want clearly to demonstrate trends in results. Use tables where you want to present your data with accurate values. Consider which form of presentation might be appropriate for your data when it is simple and when it is complex, when it is new and when it is repetitive.

Ordering data in tables

There is more than one way of ordering your data within a table. If your reader has sufficient knowledge of the type of data you are presenting, you can arrange your information so that the patterns and exceptions are easily seen. If you can't assume your reader has this knowledge, supply a sentence or two clearly interpreting the information presented. To achieve this clarity, think carefully about the ordering of your data, rather than putting it down in the first format which comes to mind. For example, when presenting tables these are some points to consider:

- Decide to what degree of accuracy you will present your figures. Depending on the purpose of your tables and the precision of your experiment, you may be able to round off your figures without losing any vital information. Your reader may do this anyhow to understand your table easily.
- Consider whether to present your data primarily in columns so that your reader's eye is led down the page, or in rows across the page. Which form makes it easier to see the patterns and exceptions in the data presented? In which form will the table fit most easily on the page?
- Decide whether to include aids such as averages, columns or rows, totals, maxima or minima, or percentages to help your reader interpret your data.
- Think about how to set out and space your material, for example where and how to divide columns of figures from each other.

Amount of information

There is a limit to the amount of information you can convey in one table or figure. Often it is better to opt for several small tables or figures rather than for one large complex one. This allows you to place each one close to the relevant text, and helps your reader focus on one or two aspects of your data at a time. If you find that in a table you have frequent blank spaces or repeated data, you may need to create smaller tables.

Labelling

To label your figures or tables:

- number them in consecutive order
- give each one a title which is precise but concise, and a legend to explain the elements it contains

- if you find yourself developing a complex system of legends and footnotes for a large table or figure, consider whether to present the data in several smaller formats
- specify the units used in tables for the headings for columns and rows, so that each entry in the column or row need be a number only
- ensure that your reader can easily see if each heading refers to a column or a row, and
- indicate units and magnitudes clearly on the axes of a graph or chart.

Table 14.1 A sample table

Comparison of lecturers' and students' perceptions of understanding of assessment criteria, grading and requirements for answering the essay question.

	Very Well Understood	Moderately Well Understood	Not Well Understood
Criteria			
Lecturers (N=19)	15 (79%)	4 (21%)	0
Students (N=125)	49 (39%)	42 (34%)	34 (27%)
Grading			
Lecturers (N=19)	8 (40%)	9 (45%)	3 (15%)
Students (N=125)	37 (31%)	55 (46%)	27 (23%)
Requirements for answering			
Lecturers (N=19)	14 (67%)	7 (33%)	0
Students (N=125)	20 (15%)	77 (59%)	34 (26%)

Source: Ross Brooker and David Smith, 1996, *Higher Education Research and Development*, vol. 15, no. 2, p. 171

Note that the author has:
- presented the data as raw data and as percentages
- arranged the data primarily in columns
- presented the pattern headings at the top of the table and the comparison headings at the side
- supplied the numbers using N, and
- given an explanatory title for the table.

Presenting data in tables and figures is an integral part of communicating your findings from practical work. In student practical sessions you may have little latitude to opt for different forms of data presentation. But when you design experiments yourself, have someone who knows your subject look at your initial data presentation to see what it conveys to them. Try different formats and ordering of your data to see which one conveys most precisely what you want to say. Data presentation is a complex skill, and this section touches on only a few of the basic points. To learn how to convey information as concisely and unambiguously as possible, find people who are skilled in the use of data presentation techniques, and work with them on the results of your own experiments.

Writing styles and conventions

… execrable writing … is the product of shoddy thinking, or careless condescension, or of pretentiousness. (*F. Peter Woodford*)

Your writing style in scientific and technical reports is likely to be shaped by conventions about what 'scientific' thinking is. For example, you are usually expected to avoid using 'I' or 'we' when describing what you did or found because scientists are supposed to be impartial observers. Become familiar with the range of techniques available and practise these often so that they become part of your writing repertoire. Whatever conventions and style you choose, use them to help you report your findings more clearly, rather than to impress your reader or hide ignorance. The principles which underlie all successful communication also apply to scientific writing. Be lucid and unambiguous, and ask yourself:

Exactly what do I want to say?

Why do I want to say it?

How can I say it most effectively?

To whom am I saying it?

Style

Reports should describe concisely and accurately what happened in an experiment or in field work—they should not be written in a narrative or story-telling style. Events are usually presented in chronological order or in order of significance, and the description should develop logically, step by step. Write most of your report in prose, and be careful of over-using formulae and other abbreviations when the information they convey could easily be expressed in words.

Language

The language you use should be neither too technical nor too elementary. Your level of writing should be aimed at whoever will read your report and you should:

- define any new words or mathematical symbols when you first use them
- use technical terms accurately (for example, 'constantly' and 'efficient') and avoid careless use of words which can have a technical meaning (such as 'parameter' or 'factor')
- use chemical and pharmacological names rather than unfamiliar trade names
- write scientific names, proper names, numerical data, equations and formulae correctly, and
- opt for familiar, short or concrete words rather than unfamiliar, long or abstract ones.

I am a Bear of Very Little Brain, and long words Bother me. (*A.A. Milne*)

Conventions

Check with your teacher which conventions you are expected to follow in a report. Some examples follow.

- Are you expected to use passive tense rather than active? For example, are you expected to write 'pH4 was needed by the enzyme' (passive) instead of 'the enzyme needed pH4' (active)? Using the passive tense does not in itself make your writing more scholarly, and active tenses generally make your writing more direct.
- Are you required to use past tense when describing your methods and reporting your results? Are you expected to use the present tense when stating facts which are generally agreed upon?
- Are some numbers to be written in words and some in figures? How are times and dates to be recorded?
- Will you number your report sections and sub-sections consecutively as in '2.1.1.', '2.1.2.', '2.1.3'?

To cite *references*, it is customary in scientific reports to use the author's name and the year of publication in the body of your text, rather than using footnotes. For example:

'According to Brown (1959) ...'
'Recent studies (Black, 1975; White, 1976) show that ...'
'After a thorough training, 'The student can no longer write; he pontificates' (Woodford, 1967).'

For references you cite but have not seen in the original:
'The mouse ran up the clock (Green, cited by Blue, 1971) ...'

If you refer frequently to other research literature, the text may become so cluttered with bracketed references that it is difficult to read. In this case list all references at the end of the text (alphabetically or in order of appearance) and number each item. To cite one of these references, quote the number of that reference in your text. For example:

'The mouse ran up the clock [31]'

or

'The mouse ran up the clock (31)'.

See Chapter 15, 'Using Conventions', for detailed information on correct referencing, including citing online references.

Grammar, spelling, punctuation

If poor grammar, spelling and punctuation prevent you communicating clearly, work on these with the help of a good reference text on the subject (see 'Further reading' for this chapter, and 'Grammar, spelling and punctuation', Chapter 15). Find a patient friend who is proficient in these skills and willing to proofread your work.

Sentences and paragraphs

Keep your sentences short and simple if in doubt about their length. Construct your paragraphs so that each one contains one idea (see 'The body of your essay', Chapter 14). If you have trouble writing coherent sentences and paragraphs, work with someone who will help you improve these skills. Read and analyse plenty of well-written articles to get the feel of effective writing—*Science* and *Nature* are good sources of these.

Editing the report

When your report is finished, set it aside if you have the time, so that you can come back to it with something of the approach of a person reading it for the first time. While it is set aside, think about what you have written and make occasional corrections—but allow yourself some distance from it before you prepare your final version.

Check through the contents of your report. If some of your report seems irrelevant or too detailed, prune it ruthlessly. See if you have covered all the points in 'As you write'. For example, have you:

- recorded all experimental information such as strength of solutions, ambient temperature, specification of instruments
- put units against all your measurements and results
- defined all symbols
- checked your calculations
- compared your results with expected or established results, and
- dated your work?

Look at your writing style. Be prepared to replace an inappropriate word and to rewrite a clumsy sentence or paragraph. Proofread your report for mistakes or omissions in details such as spelling, grammar and punctuation, or ask someone else to read your work to point out incorrect details and to suggest ways in which you can polish your writing style. When you have edited the content and style of your report, produce a clean, legible copy (see 'Presentation', Chapter 15).

Writing a scientific report involves putting words on paper, but it also involves thinking about and planning what you want to say as you take notes during an experiment or field work, as you begin to draft your whole report, and when working on your final draft. As you try to express exactly what you want to say, the process of writing itself can set off new ideas and make you look again at old ones. And remember, writing a report is you communicating about your work to your reader.

Questions and mistakes

Many students see experiments and practical work as exercises to be gone through to find the Right answers. Yet any real learning for you as an individual follows from the questions you ask for information, because you want to know. Following procedures laid down by someone else to answer a question asked by someone else inevitably leads to someone else's answers. You can learn from someone else's answers—but only if their answers have a connection with your questions (see Chapter 4, 'Asking Your Own Questions').

You interpret the results of an experiment according to the hypothesis being tested, and according to what you expected to find. The way a question is asked, a problem stated or an hypothesis worded influences the results you are likely to come up with. Even researchers who start with the same hypothesis and arrive at similar results can and do interpret those results to reach considerably different conclusions. Their results and conclusions are then interpreted by other researchers in the light of their own hypotheses and findings and opinions. To discover how scientific research has developed in an area, and just how shaky 'facts' can be, take a paper on a specific topic and read through the originals of any studies cited in that paper. Read these original studies carefully, and compare their actual findings with the way in which these findings have been cited in the later paper. It is not uncommon to find noticeable discrepancies between the two.

> School books even more rarely tell us how thinkers of the past have gone about trying to answer their own questions, and still more rarely, what mistakes they made along the way. A graduate student in Psychology suggested one day to a noted professor in that field that there should be

a publication in which psychologists would write about their mistakes, the hunches that had not worked out, the experiments that had not proved what they meant to prove; or didn't prove anything. The professor agreed that such a publication would teach students a great deal about the doing of psychology. But, he said, there was no use even thinking about such a publication, because no-one with a reputation to defend would ever put anything in it. So we find it hard to find most of our mistakes because we are so rarely told how the do-ers of the past came to make and later find theirs. (*John Holt*)

If, at the end of an experiment or field work, you have not found the answers you expected, if your results are inconclusive or point to other answers, don't automatically think you have failed. Think about what you did and try to discover why your results were inconclusive or unexpected. If you made a mistake, acknowledge it. If your work could be improved, suggest how this might be done. If you discover related questions, or areas to be explored for a more complete answer, suggest these as part of your report. Don't try to hide your unexpected or inconclusive results, or distort them to produce the Right answers. You can learn much by analysing your mistakes.

■ ■ ■ ■ ■

You can learn as much from writing a report of observations made in the laboratory or field as you can from doing the practical work about which you write. The challenge of trying to describe your work accurately, logically and lucidly for someone else to read and understand should make you think about what you actually did. It will also help you critically evaluate other people's reports. In serious research, describing your work helps you think about how to design and conduct experiments or a set of observations, about the disciplines in which you are working and writing, and about the strengths and limits of scientific knowledge. What do you think science is all about? Or technology? Your answers to these questions will shape and be shaped by the reports you write about your scientific and technical work.

Further reading

Booth, Vernon, 1993, *Communicating in science: Writing a scientific paper and speaking at scientific meetings*, 2nd edn, Cambridge University Press, Melbourne.

Council of Biology Editors, 1994, *Scientific style and format: The CBE manual for authors, editors and publishers*, 6th edn, Cambridge University Press, Melbourne.

Eunson, B., 1994, *Writing and presenting reports*, John Wiley, Brisbane.

Kumar, R., 1993, *Writing a research proposal: Some guidelines for beginners*, Curtin University of Technology, Perth.

Lindsay, David, 1984, *A guide to scientific writing*, Longman Cheshire, Melbourne.

Northey, M. & Knight, D.B., 1992, *Making sense in geography and environmental studies: A student's guide to research, writing, and style*, Oxford University Press, Toronto.

O'Connor, M., 1991, *Writing successfully in science*, Chapman & Hall, London.

Silyn-Roberts, H., 1996, *Writing for science: A practical handbook for science, engineering and technology students*, Addison Wesley Longman, Auckland.

Weissberg, R. & Buker, S., 1990, *Writing up research: Experimental research report writing for students of English*, Prentice Hall Regents, Englewood Cliffs, NJ.

CHAPTER 15

USING CONVENTIONS

'... besides that's not a regular rule; you invented it just now.'
'It's the oldest rule in the book,' said the King.
'Then it ought to be Number One,' said Alice. (*Lewis Carroll*)

When using conventions in your written assignments it is useful to understand their purposes rather than simply following rules. For example, the standard conventions used by most Western publishers serve as a shorthand to make writing and reading easier. Much of this shorthand has its origins in the reporting of scientific research where the reader needs to be able to follow up references to understand or evaluate a report fully.

Referencing is an integral part of academic debate, and skilful use of references shows an awareness of the nuances in a particular academic dialogue or controversy. If you are new to academia you may be mostly concerned to reference correctly, especially when you are inevitably confronted with different teachers expecting different referencing formats. In this case, learn the basic elements for referencing and other conventions so that you can adapt these as required—and remember that your longer-term aim is to participate in critical debates.

If citing a reference or paraphrasing an idea in a piece of academic writing, acknowledge your source and give full details of the reference. For example:

Savage, Jo, 1998, *The Film 'Fangs'*, Wolf Publications, Alaska, p. 54.

It may seem unimportant and pedantic to have to follow the academic conventions. However, if you omit any of this information (for example, if you refer only to 'Savage's book on the movie *Fangs*), your reader has to ask for further information to know how recent the book is, exactly who the author is, the book's title, where the book was published, and precisely on which page in the book to find the cited reference.

Individual academic disciplines, publications and individual teachers frequently adopt their own variations of the standard conventions. The essential elements are the same but the formatting details may vary considerably. Whichever format you use, be *consistent* and *accurate*. Check with a teacher about the conventions you are expected to follow in your respective discipline, program, course or assignment, and find out your teacher's personal preferences in these matters.

Either stick to tradition or see that your inventions be consistent. (*Horace*)

But don't let the punctilious observance of correct conventions become the focus of your writing. Use them as necessary to help you communicate more clearly—and if in doubt about which one to use or whether to use them at all, rely on your common sense to convey clearly and accurately to your reader what you want to say.

This chapter outlines why and how to use quotations, references and bibliographies and is based on the conventions set out in the Australian Government's *Style Manual*.[1] The chapter also looks at the question of plagiarism, and at some conventions for presenting an assignment.

Most of the examples in the chapter are taken from material written about the sea, a place where human conventions are subservient to nature.

Quotations

I might repeat to myself, slowly and soothingly, a list of quotations beautiful from minds profound; if I can remember any of the damn things. (*Dorothy Parker*)

Why use quotations?

Quotations can be useful:

- to express a thought or concept succinctly
- to illustrate a point you want to make
- to convey the flavour of a work, or
- to analyse in depth the exact words of an author.

How to present quotations

Long quotations

These should be set apart from the main body of your writing so that they are easily identified. If a quote is longer than about twenty words, two complete sentences, or several lines of text, it is usual to apply most of the following conventions and not to use inverted commas (quotation marks).

- introduce the quotation with a colon
- miss a line above and below the quotation
- indent from the left (some authors indent both sides)
- use single-spaced typescript when the rest of the text is double-spaced
- reference the information as required (using either the author–date or footnote systems described in this chapter).

For example:

- In his book *Sailing to the Reefs*, Bernard Moitessier (1971, p. 83) discusses the motivation behind single-handed sailing:

  > And it is, I believe, this need not simply for novelty, but for physical and spiritual cleanliness which drives the lone sailor towards other shores; there, his body and mind are freed from their terrestrial ties and bondage, and can regain their essence and integrity in the natural elements which the ancients deified.

  This description captures the spirituality of the experience …

  - A familiar children's poem describes an unusual sea voyage:
    The Owl and the Pussy-Cat went to sea
    In a beautiful pea-green boat,
    They took some honey, and plenty of money,
    Wrapped up in a five-pound note.[2]

Short quotations

These are usually integrated into your text as part of a grammatically complete sentence and are enclosed by either single or double quotation marks. For example:

- Truly immersed in the experience, 'one forgets oneself, one forgets everything, seeing only the play of the boat with the sea, the play of the sea around the boat' (Moitessier, 1975, p. 52) as the present takes priority over all else.

If quoting a couple of lines of poetry within your text, you need not set them apart and can indicate the division between the lines with an oblique. For example:

- The single-handed sailor knows the power of being 'Alone, alone, all, all, alone, / Alone on a wide, wide sea!'[3]

All quotations

In all quotations, the punctuation must be the same as in the original. This includes items such as capital letters, and inverted commas. If you wish to highlight a word or phrase in the quotation by underlining, bolding or using italics when none was used in the original, this must be indicated to the reader by adding in square brackets the words 'my emphasis' or 'emphasis added'. For example:

- Yet the neatness of a copy does not devalue a diary, because, paradox-ically, formality was part of the *genre*, and even diaries written at sea had aspirations beyond that of a briefly scribbled note [emphasis added].

If you choose to abridge a quotation (that is, omit any words or phrases), the convention is to use three dots to show that something has been left out. Note that the meaning and intent of the original must not be altered. In the process of abridging a longer quote, you may have to change the punctuation or the grammar so that the quotation still makes sense. In this case, the convention is to indicate your additions within square brackets as in the following examples:

- To working people who were unable to work for wages while at sea the purchase of a notebook ... represented a costly investment to preserve an account of the voyage.

- All diaries aspired to the status of the printed book, and the notebooks ... in which diaries were kept show a common ambition among diarists [at sea] to produce a lasting memento [of their voyage].

If you wish to draw the reader's attention to an error or indiscretion in the writing of another author, use the word *sic* (Latin for 'thus') within brackets to indicate that those were the exact words of the author and that the mistake is not yours. In the following example sexist language has been signalled:

- Only comparatively recently has a need been felt to retain documents produced by working people. The result is that the archival collections of shipboard diaries are skewed towards the writings of middle class men [*sic*] ...

Paraphrasing and plagiarism

With just enough of learning to misquote. (*Lord Byron*)

When you paraphrase, you re-express another person's thoughts in your own words and acknowledge their source. You plagiarise if you take someone else's thoughts and writings and present them as your own. Plagiarism also has a cultural basis in that modern writers and researchers in the Western tradition expect to be fully acknowledged if their ideas or their work are referred to in any way. This differs from some cultures where it is accepted that you are showing respect for authorities by copying their words. In Western higher education, failure to acknowledge or cite another person's work is called plagiarism and is treated very seriously in universities and colleges.

Plagiarism often results in an unsatisfactory piece of work because, for example, your writing style differs awkwardly from that of the plagiarised piece, or the section you have copied is not exactly relevant to your overall argument. You may not be aware that it is unacceptable to copy from a source without acknowledgment, and may inadvertently include in your own work phrases, sentences or paragraphs from another source. More extreme forms of plagiarism (cheating or stealing) occur when a student copies, with or without minor changes, large sections of an article or chapter or another student's essay. Collusion, which is another form of cheating, occurs when a student has another person complete for them some assessable work such as an exam or assignment. Collusion differs from collaboration in that the intention in the former is to deceive the teacher who will assess the work.

In many instances, teachers are familiar with the relevant source material and can easily diagnose a case of plagiarism. Otherwise, they may ask another teacher to read your work, make a thorough search for the original source, or discuss the paper with you. If plagiarism is confirmed, there are several possible courses of action for a teacher. You may be asked to write another paper, the piece of work could be failed, or work completed out of class might be disregarded and you may be expected to sit for an exam. Sometimes official disciplinary action is taken and in serious cases a student may be expelled from the institution. In any case, reading the work of a student who has plagiarised someone else's words and ideas is a disheartening experience for a teacher.

> Lies were such small things, like stones that you pitched into the water. The stones disappeared, but the water rippled out into ever widening circles that you couldn't ever catch and put back. (*Ivy Baker*)

How to avoid plagiarising

- You may be tempted to plagiarise if you are not confident about your knowledge of a subject or your writing ability, or because you feel pressured by too much work. If so, talk about these difficulties with someone who can help you (and use any relevant sections of this book) rather than resorting to plagiarism and being confronted with the same problems later on.
- If you have so much work to complete that plagiarism seems to be an option, check to see if other students in the course are having workload problems. If so, collectively approach your teacher. If not, see your teacher individually.
- When taking notes from material, read a section, put the reference aside and express the idea in your own words (see 'Notemaking and/or underlining', Chapter 9). If you copy any words exactly, put them in quotation marks; or if you want to closely rephrase another writer's words, clearly identify the beginning and end of paraphrasing. In both cases note the page reference.
- When writing, put quotes in inverted commas or indent longer quotes. For quotes or paraphrases, use footnotes, endnotes or textual references to acknowledge the source. You can indicate clearly where a paraphrase begins by acknowledging the author immediately before in your text, for example, 'Humphries says ...'. If you take an opinion from someone else, don't disguise it by using the passive tense, such as 'It has been said that ...'. If you use factual information, for example statistics that are not common knowledge, acknowledge the source.
- If you are a student from a culture where quoting authorities is acceptable, make certain that you understand referencing conventions.

References

Why include references?

References are used:

- to give the source of a quotation, paraphrase, or idea so that your readers can locate and refer to this item if they want to
- to give the source of authority for a 'fact' which a reader might question as true
- to make a cross-reference to another part of your text
- to lend authority or support to your ideas, or
- to demonstrate the breadth of your research on the topic.

How to reference material

Unfortunately for new students, there are a large number of referencing styles used in different academic disciplines. However, these are usually variations of the author–date system (also known as 'the Harvard system', 'included references', or 'adjacent referencing') or the numbering (or footnote/endnote) system.

The author–date system uses author–date citations within the essay; and the full details of all the references cited in the text are listed alphabetically by surname in a reference list at the end of the essay.

The footnote/endnote system uses consecutive numbers (either in superscript or bracketed) in the text for each reference; and the full referencing details are listed in numerical order either at the foot of the page or at the end of the essay.

Author–date references

Author–date references within a text enable a reader to continue reading your text smoothly, for example:

- In his book *Sailing to the Reefs*, Bernard Moitessier (1971, p.83) discusses the motivation behind single-handed sailing.

These textual references may be used in conjunction with footnotes or endnotes which comment on your text. This system is the accepted form of referencing in most scientific disciplines and in many disciplines in the social sciences and humanities. These references give the author's surname and the year of publication, and need to include page numbers for quotes or for references to a specific item in a source. Note that paraphrases are cited in the text in the same way as direct quotations. For example:

- Bernard Moitessier (1975, p. 4) describes sailboats as living creatures. Sailboats are sometimes described as living creatures (Moitessier 1975, p. 4).

Note that the relevant page numbers have a comma between the year and 'p.', as above (or 'pp.' where several pages are involved).

The details involved in citations using the author-date system vary depending on, for example, whether the Harvard or American Psychological Association (APA) is employed. The following selective list (in Harvard style) is not meant to be exhaustive:

- Only the author's surname is included in a textual reference, unless initials are needed to distinguish two authors with the same surnames.

  The theory was first propounded in 1970 (Larsen, A.E. 1971), but since then has been refuted; M.K. Larsen (1983) is among those most energetic in their opposition.

- If you refer to more than one publication in a year by the same author, distinguish these with letters after the year:

  1978a and 1978b.

- If you cite more than one author in the same sentence, present them in either of the following ways.

  According to these two authors (Moitessier 1975; Letcher 1974),
  According to Moitessier (1975) and Letcher (1974), ...

- If a work has two authors, use either of the following formats.

  As the authors (Pardey & Pardey, 1979) argue in their book ...
  Pardey and Pardey (1979) argue that ...

- If a work has more than two authors, use the abbreviation *et al.* after the first author's name in the citation in the text.

  Adamson *et al.* (1988) contend that leadership cannot be eliminated entirely but will become 'covert' (p. 236).

- In the reference list at the end of the assignment give names of all authors in full.

  Adamson, N., Briskin, L. & Mc Phail, M., 1988, *Feminists Organizing for Change*, p. 236.

- For works with no publication date, follow the author's name with (n.d.).

  Johnson (n.d.) has suggested ...

- For works with no author, cite the title in the text and in the reference list.

  ... as stated in Phillip's report (*The Voyage of Governor Phillip to Botany Bay*, 1790)

Footnotes

These allow for more information on the same page about your source than is possible in a textual reference. As well as being used to acknowledge a source in detail, a footnote may comment on or support what you have written in your main text.[4]

Footnotes appear on the same page as the reference. A number follows after the quotation or paraphrase you are referencing and is repeated at the foot of the page.[5] Footnotes may be numbered consecutively throughout your text or numbered separately for each page, section or chapter.

The first time you acknowledge a particular book in a footnote give whichever of the following details are applicable, so that your reader can locate the work if they want to (while noting that the order of these details may vary according to the referencing style adopted):

- the author/editor's name (surname last)
- the year of publication
- the title of the book (underlined or italicised)

- the translator/illustrator/reviser's name
- the publication details (edition, publisher, place), and
- the page reference.

For example:

> Francis Chichester, 1967, *Gipsy Moth Circles the World*, Hodder and Stoughton, London, p. 67.

- For immediately consecutive footnotes referring to the same source, in the second or subsequent footnotes use only the author's surname and the new page numbers. For example:

1 David Lewis, 1969, *Children of Three Oceans*, Collins, London, p. 60.

2 Lewis, p. 66.

- If there is more than one item by the same author, give the author's name in each case and follow it with the title and page numbers of the individual item.
- If there is more than one author with the same surname, give forenames also.

Endnotes

These serve the same purposes as footnotes. If too much space would be taken up in your text with numerous, lengthy or complicated footnotes, use endnotes. They can be easier for your reader to refer to and can be easier to lay out in the final draft of an assignment. However, as with footnotes, if you have too many endnotes in relation to the length of your assignment, consider whether the assignment is adequately planned.

When compiling endnotes, all reference notes that would have appeared as footnotes are collected at the end of your assignment. Number these references consecutively throughout your text, and apply the same rules of abbreviation to them as to footnotes. It is useful for your reader if endnotes can be detached from your text for easier reference, and if they are headed 'References' to distinguish them instantly from a bibliography.

Table 15.1 Abbreviations and contractions

app.	— appendix
bk, bks	— book (s)
©	— copyright
c. (*circa*)	— about a certain date [as in 'c. 1901']
ch., chs (or chap., chaps)	— chapter(s)
col., cols	— column(s)
diss.	— dissertation
ed., eds	— editor(s)

edn	— edition
et al. (*et alii*)	— 'and others' [used when a book has several authors, as in 'P. March et al.'].
et seq. (*et sequentes*)	— 'and following'[as in 'pp. 64 et seq.']
f., ff.	— 'and the following' [to refer to page numbers as in 'pp. 30 ff.']
facsim.	— facsimile [that is, an exact copy of writing, printing, picture]
fol., fols	— folio(s)
front.	— frontispiece
ibid. (*ibidem*)	— 'in the same work' [as previously cited]
ill., ills	— illustrator(s)
loc. cit. (*loco citato*)	— 'in the same place (already) cited' [that is, in the same passage referred to in a recent reference note]
ms, mss	— manuscript(s)
n., nn.	— note(s) [as 'p. 56, n. 3' or 'p. 56 n.']
n.d.	— no date [of publication]
n.p.	— no place [of publication]
op. cit. (*opere citato*)	— in the work [recently] cited
p., pp.	— page(s)
passim	— 'throughout the work' [rather than on specific pages]
q.v., qq.v. (*quod vide*)	— 'which see' [used in cross referencing]
rev.	— revised [by], reviser
[*sic*]	— 'thus so' [to guarantee exact quotation when the reader might doubt this]
trans., tr.	— translator, -ion, -ed
v., vv.	— verse(s)
viz. (*videlicet*)	— 'namely', 'in other words' [usually after words or statements about to be elaborated]
vol., vols	— volume(s)

Reference lists and bibliographies

Why include a reference list or bibliography?

You must include a *reference list* for all assignments, whether written, oral, taped or audiovisual, to provide full details of the works you refer to in your text. A reference list consists of the full referencing details of all publications cited in the text of your essay or report. In the author-date or Harvard system, this list is always alphabetically arranged according to the authors' surnames.

If you also provide a *bibliography* this enables you:

- to provide a complete or selected list of the sources you consulted in preparation for writing an assignment but which you have not necessarily cited in the text, and

- possibly to provide annotations, that is, brief commentaries on your sources.

A bibliography can also be a self-contained work which gives an exhaustive list of items on a topic.

If you have used fully detailed footnotes or endnotes (that is, you have used footnote/endnote referencing), you may not need to provide a reference list. However, it can be useful for your reader to see all of your sources listed alphabetically, and you may be expected to prepare a bibliography as well.

How to present a reference list and bibliography

Book entry
The basic format for these entries is:

- author or editor's name (surname first)
- year of publication
- title (underlined or italicised)
- the translator, illustrator or reviser's name
- publication details.

For example:

> Colgate, Stephen, 1978, *Fundamentals of Sailing, Cruising and Racing*, W.W. Norton and Company, New York.

An article, chapter, or anthology item
The basic format for such entries is:

- author or editor's name (surname first, followed by forename or initials)
- year of publication
- title of article, chapter or item, possibly enclosed by inverted commas (do not use inverted commas if following the Harvard style or the author-date system)
- author or editor of the book in which the chapter or item is found
- title (underlined or italicised) of the periodical, book, anthology or newspaper from which the item was taken
- publication details of periodical or book (include publication details for overseas periodicals), and
- page numbers of article, chapter or item.

For example:

> Burke, K. M, 1979, 'A Dream in Ice and Snow', *Cruising World*, Newport, Rhode Island, vol. 5, no. 1, January, pp. 60–63.

Additional points

- Publication details are as follows:
  - periodical: place (if overseas), volume number, issue number (if pages are numbered afresh for each issue), date
  - book: edition (if not the first edition), place, publisher, date.
- If there is more than one entry for an author, list these entries in chronological order of publication.
- Bibliography entries may be classified into groups according to topic or the nature of the material, for example:
  - 'Primary Sources' and 'Secondary Sources'
  - 'Books' and 'Articles'
  - 'Items from Newspapers' and 'Personal Conversations'.
- The heading of a bibliography should indicate its scope, for example, 'Selected Bibliography', 'Brief Annotated Bibliography' or 'A General Bibliography'.

Table 15.2 Reference list or bibliography entries

Books

One author

Van Dorn, William G., 1974, *Oceanography and seamanship*, Dodd, Mead and Company, New York.

Two authors

Pardey, L. & Pardey, L., 1979, *Seraphyn's European adventures*, W.W. Norton and Company, New York.

Three or more authors

Pariser, E.L. *et al.*, 1978, *Fish protein concentrate: Panacea for protein malnutrition?* M.I.T. Press, Boston, Mass.

Repeat entry by same author

Letcher, John S. Jr., 1974, *Self steering for sailing craft*, International Marine Publishing Company, Camden, Maine.

—— 1977, *Self-contained celestial navigation with H.O. 208*, International Marine Publishing Company, Camden, Maine.

Author and translator

Moitessier, Bernard, 1975, *The long way*, trans. William Rodarmor, Doubleday and Company, New York.

Editor

Kemp, Peter (ed.), 1976, *The Oxford companion to ships and the sea*, Oxford University Press, London.

Unknown author

The voyage of Governor Phillip to Botany Bay, 1790, London.

Corporate author

Naval Training Command, 1972, *A navigational compendium*, 2nd edn, Government Printing Office, Washington, D.C.

Article (unsigned) from reference book
'Oceanography', 1968, *Encyclopedia of the sciences*, 2nd edn, Sill, W.B. & Hoss, N. (eds), Grosset & Dunlop, New York.

Excerpt from book not read in original but seen reproduced in another book
Robertson, Dougal, 1973, 'Sunk by a Whale' in *Survive the savage sea*, Elek Books, London, in Stevenson, Ralph (ed.), 1978, *Small boats and big seas: A hundred years of yachting*, David McKay Company, New York.

Chapter of a book where both are by the same author
Crealock, W.I.B., 1955, 'Stainless steel and panties', *Cloud of islands*, David McKay Company, New York.

Article from edited book (author and editor different)
Fuller, R. Buckminster, 1970, 'Formula for a floating city' in Dunstan, M.J. & Garian, P.J., (eds), *Worlds in the making*, Prentice-Hall, New Jersey.

Journals, newspapers
Article from journal
Lundberg, Madeleine, 1979, 'Eugenie Clark: Shark tamer', *Ms*, VIII, 2 August, pp. 12–21.

Article from newspaper
Heydon, Neville, 1980, 'Right port for Jan', *The Mercury*, Hobart, 14 February, p. 1.

Oral information
Information from a lecture
Macbeth, J.W., 1991, 'Participant research: Ocean cruisers, a study of a deviant subculture', Lecture, Murdoch University, 4 June.

Information from a television or radio program
'Voyage to the ice', 1978, Australian Broadcasting Commission, Sydney, 27 September.

Personal conversation
Driscoll, John, 1978, personal conversation with author.

Interview
Fletcher, Dorothy, 1978, interviewed by Jim Macbeth, 9 September.

Electronic sources
Document available by World Wide Web
McGrady, J.F., 1997, *Sailing the dream* : *An autobiographical odyssey—Querencia chronicles*, [Online], available World Wide Web, URL: http://www.coconutinfo.com/sailingthedream/cover.html (Accessed 11 December 1997)

Article from online database
Logan, D., 1995, 'The known and unknown wind in sailors lore and mythology', *Parabola*, 20 (1) 34–6, [Online], available Expanded Academic Index InfoTrac Search Bank, Elec. Coll.: A16624769

Document obtained through computer service
Cylke, F.K. (ed.), 1990, *Sailing: An introduction to the wonders of sailing for blind and physically handicapped individuals* [CD-ROM] The Library of Congress, Washington DC, ERIC ED342185

Full-text journal article on CD-ROM
Ladbury, A., 1994, 'Marine underwriters predict smooth sailing in year ahead', *Business insurance*, 28 (35) 48–53, [CD-ROM] in Business periodical Ondisc, Ann Arbor, Michigan, UMI Accession no. 00899744

Article available by e-mail
Wenner, L.A., 1995, 'Riding waves and sailing seas: Wipeouts, jibes and gender', *Journal of sport and social issues*, 19 (2) 123–25, [Online], available e-mail: uncovweb@carl.org

Newspaper article on CD-ROM
Thomas, I., 1996, 'Smoother sailing for cruise liners', *Australian financial review*, Aug 14: 2, AUSTROM:ATI (Tourism) [CDROM]

Discussion list message or attached document from a bulletin board
Gray, J., 1997, *Limits of development: Tidal sea caves*, December 11, [Online], available via e-mail, Trinet discussion list, address TRINET-@Hawaii.edu

The finishing touches

You are expected to present your work clearly and to use correct grammar, spelling and punctuation in writing assignments and reports. If you are uncertain about the conventions you are expected to follow in these matters, check with a teacher and with reference books.

Grammar, spelling and punctuation

'He has got no good red blood in his body,' said Sir James.
'No. Somebody put a drop under a magnifying-glass, and it was all semi-colons and parentheses,' said Mrs. Cadwallader. (*George Eliot*)

A sound knowledge of grammar helps you write more fluently and is an important part of the writer's craft. Your ideas have less impact if your grammar, spelling and punctuation are poor, since your reader frequently has to re-read what you have written to clarify what you meant to say. To improve these skills, consult books and ask for help from other people. You may have to learn by heart the correct forms and usages, but if you can discover underlying reasons for a particular rule you remember the correct version more easily. Read your work aloud to yourself (possibly into a tape recorder) and check the grammar and punctuation of any sections which don't flow smoothly. Use the spellchecker facility of your word processing program; and if it is possible develop your own dictionary for your computer, especially if you have a learning disability which results in repeated spelling errors. If English is not your first language and you have trouble with grammar and punctuation, ask for help from a language adviser.

'I struggle through the alphabet as if it had been a bramble bush; getting considerably worried and scratched by every letter.' (*Charles Dickens*)

Presentation

The purpose of presenting work clearly is to help your reader.

- Legible writing saves your reader from eye strain and irritation. Assignments should be typed, printed or clearly written in ink. When handwriting, take care with details such as dotting your 'i's accurately or forming your 'r's clearly, as these make your writing surprisingly easier to read. If your handwriting is atrocious or if you have physical difficulties with writing, persuade a friend or a proficient typist to type your assignments for you, or learn to type yourself.
- Keep a copy in case your reader happens to lose your assignment. Save your work on both your hard disk and a floppy disk.
- Do not overcrowd each page. If your work is typed or printed from a computer, leave space on the sides and at the top and bottom. A wide left hand margin (at least 4 cm) enables your reader to write full and detailed comments.
- For easy identification, provide a cover sheet giving your name, the assignment title, course, teacher's name, and date on which the assignment is due and the date of submission. The cover sheet may also include an abstract or synopsis (see 'Report genres', Chapter 14).
- Number the pages.
- Write or type on only one side of the paper, particularly if you write in ink or on lightweight paper. However, as this is environmentally wasteful, if you wish to save paper explain this to your teacher.
- Secure all pages firmly together. Any appendices to which the reader will refer frequently should be detachable (for example, endnotes or tables of results).
- To help your reader understand the structure of a long assignment you may decide to provide a contents page. This could be accompanied by a list of any diagrams, graphs or appendices.

■ ■ ■ ■ ■

No publication, whatever its nature, should be expected to follow slavishly any set of rules—by whomsoever prescribed—if to do so would have an adverse effect on the text as a whole. What counts above all is consistency of approach and treatment; and for that reason, discretion, sensitivity and sheer common sense should always prevail in writing and editing. (*Australian Government Publication Service*)

Use conventions to help you say what you want to as lucidly as possible. Don't worry about the correct form of academic conventions so much that they prevent you from writing effectively. Become familiar with the basic conventions and their purposes, check which forms to follow for a particular piece of work, and then rely on your common sense to convey what you want to say to a reader. If you have trouble with using any convention, find yourself an efficient proofreader and work at overcoming your difficulties.

List of sources used for author–date references in this chapter

Hassam, A., 1995, *No privacy for writing: Shipboard diaries 1852–1879*, Melbourne University Press, Carlton.

Letcher, John S. Jr., 1974, *Self steering for sailing craft*, International Marine Publishing Company, Camden, Maine.

Moitessier, B., 1971, *Sailing to the reefs*, trans. Rene Hague, Hollis and Carter, London.

Moitessier, B., 1975, *The long way*, trans. W. Rodamor, Granada, London.

Pardey, L. & Pardey, L., 1979, *Seraphyn's European adventures*, W.W. Norton and Company, New York.

Further reading

American Psychological Association, 1994, *Publication manual of the American Psychological Association*, 4th edn, APA, Washington.

Australian Government Publishing Service, 1994, *Style manual: For authors, editors and printers of Australian Government publications*, 5th edn, AGPS, Canberra.

Bate, Douglas & Sharpe, Peter, 1990, *Student writer's handbook: How to write better essays*, Harcourt Brace Jovanovich, Sydney.

Bailey, R.F., 1984, *A survival kit for writing English*, 2nd edn, Longman Cheshire, Melbourne.

Bullock, A., Stallybrass, O., & Trombley, S., 1988, *The Fontana dictionary of modern thought*, 2nd edn, Fontana Press, Glasgow.

Chapman, Robert L. (ed.), 1994, *Roget A to Z*, Harper Collins, New York.

Collins, 1987, *Cobuild English Language Dictionary*, Collins, London.

Collinson, D., Kirkup, G., Kyd, R. & Slocombe, L., 1993, *Plain English*, 2nd edn, Open University Press, Milton Keynes, Bucks.

Eagleson, R.D, Jones, G. & Hassall, S., 1990, *Writing in plain English*, AGPS, Canberra.

Gibaldi, Joseph & Achtert, Walter S., 1988, *The MLA handbook for writers of research papers, theses, and dissertations*, 3rd edn, Modern Language Association of America, New York.

Landau, Sidney I. & Bogus, Ronald J., 1987, *The Doubleday Roget's Thesaurus in dictionary form*, Doubleday, Sydney.

Li, X. & Crane, N. B., 1993, *Electronic style: A guide to citing electronic information*, Meckler, London.

Macquarie University, 1997, *The Macquarie dictionary*, 3rd edn, Macquarie Library, Sydney.

Murray-Smith, Stephen, 1990, *Right words: A guide to English usage in Australia,* Penguin, Ringwood.

Peters, Pam, 1996, *The Cambridge Australian English style guide*, Cambridge University Press, Melbourne.

Turabian, Kate L. 1987, *A manual for writers of term papers, theses, and dissertations*, 5th edn, The University of Chicago Press, Chicago.

University of Chicago Press, 1993, *The Chicago manual of style*, 14th edn, The University of Chicago Press, Chicago.

Notes

1 A range of conventions have been used in this book to provide examples for you to follow. The quotations, for example, use an endnote system (see 'Sources' at the end of this book) whereas in this chapter textual references have been used. Some of the endnotes in this chapter could easily have been presented as footnotes.

2 Edward Lear, 1943, *Nonsense omnibus*, Frederick Warne and Company, London, p. 251.

3 Ernest Hartley Coleridge (ed.), 1912, *The poems of Samuel Taylor Coleridge*, Oxford University Press, London, p. 196.

4 Lengthy footnotes suggest that your essay has not been planned with sufficient care, and they break the flow of the text for your reader. In such cases, ask yourself if the footnote information is really necessary. If it is, consider whether the information should be incorporated into the assignment or placed as an appendix to the text.

5 The quotation or paraphrase may be a word or phrase, a sentence or a paragraph.

CHAPTER 16

LEARNING FROM EVALUATION

If you want to learn to speak Italian, you learn more quickly if you live among Italians. You can evaluate your pronunciation constantly by comparing it with what you hear, and you receive instant feedback when you practise your new language skills.

If you want to take a more effective part in discussion groups, you need frequent practice in talking and listening in groups. At the same time, you need to reflect on your strengths and weaknesses as a group member, and how to improve. You can then evaluate your participation and make more use of any feedback you receive from other people in a group.

In both these instances, reflection, evaluation and feedback are fundamental to your learning. Part of the evaluation you need to do for yourself, for example, comparing your pronunciation or evaluating your group participation. On the basis of what you want to learn you appraise your learning so that your goals and your strengths and weaknesses emerge more clearly. You may discover, for example, that you want to learn more colloquial Italian so you can take part in day-to-day conversations, or you may decide that in discussions you need to practise listening carefully to other people. These discoveries provide you with further criteria for reflecting on and evaluating what you learn—and so the learning process continues.

> This chapter emphasises that evaluation—whether your own or other people's—should help rather than hinder the process of your learning. The chapter looks at the purposes of evaluation, at who evaluates your learning and how this is carried out by feedback and recorded assessment. In conclusion, we list some of the assumptions underlying the evaluation of your formal learning.

In your formal learning you both give and receive responses. If a friend asks for helpful comments on an essay, what sort of comments might you make? You could respond with the first thoughts that come into your head. You might write down your reactions in detail, confine yourself to a few pithy statements at the end of the essay, or discuss your comments with your friend. If you do discuss your comments, you will probably modify some of your criticisms as you come to understand more clearly what your friend was trying to achieve. And if you don't already realise it, you will soon come to know that your responses are subjective—they come from your preferences and beliefs which arise from your personal experiences of learning in particular cultures. Do you believe that you know how 'good' essays should be written? If you judge your friend's work according to a particular model of what is desirable in essay writing, you need to explain this model so that your friend can accept or reject it. Your comments will be more useful if you make it clear that you are giving personal reactions to the work.

When you are in a situation where your understanding of a topic is to be assessed, how would you prefer to prove what you know? What would you submit: writing you have done, other people's comments on your work, your own evaluation? Could this evidence adequately demonstrate what you have learnt? You might want to discuss what you know with the people assessing you, or to take an exam on the topic. What particular aspects of your learning would you want to be tested? Who do you think could best assess these? Answering these questions involves thinking about your reasons for learning. These reflections in turn might lead you to ask if you wanted or needed someone else to assess your knowledge at all, and to ask 'What are the purposes of evaluation?'.

Why evaluation?

Your objectives

One explicit purpose attributed to formal evaluation is to help you learn further, to help you progress towards your objectives (see 'Why remember?' Chapter 5). Being able to ask for and use evaluation and feedback requires that you reflect on your purposes for undertaking an assignment or a course, and about why you want to learn. Think about what you want to learn, and ask yourself how and when you want to learn. These questions are often too complex to answer fully, but unless you are content mostly to follow the goals other people set for you, you need to consider them seriously. Your purposes will probably evolve further during your learning, so re-formulate them as this happens. If your objectives are clear, you can use them as criteria to evaluate whether, what and how well you are learning.

You are likely to modify your abilities or behaviour or ideas according to the responses and evaluation you receive when you try to communicate and practise what you are learning. These changes may be slight, for instance when you learn how to pronounce a word more accurately; or they may be a new cornerstone in your learning, for instance if you gain a significant new insight into how people behave in groups. The feedback you have received then becomes an integral part of learning according to your objectives. (This contrasts, for example, with an exam at the end of a course which tests your knowledge according to others' objectives and from which you gain no feedback.)

However, sometimes you don't have enough experience and knowledge to make use of the information in a response you are given, and at other times you reject feedback because it 'feels wrong' or doesn't fit with your knowledge or world view. Being able to use other people's responses to your learning depends on being ready for them.

Proving your knowledge

A schoolgirl answered the question 'In what countries are elephants found?'
'Elephants are very large and intelligent animals, and are seldom lost.'
(James Agate)

Another explicit purpose of formal evaluation is proving your knowledge to satisfy other people's objectives. These people are usually teachers who directly assess your work, and they also include academic and administrative committees within a university or college, professional bodies, and prospective employers. Their objectives are grounded in particular cultural expectations of higher education.

When you begin a program, course, or assignment, the objectives your teachers have planned for it should be clearly formulated. These objectives should preferably be set down in writing so you can refer to them, and you should be able to discuss them with your teachers and other students. When teachers don't set out clear objectives, this may be because they are unaware of them beforehand and/or because they have not thought them through in detail. Teachers may also choose to conceal their aims. For example, early in a course you may be given a written assignment to introduce you to a basic area of knowledge and at the same time to diagnose your writing abilities. To test you more 'effectively' you may not be told about the second objective.

Like you, teachers often develop new objectives as a program or course progresses, perhaps as implicit purposes become obvious or in response to the particular group of students taking the course. As new objectives emerge, they should be discussed with you. To decide whether or not you accept your teachers' objectives, be clear about your own.

Teachers often use their evaluation to judge if you are ready to move on to what they consider more difficult material. This use of evaluation is important in subjects which teach a sequence of physical skills, where a thorough knowledge of the preliminary steps is necessary to cope with the more demanding ones. This sequential model is often applied to intellectual learning, and sequences are constructed according to particular models of a body of knowledge. For example, unless you understand and can do what a teacher defines as elementary grammar, you are not permitted to move to more advanced language courses. These sequences are not necessary for you to learn a subject—they are not inherent in the material. You can take structured courses in Italian which formally evaluate your learning at various stages; but you can learn Italian by living in Italy and immersing yourself in the language.

> ... reading, unlike dancing, is not a muscular act, and it is a serious mistake to treat it like one. The dance master must stretch and strengthen the student's muscles so that the student may make the next movement, and without injury. But one cannot injure oneself with a difficult thought. (*John Holt*)

Who evaluates your learning?

It is much more difficult to judge oneself than to judge others. (*A. de Saint-Exupéry*)

Who gives you feedback on your learning?

Who formally assesses your work?

You should be the first person to evaluate your work. Make your evaluation more than a passing thought or a casual comment to a friend. Take time to reflect. Compare what you have learnt with your objectives and with the aims of a program, course or assignment. Other people can help you reach your objectives by evaluating your learning with these objectives in mind. However, you should be the person who knows your objectives, abilities and previous learning best, so by these criteria you are the best person to decide how well you are learning. If when you hand in an assignment you also submit a brief written evaluation of the piece, your teacher is more able to provide you with comments to help further your learning.

A discussion or study group to which you belong can give you feedback on work such as an essay plan or a seminar presentation (see 'Share your writing', Chapter 12). The group may formally assess some or all of your work. This alternative to more traditional assessment requires thorough planning to work well, but people in groups which undertake this collective responsibility gain a great deal from their involvement in each other's learning. If you are willing to have your world view with its biases and assumptions challenged you might actively seek comments from a group with a diversity of ideas.

An adviser whom you seek out to be your sounding board can provide you with help ranging from correcting spelling errors in a report to giving a detailed critique of a major assignment. This adviser might be a sympathetic teacher, a learning adviser, a language adviser, a member of an online study group, a student who has previously taken the course, or a friend.

A teacher with whom you work in a course is usually responsible for formally assessing your work, sometimes in collaboration with you or other teaching staff. The amount of informal feedback teachers give you varies according to their teaching styles—and to your willingness to ask for comments.

> I wrote my name at the top of the page. I wrote down the number of the question '1'. After much reflection, I put a bracket around it thus '(1)'. But thereafter I could not think of anything connected with it that was either relevant or true. ... It was from these slender indications of scholarship that Mr Welldon drew the conclusion that I was worthy to pass into Harrow. It is very much to his credit. (*Winston Churchill*)

Ideally the person who comments on your writing and work should be someone you find stimulating as a thinker. They should also be someone you respect, whether or not they share many of your assumptions and beliefs. Your commentator also needs to be easily accessible. Your official teacher may be difficult to find or talk to, or may give you little or no feedback on your work. Make an appointment or send an e-mail indicating the timeframe in which a reply would be useful to you. Formulate a clear question or idea to discuss, and ask for comments on particular aspects of your work (see 'Approaching teachers', Chapter 3). If your attempts don't change the situation, find another person or group of people with whom you can discuss your learning. If your teacher is the person who formally assesses your work, you still need to be prepared to approach her or him if you want to discuss or question an assessment you are given.

How is your learning evaluated?

Your own evaluation

Making your own written evaluation of your work enables you to look at your learning in relation to what an assignment, course or program has given you and what you have put into it. Since your life cannot be neatly segmented as if it was an orange, in a self-evaluation for a particular subject or piece of work you inevitably comment on your informal learning, on your approach to studying, and on the relevance of other work or other courses.

This may sound like a lot of writing. In fact self-evaluations can vary in length from a couple of paragraphs about a specific assignment to several typewritten pages about a course to three months of diary entries about your tertiary study. The guidelines in Table 16.1 were used by students preparing a written self-evaluation for a half-hour discussion with their teacher at the end of a course. They may suggest to you some ideas for evaluating your own learning.

You might choose to build up a learning portfolio during your formal education. This can give you a sense of how your learning develops, and can serve as a file from which to choose material when applying for entry to a particular course, an honours or postgraduate program, or a future job.

What might you include in a learning portfolio?

- Items you have written about yourself as a learner—your aims, your questions, your enthusiasms (see 'Learning journals or logs', Chapter 12). Your self-evaluations are an important part of this.
- Selected pieces of work you have completed, along with comments and assessments by yourself or others.
- Material connected with you as a learner, material such as drawings you have done in response to an idea, items of information you want to follow up, articles which have been particularly significant for you.
- Descriptions of your involvement in a paid job or voluntary work which is an important part of your learning.

  His [sic] 'noteworthy contribution' is an essential step demonstrating a student's readiness for a degree. This may be a work of art, a research finding, or a community service. It will be intended to show that the candidate for a degree is more than a consumer of what earlier scholars, creative artists, and social leaders have given to him [sic]. (*University Without Walls*)

Table 16.1   A self-evaluation

Imagine you are writing for someone you will meet in the future. This unknown person wants to know about you and your work during the course.

- What were your goals when you started the course?
- What strengths did you feel you possessed?
- What were your weaknesses?
- How did you apply your strengths?
- How did you try to overcome your weaknesses?
- What work did you accomplish in quality and quantity (for example, in assignments or for tutorials)?
- How much recommended reading did you do for the course and for tutorials?
- What reading did you do beyond recommended readings (author, title, and any comments)?
- What ideas came from your 'outside' reading, and how did they relate to the course?
- What do you feel you learned:
  - about tutorials
  - about university or college
  - about yourself
  - about improving your ability to learn, and
  - about directions you want to pursue in future learning?

A self-evaluation should not be a compilation of your real or imagined shortcomings, or a prosaic listing of the number of books read and lectures attended. Write about your strengths as well as your weaknesses. Evaluate your learning so that if you read the evaluation again in a couple of years' time it would tell you about this one aspect of yourself. Your evaluation is not a formal course assignment to be judged, and will be next-to-worthless if you are not honest with and about yourself.

Other people's evaluations

Imagine what you would do in one of the following situations, and discuss this with friends if you can.

- You have spent two weeks carefully preparing and writing an assignment. When it is returned, you skim through the pages and find the only comment on the final page—'Pass. Satisfactory work'. You would like to ask the tutor for further comment but don't feel as if you know him well enough. What do you do?
- If asked to record an assessment of a friend's essay in an official student file, on what would you base your assessment?
- You are in your first year at university or college, and you are told that selected first year courses will be assessed only on a Pass/Fail basis. How does this assessment method affect your choice of courses?

Your teacher may give you feedback during a course to help you improve (formative assessment), or they will give you an assessment which will contribute to your final grade (summative assessment). Feedback may be officially recorded or informal and unrecorded.

1 Unrecorded feedback

A person giving you feedback on your learning should give you constructive comments on both the strengths and the weaknesses as they perceive them, rather than merely demonstrating your seeming inadequacies or rating your work according to apparently 'objective' criteria. You may not be ready to understand and use all such comments, but you should be able to find them when you need them and you should be able to decide how detailed any responses need to be. Ask for the feedback you want—you can't expect a teacher to know this exactly. If possible, ask for feedback from the person you think might give you the most useful responses for a specific piece of work.

What form might feedback and comments take? Ideally this depends mostly on what you need. In formal education, the comments might be written or oral. They might be given ad hoc, or structured according to specific criteria or the requirements of situations such as a seminar. They might be part of a required individual consultation with your teacher at the end of a course, or given when an assignment is returned to you. In online courses you might receive feedback from an e-mail discussion list or when working collaboratively on the draft of an assignment.

Formative feedback needs to be given in a way you understand. For example, if you ask for an idea to be clarified, you need an explanation which gives you more information but doesn't overwhelm you with detail, or if you have used a word inaccurately, you need to see it in different contexts so that you understand its correct meaning.

Feedback is most useful if given immediately or when you want it. For example:

- if a friend shows you how to throw a frisbee after you have made several unsuccessful attempts
- if a teacher gives you useful hints when you are attempting to remember the proof of a theorem, or
- if you ask for comments and discussion on a seminar paper immediately after delivering it.

When a batch of work is due your teacher should have set aside time for commenting in some detail on each piece submitted; your responsibility is to hand the work in on time. Ask your teacher when your work will probably be available. If it hasn't been returned by this time, ask again when you can expect it back. It is particularly important to ask for prompt comments if you need them to proceed with your next assignment, or if you are a distance student for whom the return of work is already slow because of mailing time.

2 Recorded assessment

> For most of the students, the competitive grade has come to be the
> essence. The naive teacher points to the beauty of the subject and the
> ingenuity of the research; the shrewd student asks if he is responsible for
> that on the final exam. (*Paul Goodman*)

Recorded assessment may include formal, structured comments, but more usually it consists of a letter grade, a percentage or a pass/fail mark. The effect of grades and percentages on students' learning is controversial. Some people argue that grades and percentages enable student performances to be ranked more efficiently and objectively and that future employers will look only at grades and ignore comments. However, others argue that grading creates pressures which hinder learning, and that at least some aspects of student learning (such as discussion group participation or introductory courses) should not be graded. Some educational theorists argue that students should have a substantial input into any recorded assessment of their own learning.

Recorded summative assessment may be based on continuous assessment and/or on a major final paper or exam. 'Continuous assessment' refers to frequent cumulative assessments of your learning by methods such as weekly laboratory reports, regular seminar papers, monthly assignments or a combination of these. It may be used on its own or in combination with a major final assessment.

Educators debate the value of both forms of assessment. For example, if your work is assessed only or mostly at the end of a course, you may receive little feedback on your learning during a course, you have no formal indication of your progress until the end, and it is difficult to convey your total understanding of a subject in one final assessment.

Criteria and standards

When teachers evaluate your learning, they usually do so in comparison with certain criteria. These include:

- your previous knowledge or work in an area
- the work of other students on a topic or subject area
- specific standards determined by one or more of the teachers involved in a course
- the educational/cultural models and preferences of an individual teacher who directly assesses your work, and
- the requirements of professional organisations.

As well as academic standards, the evaluation of your work is shaped by administrative requirements. These may include demands for assessment methods which require minimum staff time or for results which can be recorded in a particular computer format. They may reflect a desire to conform to practices in other institutions and the implicit expectations of employers and professional organisations.

For each program, course or assignment, you need to know how you are to be assessed and the standard you are expected to reach to pass or achieve a particular grade or percentage.

You need to know as early as possible:

- what work you are expected to complete, and when
- whether you must pass each assignment in a course (or each course in a program), or whether you can fail one or two of the individual assignments/courses and still gain an overall pass
- whether results are given as a Pass/Fail, a grade, a percentage and/or comments
- who assesses your work
- what degree of choice you have in the four previous points
- whether you are able or expected to contribute to the assessment of your work, and
- whether you can appeal against or record a dissent from an assessment in your official file and if so how.

The academic criteria used to arrive at a recorded assessment should reflect the objectives of an institution, a program, a course and an assignment (see 'Expectations of assignments', Chapter 6). For example, if you are expected to display knowledge about a particular topic or to write cogently, the assessment criteria should explicitly take account of this. Such criteria should be available to you so that you can check them against your objectives, know what is expected of you, and plan your work schedule ahead of time.

> ... students have to play an academic game to succeed. The rules of this game are determined by personal and organisational requirements of the course as they see them. These perceived requirements frequently conflict with aims explicitly stated by teachers. Teachers say they want students to have critical minds, but they feel threatened if they do. Teachers say they like students to write thoughtful answers in examinations, but they award marks on the basis on regurgitated 'facts'. (*Donald Bligh et al.*)

Recorded assessment based on other people's aims inevitably means that you have to do a certain amount of guessing about what you are expected to learn. And when you are also required to compete with other students in your guessing, it is only fair that the rules of this guessing game are made as explicit as possible. This is particularly important where teachers have more than one criterion for assessment. For example, an assignment may be graded according to the content you select and your use of quotations and general writing style. If the result is recorded by a single letter grade, the letter you are given can't tell you how well you have done on each of the criteria. Neither does it indicate how your teacher averaged or added up your performance for each criterion to arrive at a single grade. To learn from evaluation it is vital that you know explicitly why your teacher chose the particular letter grade, and that you receive comments or grades for each of the criteria involved. If recorded assessments are to mean anything useful to you, they must be accompanied by detailed comments. Hopefully, recorded assessments are formalities which follow on from the comments you are given, but this seems rarely to be the case. Why?

The criteria used in assessment may be explicitly set out, widely accepted and clearly defined in an individual teacher's mind, but this doesn't make the use of these criteria objective. In practice, the individual teacher adopts some of the cultural and discipline-based guidelines used for evaluating learning in an area and combines these with a personal preference for certain academic conventions. And when applying these methods and criteria to your work, a teacher arrives at a result partly because of the feeling that your work evokes at the time. All students are familiar with the game of trying to uncover the subjective approaches that each teacher brings to assessment—and with the hope that their particular piece of work appears at the most favourable place in the pile of assignments to be marked.

> After some years it began to happen that I would find myself in the middle of writing a comment and begin to wonder whether it could really be trusted, whether it was really useful. Perhaps I was telling someone about his flowery and wordy diction. His diction was indeed wordy and would be called flowery. But I began to wonder if this was *why* I was complaining about it. I sometimes found myself suspecting it was something else I couldn't put my finger on that bothered me but floweriness was more available. If I were in a different mood or the paper were in a different place in the stack, perhaps I wouldn't have made the comment I did. (*Peter Elbow*)

Some underlying assumptions

When assessing your work, individual teachers bring to the evaluation process many assumptions which are integral to a particular educational culture (see 'Tertiary institutions and you', Chapter 3). Since these assumptions are often not made explicit, it may not seem necessary or desirable for you to understand or question them. If you come from another educational system, you might find it more difficult to uncover these implicit biases. However, understanding the cultural assumptions underlying evaluation can demystify the evaluation process; and questioning them can help you use evaluation for your learning purposes instead of blindly following someone else's. What are some of these assumptions?

Students should be evaluated by formal institutions

> I look upon social and professional life as a continuous examination ... In ordinary scholastic examinations marks are allotted in stated proportions to various specified subjects ... The world in the same way, but almost

unconsciously, allots marks to men [*sic*]. It gives them for originality of conception, for enterprise, for activity and energy ... and much besides of general value, as well as for more specially professional merits ... Those who have gained most of these tacit marks are ranked, by the common judgement of the leaders of opinion, as the foremost men [*sic*] of their day. (*Francis Galton*)

In Western society, compulsory education in primary and secondary schools is seen as inevitable and desirable. As part of this belief, it is assumed that one of the purposes of formal education is to evaluate and grade students according to the knowledge they are judged to have acquired and the characteristics they are deemed to have displayed. Teachers, for example, may define a child as 'hyperactive', 'promising', 'lazy', 'a problem child', 'a tomboy', or 'too sensitive', or a child may be placed in stream A or stream E, or in a 'professional' or 'academic excellence' class.

In universities and colleges, evaluation and grading is continued in a specialised way. Tertiary education is often seen in itself as desirable in terms of intellectual and social status, if not always in terms of usefulness, and this is reflected in approaches to evaluation. Where and what you study has a further effect on this status. Are you attending a technical college or a relatively new university? Are you training as a surgeon or a primary school teacher or an accountant? Are you planning to do postgraduate work, or are you studying for a diploma? Courses such as veterinary science or commerce may be seen as 'relevant', or as 'too job-oriented'. Subjects such as politics and literature are sometimes seen as 'real' and 'people-oriented', and sometimes as 'airy-fairy'. The area in which you enrol is often taken as an indicator of your status.

> 'I've been to a day-school, too,' said Alice. 'You needn't be so proud as all that.'
> 'With extras?' asked the Mock Turtle, a little anxiously.
> 'Yes,' said Alice: 'we learned French and music.'
> 'And washing?' said the Mock Turtle.
> 'Certainly not!' said Alice indignantly.
> 'Ah! Then yours wasn't a really good school,' said the Mock Turtle in a tone of great relief. (*Lewis Carroll*)

Evaluation is best done by teachers

In universities and colleges, it is usually assumed that people who have researched and published in a subject can also teach that subject, whether or not they are trained as teachers. It is further assumed that teachers can and should evaluate students' learning in the subject. Correspondingly, any evaluation you as a student make of your own formal learning is usually seen as less satisfactory than a teacher's, or your evaluation is ignored altogether.

Who decides what is worth learning and why and how this learning is to be evaluated? These decisions are made by an individual teacher, a group of teachers, administrators, other educational institutions or—at a fundamental level—society in general. An individual teacher may decide if you deserve to pass a course which leads to your becoming a doctor; but that teacher is mostly making that decision on behalf of other people. Those people include a professional medical association which sets down standards for doctors, patients who expect certain skills in doctors, and government bodies which make decisions about the number of doctors needed.

Learning can be reliably graded

Along with the assumption that teachers are the best people to evaluate your learning goes the assumption that there are reliable methods which teachers can administer to grade learning, methods such as examinations and tests, essays and reports. Many people disagree about the value of these methods, but they are used frequently because they are familiar and because they produce quantitative 'results'. Too little consideration is given to whether the methods test what they are supposed to, or to alternatives such as self-evaluation or collaborative assessment. Very little thought is given to whether learning can or should be graded at all.

Evaluation can be objective

> Objectivity, in short, has the logical status of a myth: it builds up one sense of reality rather than others. It is a myth whose attainment and maintenance demands of its subjects a rigorous and continued asceticism ... (*Michael Novak*)

It is impossible for any human to be objective, yet humans make decisions about the purposes, methods and criteria of evaluation and often assume that they are being objective. In practice their decisions are based on an array of beliefs and assumptions such as what 'education' can be, what type of student is being assessed, what a university or college should be, which knowledge is valuable, and whether such knowledge can or should be evaluated.

The criteria by which your learning is evaluated may appear to you to be objective. These criteria are often taken for granted, and most people who use them arrive at results they believe to be valid. These criteria appear even more objective when they are elaborated in a system of precedents and percentages, examinations and 'weighted averages', 'full-time equivalent students' and confidential files. How else, it is argued, is a teacher or employer to know the 'good' students unless students have mostly A's or firsts on an official record, unless a student has produced a thesis on an acceptable topic, or has completed all the work set for a course? It is easier and more 'economical' in the short term to deal with the results of a system than with complex individuals. But problems arise when evaluation is claimed to be purely objective, or if the stated bases of evaluation differ from what students see as the real bases. As a student you need the opportunity to disagree with subjective assessments of your learning and to have an impact on these assessments.

Some teachers help with this because they acknowledge and attempt to spell out the assumptions, criteria, biases and beliefs by which they evaluate your learning. They don't assume that a practice which has 'always' been carried out, or which is used 'everywhere else' or is 'efficient' is thereby the best and only valid system. These teachers don't attempt to judge your work by immutable standards of what Physics or History is all about. You as a student then have the opportunity to accept, reject or negotiate these teachers' decisions about your work according to your own reasons and needs for learning.

Experts know when students should fail

What if a piece of your knowledge is formally assessed and you are told that you don't know what you were expected to know—if you are given an E, or a Fail, or 45%? Many students assume that there is little they can do. If you care about that particular area of knowledge, you would probably try to find out what it is that you apparently don't know. You might ask yourself if you agree with the assessment. How would you decide? You could ask for the explicit criteria on which the assessment was based, but even then it could be difficult to decide if you agree unless you are dealing with a tangible physical skill like the ability to walk a straight line. What if you find that you disagree with the criteria? Do you challenge them?

Whatever you do, you will undoubtedly have to handle the implanted idea that you don't know. Do you fight it? Probably not, because teachers are people who know. Do you question a Fail on a university or college paper? Only if you have considerable confidence in your ability to write, to think and to understand, and if you are not overawed by the authority of teachers and institutions. Can you learn from a Fail, apart from the unhappy fact that you have been classed as a failure? If you expected to pass or if you have to pass, you might try to find out why you failed and use this to help you pass. Otherwise you probably accept the verdict, and try again or drop out.

This is the power of evaluation in formal education—that those who lose accept that they deserve to lose. Why? Because all of us are taught from our first day at school that there are experts who know—doctors, judges, priests, scientists, football heroes and test pilots. And teachers are the experts who know when students should pass and when they should fail. We all know that we should learn and to do so we have to go to school and then on to university or college if we want to learn some more. And teachers know what we should learn and when and how and why. As students, our job is to try to find our way through the maze of formal education, to discover the Right way to learn. We develop our own likes and dislikes among individual teachers and subjects, but we don't question the basic rules of the competition.

> School is ... a training for later life not because it teaches the 3 Rs (more or less), but because it instils the essential cultural nightmare fear of failure, envy of success, and absurdity ... (*Jules Henry*)

■ ■ ■ ■ ■

To have been accepted as a student in a tertiary education institution means that you are accepted as a potential winner. The chances are high that as a new student you accepted most of the assumptions, purposes and criteria by which the decision was made. Whether you continue to accept any or all of them is one of the most fundamental decisions you can make as a tertiary student, and depends on how much you question and reflect on what learning is for you.

What are your assumptions about learning and formal education?

What do you want to learn?

How do you want to learn?

Why do you want to learn?

Further reading

Boud, David, 1986, *Implementing student self assessment*, Higher Educational and Research Development Society of Australasia Green Guide, HERDSA, University of New South Wales.

Lindsey, Crawford W., 1988, *Teaching students to teach themselves*, Kogan Page, London.

Rowntree, Derek, 1977, *Assessing students: How shall we know them?* Harper and Row, London.

APPENDIX

Appendix

DISCRIMINATION – SEXIST LANGUAGE AND ATTITUDES

Discrimination legislation has often been concerned mostly with stereotypes based on sex, sexual preference, disability or race. Some other stereotypes commonly perpetuated in our culture relate to a person's age, religion, politics, economic circumstances and occupation. Trying to counter such stereotypes may been dismissed as 'politically correct'. However, in any society there are always a range of discourses which constrain and enable ways of speaking and writing; and some of these discourses are more privileged than others and more difficult to identify. The discourses labelled 'politically correct' are among those developed by less powerful groups (such as women and Aboriginals) as part of their attempts to gain more equal opportunities.

Using language which depicts people according to stereotypes is undesirable for a couple of reasons.

1 It shows a lack of awareness of our biases and prejudices. We can never be totally objective, and it is essential to our learning and communicating that we are as honest as possible about our particular forms of subjectivity.
2 It reveals insufficient thought and care about what we are communicating. Some manifestations of the shoddy use of language are unsupported generalisations, terms which are not defined clearly, and clichés.
   • 'Australians are easy-going'. Does this apply to all, most, many or a few? Has this general statement been supported and explained?
   • In 'a neurotic woman' or 'the average Italian'; 'neurotic' and 'average' are both terms which have precise meanings in certain disciplines. Has their meaning in the particular context been defined?
   • The phrase 'a career woman' is sometimes used to describe a woman seriously interested in her work, or 'a dole bludger' to describe someone who is unemployed. Why have these clichés been used?

In this appendix we look at sexist language and attitudes as an example of discrimination.

Avoiding sexist language

Sexist language is based on stereotypes which assume that being biologically male or female implies a whole range of associated characteristics. Occasionally it is relevant to describe a woman as petite or a man as husky, or to describe a female person as someone's wife or mother; but all too often adjectives such as these form part of a description in which they are irrelevant.

'Janet Smith, a petite brunette, has just become the first woman truck driver for the company.'

'Henry Jones, a husky ex-footballer, today graduated as a male nurse.'

One useful test for sexist language is to substitute mention of a woman where a man is mentioned and vice versa. Would you write 'Fred Smith, a tall redhead who is married to a typist, was today awarded his second gold medal'? How do you react to reading 'The stockbroker should at all times protect her clients' interests'?

Pronouns—'he'? 'him'? 'his'?

'He' is commonly used to refer to both females and males; for example, 'The best time to teach a child maths is when he is about 2 years old.' This convention limits our view of reality. Studies have shown that children literally think of a male when they read or hear the word 'he', and many people who argue for the use of 'he' as a convenient shorthand to include both sexes object to the suggestion that 'she' might serve the same purpose. There are alternatives to using only 'he', 'him', and 'his'.

- Change from singular to plural:
  This monograph is for teachers concerned with improving their communication with their students ... The intention of the authors is to share experiences with teachers who may find some of them helpful in their own situations.
- Re-word to eliminate unnecessary gender pronouns:
  This monograph is for a teacher concerned with improving communication with students ... The intention of the authors is to share experiences so that a reader may find some of them helpful in teaching situations.
- Replace the masculine pronoun with 'he or she', 'him or her', 'her or his', or with 'he/she', or 's/he', or with 'one' or 'you'.

'Man'?

The word 'man' has an ambiguous double usage—to refer to a male person and to describe humanity in general. As with the use of 'he', the word 'man' creates a male image. When we read of 'man the hunter' we visualise a male adult and forget about the women (and children and elderly people) who are supposedly part of the total picture.

Instead of:	Consider:
man or mankind	humanity, human beings, people, the human race, men and women
manpower	human resources, human energy, workers, workforce
the man in the street	a typical person, the average person, lay person
manmade	synthetic, artificial, manufactured, constructed
chairman	chairperson, the chair, leader, co-ordinator, convenor.

Apples are apples and oranges are oranges; but apples and oranges are fruit. (*Without Bias*)

'A man's job'? 'Woman's work'?

Our language is based on assumptions, frequently outdated, about the occupations of women and men (for example, nurses are assumed to be female and doctors male). Women are categorised primarily as mothers and wives, despite the high proportion of women who are in the paid workforce. We read newspaper headlines such as 'Rebel mum of three suicides in cell' to describe the prison death of a prominent political activist and journalist; or 'Dr Samuel Keep, a leading physician, and his wife Margaret' is used to introduce two doctors who are married. Women should be treated as people in their own right, and women in traditionally masculine fields (or men in traditionally feminine fields) should not be singled out.

Instead of:	Consider:
'Anna Clarke, career girl' to describe a woman who takes her work seriously	describing the woman's occupation 'Anna Clarke, teacher' or 'Anna Clarke, engineer'
terms such as 'male secretary', 'lady executive' or 'woman doctor'	the terms 'secretary', 'executive' or 'doctor' to apply to both men and women
workmen	worker, labourer, employee or staff member
author or authoress	author
waiter or waitress	steward or attendant
the lady of the house, housewife	the consumer, home maker, housekeeper
cleaning lady, cleaning woman	domestic help, cleaner.

Names

Different attitudes of men and women are reflected in the inconsistent use of forenames and surnames, for example, 'Peter Braithwaite and Miss Smith', 'Braithwaite and Janet Smith'. The use of titles also reveals attitudes, for example, 'Dr White and Alison Black' (instead of 'Dr Black'). One of the most common examples of discrimination by title is that the title 'Mr' refers to both married and single men while the terms 'Mrs' and 'Miss' are used for women, thus assuming that marital status should be an important part of a woman's identity, but not a man's.

Instead of:	Consider:
Peter Braithwaite and Miss Smith	Mr Braithwaite and Ms Smith, or Peter Braithwaite and Janet Smith
'Dr Tom Jones and Ms Margot Thomas recently published a book on marine biology. Margot is now doing further research on this topic. Dr Jones is acting as her assistant.'	'Ms Margot Thomas and Dr Tom Jones recently published a book on marine biology. Ms Thomas is now doing further research on this topic. Dr Jones is acting as her assistant.'

Put-downs

Patronising descriptions of women are unnecessary and are often clichés.

Instead of:	Consider:
the girls, the ladies, the fair sex, the weaker sex	the women
the missus, the wife, the little lady, the better half	wife (or refer to the woman concerned by her name)
chicks, birds, girls	girls (for younger women), women
libbers	feminists, liberationists

- Issues that seriously concern women should not be considered as trivial or funny, for example, the use of 'Ms', discrimination in employment, or rape.
- Jokes which are based on stereotypes of both women and men are offensive to many people, for example, jokes about incompetent women drivers, frustrated spinsters, gossiping housewives, men-hating 'women's libbers', hen-pecked husbands, helpless house-husbands, effeminate males.
- Referring to 'men and ladies' instead of 'men and women' or 'ladies and gentlemen' is discriminatory.
- Don't always refer to 'men and women' or 'he and she'; use 'women and men' or 'she and he' as well.
- Avoid talking about 'man and wife'; instead use 'partners', 'husband and wife', 'a man and a woman' or 'a couple'.

    Identity
    'Who's she?' they asked
    and straight away
    I answered back,
    'She's Brian's wife'.

Why say it so?
Why not just say
'She's Josephine'?
A rose by any name
should smell as sweet.
But Josephine's a sweeter name
by far, than
'Brian's wife'
or 'Jenny's mum'
or 'Noelene's friend'. (*Brian's Wife Jenny's Mum*)

Male and female characteristics

- Instead of assuming that only women can be gentle, compassionate or sensitive and only men can be decisive, logical, assertive, strong, or adventurous, think of these qualities as human rather than sex-based. Similarly, avoid the assumption that only women are passive, helpless or emotional and only men are insensitive, angry or ruthless.
- Women who don't comply with the stereotype of a passive female and men who don't conform to the image of an aggressive male are often described in a negative way.

Instead of:	Consider:
a pushy woman	a powerful woman
a gossiping woman	a talkative woman
an effeminate man	a gentle man
an hysterical woman	a woman who is upset
an aggressive woman	an assertive woman

Avoiding sexist attitudes

Sexist language is a subtly pervasive yet tangible way of perpetuating stereotypes. Sexist attitudes are equally pervasive and subtle. The following are some instances of sexist attitudes which you are likely to find in written material.

- **The 'invisible woman'** attitude occurs when women as part of a group of people or society are ignored or rarely included in writings about that group or society. For example:
  - in writings on human evolution, where only hunting societies and the activities of male homo sapiens are considered, with little or no reference to the female of the species
  - in gender-blind statistics which give figures for the amount of unpaid domestic work but fail to break these figures down according to gender

- in children's books, where the majority of characters in stories and illustrations are often male, and
  - in anthologies, where most or all of the writers represented are male.
- The **'token woman'** position is evident when individual women are described because they are unusual but the majority of women are still ignored. This occurs, for example in history texts which include descriptions of the life of a woman who is prominent as a social reformer (such as Elizabeth Fry) or a pioneer in a traditionally male field (such as Elizabeth Blackwell), but which neglect the 'ordinary' female contemporaries of these women.
- The **'patronised woman'** approach occurs when a special section is allocated to women without a corresponding section for men, for example, a book index which has an entry under 'Women' but none under 'Men'.
- **Stereotypes** of women and men are common. Examples include:
  - sociology texts which assume that women are wives and mothers and that men are breadwinners, and
  - career information brochures which assume that women are nurses and men are doctors, or that females have no serious work interests.

Instances of these attitudes can also be found when discrimination is based on grounds other than sex. For example, the 'invisible' ethnic group; the invisibility of people in poverty; the 'token' black or 'working-class' representative; the patronised handicapped person or religious sect; stereotypes of homosexuals or of elderly people or of socialists.

■ ■ ■ ■ ■

In writing, reading and speaking, being aware of discriminatory attitudes or language in ourselves and in others requires that we question and evaluate what is communicated. The discriminatory thought patterns of many academic disciplines need to be redressed, but these changes are not just exercises to be followed in the interests of scholarly rigour. They are changes which involve an awareness of the world views that we bring to our learning, changes in who we are and how we see the other human beings with whom we live. Such changes can only be achieved by consistent and conscious effort because our discriminatory attitudes and language are part of who we have learned to be.

Further reading

Curriculum Development Centre, 1975, *Guidelines for writers*, CDC, Canberra.

Hill, Robert, (n.d.) 'Understanding inequality' in Terry Lovat (ed.), *People, culture and change*, Social Science Press, Wentworth Falls.

International Association of Business Communicators, 1977, *Without bias: A guidebook for nondiscriminatory communication*, IABC, San Francisco.

Lakoff, Robin, 1975, *Language and woman's place*, Harper and Row, New York.

McGraw-Hill Book Company, 1974, *Guidelines for equal treatment of the sexes*, McGraw-Hill, New York.

Miller, C. & Swift, K., 1981, *The handbook of non-sexist writing for writers, editors and speakers*, Women's Press. London.

Poynton, Cate, 1985, *Language and gender: Making the difference*, Deakin University Press, Geelong, Victoria.

Random House, 1976, *Random House guidelines for multi-ethnic nonsexist survey*, Random House, New York.

QUOTATION SOURCES

1 You

Gay Gaer Luce, 1973, *Body time: The natural rhythms of the body*, Paladin, St. Albans, England, p. 177.

Evelyn Waugh, 1928, *Decline and fall*, Chapman and Hall, London, p. 143.

Virginia Woolf, 1929, *A room of one's own*, Harcourt, Brace and World, New York, p. 18.

Gayle Olinekova, 1982, *Go for it*, Simon and Schuster, New York, p. 142.

Fred Morgan, 1972, *Here and now II: An approach to writing through perception*, Harcourt Brace Jovanovich, New York, p. 3.

Liz Carpenter, 1977, in 'The all-American complaint "If I only had the time..." ', *Ms*, January, p. 48.

Marie Bashkirtseff, quoted in Jean Webster, 1912, *Daddy-long legs*, Scholastic Inc., Apple Paperbacks, New York, p. 75.

Peter Hoeg, 1993, *Miss Smilla's feeling for snow*, Flamingo, Harper Collins. p. 9.

Michel Foucault, quoted in Rux Martin, 1988, 'Truth, power, self: An interview with Michel Foucault', October 25, 1982. In L.H. Martin, H. Gutman & P.H. Hutton, (eds), *Technologies of the self: A seminar with Michel Foucault*, Amherst The University of Massachusetts Press, Massachusetts, p. 14.

S.B. Simon, L.W. Howe & H. Kirschenbaum, 1972, *Values clarification: A handbook of practical strategies for teachers and students*, Hart Publishing, New York, pp. 13–14.

Jean Webster, 1912, *Daddy-long-legs*, Scholastic Inc., Apple Paperbacks, New York, p. 22.

Eight-year old girl, in Hazel Edwards (ed.), 1975, *Women returning to study*, Primary Education, Richmond, Victoria, p. 43.

Margaret Norton, in Allan Hall (ed.), 'Worse verse' from the 'Look!' pages of *The Sunday Times*, Times Newspapers, London, undated and not paginated.

William Shakespeare, *Hamlet*, Act I, Scene iii, p. 58.

2 Planning when and how you study

Jerome K. Jerome, 1947, *The idle thoughts of an idle fellow*, J.W. Arrowsmith, Bristol, p. 51.

Western proverb.

Norton Juster, 1962, *The phantom tollbooth*, William Collins, London, p. 24.

Anon.

Edwin C. Bliss, 1977, *Getting things done: The ABCs of time management*, Macmillan, Melbourne, pp. 32–3.

Lewis Carroll, 1970, *The annotated Alice: Alice's adventures in wonderland and through the looking-glass*, revised edn, Penguin Middlesex, p. 304.

Vivienne, in Hazel Edwards, p. 26.

Lewis Carroll, p. 322.

Barbara Sher, 1979, *Wishcraft: How to get what you really want*, Ballantine Books, New York, p. 213.

3 Becoming an independent student

Craig McInnis & Richard James with Carmel McNaught, 1995, *First year on campus: Diversity in the initial experience of Australian undergraduates*, A commissioned project of the Committe for the Advancement of University Teaching, Centre for the Study of Higher Education, Melbourne University, p. 121.

Ian Lowe, 1990, 'The dying of the light', *The Australian universities review*, vol. 33, nos. 1 and 2.

Harold Taylor, 1969, *Students without teachers*, McGraw-Hill, New York, p. xii.

Craig McInnis, p. 69.

Jean Webster, p. 79.

Stephen D. Brookfield, 1989, *Developing critical thinkers: Challenging adults to explore alternative ways of thinking and acting*, Jossey Bass, San Francisco, p. 14.

Paul Jewell, 1992, 'Snake oil, sophistry and sterile syllogisms', in Paul Jewell (ed.), *On the same premises: Proceedings of the second national conference on reasoning*, Flinders University 1991, Flinders University Press, p. 3.

Stephen D. Brookfield, p.7.

Lewis Carroll, p. 88.

L. Harasim, S.R. Hiltz, L. Teles & M. Turoff, 1996, *Learning networks: A field guide to teaching and learning online*, The MIT Press, Massachusetts Institute of Technology, Cambridge, Massachusetts, p. 3.

Peter Hoeg, p. 298.

Michael Deakin, 1973, *The children on the hill: The story of an extraordinary family*, Quartet Books, London, p. 27.

F.R. Leavis quoted in J. Wyatt, 1990, *Commitment to higher education: Seven west European thinkers on the essence of the university*, Society for Research into Higher Education and Open University Press, Bucks, p. 82

Theodore Roszak, 1996, 'Dumbing us down', *New Internationalist*, Dec 1996, p. 13

E.P. Thompson, 1967, 'Time, work-discipline and industrial capitalism', *Past and present: A journal of historical studies*, vol. 38, December, p. 50.

Michel Foucault in Martin L. H., Gutman, H. & Hutton, P.H., p. 9.

Jean Webster, p. 103.

Peter Hoeg p. 95.

Gwen Wesson (ed.), 1975, *Brian's wife Jenny's mum*, Dove Communications, Blackburn, Victoria, pp. 164–5.

Craig McInnis, p. 47.

JITOL 'What is JITOL?' (online) September, 1997.

4   Asking your own questions

John Holt, 1977, *Instead of education: Ways to help people do things better*, Penguin Books, Middlesex, p. 20.

Brigid Ballard & John Clanchy, 1988, 'Literacy in the University: An "anthropological" approach' in GordonTaylor et al., 1988, *Literacy by degrees*, The Society for Research into Higher Education and the Open University Press, Milton Keynes, Bucks., p. 14.

Donald Sutherland, 1951, *Gertrude Stein: A biography of her work*, Yale University Press, New Haven, p. 203.

Bertrand Russell, 1964, quoted by G.M. Carstairs 'Concepts of insanity in different cultures', in *The listener*, LXXII, 1944, July 30, p. 160.

N.J. Berrill, 1958, *Man's emerging mind*, Dennis Dobson, London, p. 158.

Kurt Vonnegut Jr, 1971, *Cat's cradle*, Victor Gollancz, London, p. 150.

Jules Feiffer, 1963, 'Crawling Arnold, dramatists play service', New York, in J.M. & M.J. Cohen (eds), *A dictionary of modern quotations*, p. 72.

Stephen D. Brookfield, p. 9.

Dylan Thomas, 1954, 'Quite early one morning', New Directions Publishing, New York, quoted in Daniel G. Kozlovsky, *An ecological and evolutionary ethic*, Prentice-Hall, Englewood Cliffs, N.J., p. 7.

Lewis Carroll, p. 251.

Ronald Barnett, 1992, *Improving higher education: Total quality care*, The Society for Research into Higher Education and Open University Press, London, p. 120.

John Holt, *Instead of education*, pp. 87–8.

John Holt, 1969, *How children fail*, Penguin Books, Middlesex, England, p. 166.

Craig McInnis, p. 124.

Crawford W. Lindsey, Jr., 1988, *Teaching students to teach themselves*, Nichols Publishing, New York, pp. 63–4

5 Learning and remembering

Ogden Nash, 1972, 'Who did which? or who indeed?' in *I wouldn't have missed it: Selected poems of Ogden Nash*, Little, Brown and Co., Boston, p. 224.

Sam Keen, 1970, *To a dancing god*, Harper and Row, New York, p. 32.

Lewis Carroll, pp. 137–8.

Julia Hobson, 1996, from an interview for the video *Critical thinking in context*, Murdoch University.

Mark van Doren, quoted in Dave Ellis (ed.), 1994, *Becoming a master student*, 7th edn, Houghton Mifflin, Boston, p. 97.

Lewis Carroll, p. 149.

Patrick O'Brian, 1994, *Testimonies*. Harper Collins, read on audiotape by Patrick Tull, 1996, Stirling Audio, Bath, UK.

Hermann Hesse, source unknown.

Patsy Hallen, 1996, from an interview for the video *Critical thinking in context* quoted in the booklet *A teacher's guide to the video*, Murdoch University, p. 39.

Ronald Barnett, p. 120

J Chaytor, 1945, *From script to print*, other details unknown.

Robert Theobald, 1997, 'The future of work', *Sunday special*, ABC Radio National Sept 14.

Lewis Carroll, pp. 247–8.

Jorge Luis Borges, 1972, 'Funes, the memorious', *A personal anthology*, Picador, London, p. 33.

David Bridges, 'Transferable skills: A philosophical perspective', *Studies in Higher Education*, vol. 18, no. 1, 1993, p. 50.

Jean Webster, p. 82.

6   Choosing and analysing a topic

Lewis Carroll, p. 137.

William Shakespeare, *Henry IV*, Pt I, Scene iii, p. 41.

Norton Juster, p. 17.

Gunter Kress, 1990, 'Two kinds of power', *The English magazine*, vol. 24, Autumn, p.4.

Robert M. Pirsig, 1975, *Zen and the art of motorcycle maintenance*, Bantam Books, New York, p. 166. Originally published by *The Bodley Head*, London.

Marshall McLuhan, 1969, interviewed by Eric Norden 'Playboy Interview: Marshall McLuhan', *Playboy*, March, p. 54.

Lewis Carroll, p. 269.

7   Researching a topic

Theodore Roszak, p. 13.

Zoe Sofoulis, 1992, 'Serendipitous Ventures', *StarGuide: Study techniques and materials*, Murdoch University, Western Australia, p. 21.

David Hawkins, 1973, 'What it means to teach', *Teachers college record*, vol. 75, no. 1, September, p. 11.

Peter Hoeg, p. 120.

Theodore Roszak, p. 12.

Lewis Carroll, p. 86.

John Milton, in *The Oxford dictionary of quotations*, p. 352.

Idries Shah ('Rahimi'), 1974, *Thinkers of the East*, Penguin Books, Middlesex, England, p. 104.

Samuel Johnson, in *The Oxford dictionary of quotations*, p. 276.

8   Using libraries and other information sources

Grant Stone, 1997, Personal conversation.

Edward Gibbon, in *The Oxford dictionary of quotations*, p. 224.

A Librarian, source unknown.

University without walls: First report, Antioch College, Yellow Spring, Ohio, undated, p. 32.

Werner Heisenberg, 1959, *Physics and philosophy: The revolution in modern science*, Allen & Unwin, London, p. 75.

Joan Acker, Kate Barry & Joke Esseveld, 1983, 'Objectivity and truth: problems in doing feminist research', *Women's Studies international forum*, vol. 6, no. 4, pp. 423–35.

Nancy Lane, 1996, *Techniques for student research: A practical guide*, 2nd edn, Addison Wesley Longman, Melbourne, p. 159.

David Rothenburg, 1997, 'Caught in the web', *The Australian*, August 27, p. 40.

Stephen Brookfield, p. 184.

Edmund Carpenter, 1970, 'The new languages', in Edmund Carpenter & Marshall McLuhan (eds), *Explorations in communication: An anthology*, Jonathan Cape, London, p. 163.

Stephen Brookfield, p. 303.

Ronald Firbank, 1961, 'The flower beneath the foot', *The complete Ronald Firbank*, Duckworth, London, p. 500.

Marshall McLuhan, 1967, from the film *This is Marshall McLuhan: The medium is the massage*, USA.

Mike Cooley, 1992, 'Human-centred education' in Chris Bigum & Bill Green (eds), *Understanding the new information technologies in education: A resource for teachers*, Deakin University, Geelong.

9 Reading

W. Somerset Maugham, 1967, *The summing up*, William Heinemann, London, p. 92.

Bronwyn Mellor, Annette Patterson & Marnie O'Neill, 1991, *Reading fiction*, Chalkface Press, Scarborough, W.A. p. 21.

John M. Culkin, 'A schoolman's guide to Marshall McLuhan', *Saturday review*, p. 301.

John Neiwenhausen, 1997, 'Soundbite education', *Ockhams Razor*, ABC Radio National, June 15.

Doris Lessing, *Martha Quest*, 1970, A Plume Book, The New American Library, New York, p. 200.

Linda Harasim, p. 25

John Holt, *Instead of education*, pp. 74–75.

Doris Lessing, p. 28.

Lewis Carroll, p. 191.

Ronald Barnett, p. 39.

Bronwyn Mellor, Annette Patterson & Marnie O'Neill, p. 44.

Francis Bacon, in *The Oxford dictionary of quotations*, p. 27.

Arthur Ransome, 1976, *The autobiography of Arthur Ransome*, Jonathan Cape, London, p. 34.

Idries Shah, 1970, 'A quality must have a vehicle', *The way of the Sufi*, Penguin Books, Middlesex, England, 1974, p. 61.

Samuel Johnson, in *The Oxford dictionary of quotations*, p. 280.

Lewis Carroll, pp. 189–90.

Jean Webster, p. 36.

Lewis Carroll, p. 25.

10 Listening to lectures

Samuel Johnson, source unknown.

Donald A. Bligh, 1972, *What's the use of lectures?* Penguin Education, Penguin Books, Middlesex, England, p. 61.

Lewis Carroll, p. 122.

Lewis Carroll, p 146.

Anon., in *A dictionary of modern quotations*, p. 5.

Enrico Fermi, 1970, quoted in Anthony Smith, *The body*, Penguin Books, Middlesex, England, p. 16.

11 Participating in tutorials and seminars

Linda Harasim, pp. 4–5

Samuel Johnson, in *The Oxford dictionary of quotations*, p. 280.

Linda Harasim, p. 4.

Julia Hobson, 1996.

Lewis Carroll, p. 235.

Narayan, Uma, 1988, 'Working together across differences: Some considerations on emotions and political practice, in *Hypatia* (Summer), p. 38 in Warren, Karen J., 'Rewriting the future: The feminist challenge to the malestream curriculum' in *Feminist teacher*, vol. 4, nos. 2/3.

A student quoted in The Nuffield Foundation, 1976, *Small group teaching: Selected papers*, Group for Research and Innovation in Higher Education, London, p. 123.

Peter Hoeg, p. 37.

Allison Brown, 1997, 'Teaching "big picture" economics' unpublished paper, Murdoch University, p. 6.

Lewis Carroll, p. 158.

Cicero, source unknown.

Anon.

Allison Brown, p. 8.

A student quoted in The Nuffield Foundation, pp. 122–3.

Gwen Wesson, pp. 79–80.

Ronald Barnett, p. 198.

12 Developing your writing

Colette, 1960, *The vagabond*, trans. Enid McLeod, Penguin Books, Middlesex, England, p. 13.

V.A. Howard, 1990, 'Thinking on paper: a philosophers look at writing', in *Varieties of thinking*, Essays from Harvard's Philosophy of Education Research Center, Routledge, New York, p. 84

Kurt Vonnegut, 1980, 'How to write with style', advertisement in *Psychology today*, September, p. 58.

V.A. Howard, p. 91.

Phil Mullins, 1988, 'The fluid word: Word processing and its mental habits', *Thought*, vol. 63 no. 251, December.

Gwen Wesson, p. 109.

Peter Elbow, 1981, *Writing with power*, Oxford University Press, Melbourne, p. 14.

Arthur Ransome, p. 9.

Jim R. Martin, 1985, *Factual writing: Exploring and challenging social reality*, Deakin University Press, Geelong, p. 15.

Kurt Vonnegut, 'How to write with style', p. 58.

Oscar Wilde, 1977, 'The importance of being Earnest', *The portable Oscar Wilde*, Richard Aldington (ed.), Penguin Books, Middlesex, England, p. 481.

Ira Progoff, 'Intensive journal', unpublished handout from The personal growth and creativity program of Dialogue House Associates, 45 West Tenth St., New York, N.Y. 10011.

Anais Nin, 1966, *The diary of Anais Nin 1931–1934*, Gunther Stuhlmann (ed.), A Harvest Book, New York, p. 89.

Peter Elbow, pp. 20–21.

Linda Harasim, pp. 3–4.

13 Writing assignments

Ernest Hemingway, 1965, interviewed by George Plimpton, *Writers at work: The Paris review interviews*, Viking, New York. p. 235.

Francis Quarles, 1979, in *The Oxford dictionary of quotations*, p. 403.

Gwen Wesson, p. 81.

Russell Baker, 1972, 'At Lunch' in Joseph Frank, *You*, Harcourt, Brace, Jovanovich, New York, p. 63.

Gwen Wesson, p. 120.

Lewis Carroll, p. 95.

Winston Churchill, 1958, *My early life*, School edn, Andrew Scotland (ed.), Odhams Press, London, p. 143.

Kurt Vonnegut, 'How to write with style', p. 58.

Samuel Johnson, in *The Oxford dictionary of quotations*, p. 274.

Ken Macrorie, 1968, *Writing to be read*, Hayden Book Co., New York, p. 89.

Peter Hoeg, p. 79.

14 Writing scientific reports

F. Peter Woodford, 1967, 'Sounder thinking through clearer writing', *Science*, 156, 3776, May, p. 743.

Abraham Lincoln, source unknown.

Lorraine Marshall, 1997, *A learning companion*, 2nd edn, Murdoch University, p. 310.

Robert M. Pirsig, p. 100.

Robert M. Pirsig, p. 101.

F. Peter Woodford, p. 744.

Robert M. Pirsig, p. 102.

F. Peter Woodford, p. 744.

A.A. Milne, 1926, *Winnie the Pooh*, Methuen and Co., London, p. 48.

John Holt, *Instead of education*, pp. 99–100.

15 Using conventions

Lewis Carroll, p. 156.

Horace, 1936, 'The Art of Poetry', transl. Edward Henry Blakeney in *The complete works*, Casper J. Kraemer, Jr. (ed.), The Modern Library, New York, p. 401.

Dorothy Parker, 1939, 'The little hours', in *Here lies: The collected stories of Dorothy Parker*, Longmans, Green and Co., London, pp. 209–10.

Lord Byron, 1945, 'English bards and Scotch reviewers', 1.66, in *The poetical works of Lord Byron*, Oxford University Press, London, p. 114.

Ivy Baker, 1984, *If wishes were horses*, Bluegum, Angus and Robertson, Sydney, p. 32.

George Eliot, 1950, *Middlemarch*, The Zodiac Press, London, p. 70.

Charles Dickens, *Great expectations*, Chapman and Hall, London, undated, p. 50.

Australian Government Publication Service, 1994, *Style manual: For authors, editors and printers of Australian Government Publications*, 5th edn, AGPS, Canberra, p. xi.

16 Learning from evaluation

James Agate, in *A dictionary of modern quotations*, p. 2.

John Holt, *Instead of education*, p. 61.

Antoine de Saint-Exupèry, 1943, *The little prince*, Harcourt, Brace and World, New York, p. 39.

Winston Churchill, pp. 21–22.

University Without Walls, First report, p. 35.

Paul Goodman, 1971, *Compulsory miseducation*, Penguin Education, Penguin Books, Middlesex, England, p. 106.

Donald A. Bligh et al., 1975, *Teaching students*, An Exeter University Teaching Service Production, Devon, England, p. 91.

Peter Elbow, p. 118.

F. Galton, 1896, *Hereditary genius*, London Macmillan, pp. 49–50.

Lewis Carroll, p. 128.

Michael Novak, 1970, *The experience of nothingness*, Harper and Row, New York, p. 37.

Jules Henry, 1972, *Culture against man*, Penguin Books, Middlesex, England, p. 250.

Appendix Discrimination: Sexist language and attitudes

International Association of Business Communicators, 1977, *Without bias: A guidebook for nondiscriminatory communication*, International Association of Business Communicators, San Francisco, p. 22.

Gwen Wesson, p. 26.

REFERENCE BOOKS

Teaching learning skills

Ballard, Brigid & Clanchy, John, 1991, *Teaching students from overseas: A brief guide for lecturers and supervisors*, Longman Cheshire, Melbourne.

Fairbairn, Gavin J. & Winch, Christopher, 1991, *Reading, writing and reasoning: A guide for students*, The Society for Research into Higher Education and Open University Press, Milton Keynes, Bucks.

Gibbs, G., 1981, *Teaching students to learn: A student-centred approach*, The Open University Press, Milton Keynes, Bucks.

Habeshaw, T., Habeshaw, S. & Gibbs, G., 1989, *53 Interesting ways of helping your students to study*, 2nd edn, Technical and Educational Services Ltd, England. (See also the other seven volumes in this series for interesting ideas on teaching.)

Harasim, L., Hiltz, S.R., Teles, L. & Turoff, M., 1996, *Learning networks: A field guide to teaching and learning online*, The MIT Press, Massachusetts Institute of Technology, Cambridge, Massachusetts.

Lindsey, Crawford W., 1988, *Teaching students to teach themselves*, Kogan Page, London.

Main, Alex, 1980, *Encouraging effective learning: An approach to study counselling*, Scottish Academic Press, Edinburgh.

Marton, F., Hounsell, D. & Entwistle, N. (eds), 1984, *The experience of learning*, Scottish Academic Press, Edinburgh.

Nightingale, Peggy, 1986, 'Improving Student Writing', HERDSA Green Guide, University of New South Wales.

Nisbet, John & Shucksmith, Janet, 1986, *Learning strategies*, Routledge & Kegan Paul, London.

Webb, Carolyn, 1991, 'Writing an essay in the Humanities and Social Sciences' from Webb, Carolyn (ed.), Writing practice for university students, (series) Learning Assistance Centre, University of Sydney, Sydney.

Webb, Carolyn & Murison, E., 1991, 'Writing a research paper' from Webb, Carolyn (ed.), Writing Practice for University students (series) Learning Assistance Centre, University of Sydney, Sydney.

Student learning skills texts

Burdess, Neil, 1991, *The handbook of student skills*, Prentice-Hall, London.

Ellis, Dave (ed.), 1994, *Becoming a master student*, 7th edn, Houghton Mifflin, Boston.

Marshall, Lorraine, 1997, *A learning companion*, Murdoch University, Murdoch, Western Australia.

INDEX